THE
NEW
ROMAGNOLIS'
TABLE

THE
NEW
ROMAGNOLIS'
TABLE

Margaret and G. Franco Romagnoli

Photographs by G. Franco Romagnoli

THE ATLANTIC MONTHLY PRESS
NEW YORK

With special thanks to our children, Gian Giacomo, Marco, Paolo, and Anna, as well as our grandson Gian Carlo, the latest generational addition to our table. They all, with appreciated partners, continue to chop and mince, test-taste, and join us around our various tables to share in the little and big celebrations of living.

With gratitude also to WGBH-TV, Boston, which aided and abetted by putting the first of the Romagnoli recipes on the air.

The New Romagnolis' Table is a revised edition of *The Romagnolis' Table,* first published in 1975.

FIRST EDITION

Library of Congress Cataloging-in-Publication Data

Romagnoli, Margaret.
  The new Romagnolis' table/by Margaret and G. Franco Romagnoli:
photographed by G. Franco Romagnoli.—1st ed.
  English and Italian.
  Rev. ed. of: The Romagnolis' table. 1975.
  Includes index.
  ISBN 0-87113-214-1
  1. Cookery, Italian. I. Romagnoli, G. Franco. II. Romagnoli,
Margaret. Romagnolis' table. III. Title.
TX723.R54 1988
641.5945—dc19   87-22871

Published simultaneously in Canada
Printed in the United States of America

Design by Laura Hough

The Atlantic Monthly Press
19 Union Square West
New York, NY 10003

FIRST PRINTING

To all of you
who have shared your tables
with us

Contents

CONTENTS

Introduction

In the process of moving our residence from Rome to Boston—and vice versa, in what now seems like the periodic migrations of birds—we purchased a monastery's refectory table. It is a thick slab of chestnut wood, about three by eight feet, and one of the few pieces of furniture to follow us back and forth across the ocean. It is not unusual at all to find eight people sitting around it. Sometimes more, with a little squeezing. Food and wine are partaken of around it and, equally important, as much laughter and friendship as we can cram into every meal. It was while sitting around this table that the idea of our TV show and of this book was born. When the search for a title led nowhere, one of the TV producers knocked on the table and said: "Here it is: 'The Romagnolis' Table'!"

More than a decade has passed since the first *Romagnolis' Table* saw the light of day. Its acceptance by the public at large has been a great pleasure for us. Even though we followed it with two other cookbooks, that firstborn, so to speak, has always been closest to our hearts. But a decade is bound to bring changes. The major one in our lives has been to open a restaurant—a daring way to put our money where our mouths are. Its name and its menu are based on the book, and like the book it has been a miraculous source of new friends.

On the culinary scene, both here and in Italy, the past decade has seen many changes. The most laudable in Italy is the availability and use of ingredients once thought exotic and hard to obtain. Here in America, we applaud the recognition of the Italian cuisine as a major culinary influence, a fact that has made the availability of Italian products on the American market quite common. In Italy, as here, there has been a swing towards the new or *nouvelle cuisine* in an unexpected way, with sometimes unexpected dishes. But now the pendulum is swinging back to the regional and traditional cookery. Nouvelle cuisine's major contribution has been in giving some leeway in the interpretation, preparation, and presentation of classic dishes and in making them conform more to the economy and lifestyles of the new generations.

These basically are the reasons for this new edition. We have kept many of the recipes from the first edition—certain things do not age! We have retired some others and added many new ones, gathered in these intervening years, especially the new ones which have withstood the test of family, friends, and the restaurant.

We realize a lot of books have been written on the subject of Italian cooking, and surely many more will be. Some have been written with the sole purpose of recording the "real, true, original" recipe, and some for the veiled purpose of rebutting the former. We found most of them beautifully accomplished, elegant tomes. (Some, very few fortunately, were by foreign writers whose instant love for the Italian *cucina* exceeded their knowledge of the Italian language and dialects and led them to misinterpretations.) We hope our book will serve as a tool in your kitchen and will introduce you to some of the basic techniques involved, as well as show you how easy the preparation of Italian food can be and how varied.

Deciding on the recipes to use was not easy. A brief look at Italy's history and geography will explain, we hope, both the simplicity and the variety. The country until quite recently was a conglomerate of independent states that were, for geographical or political reasons, sealed off from each other. Give or take a few exceptions, they were agrarian states. The Italian farmer has never been rich; everybody in his large family has had to work, dawn to dusk, in the fields. There was not much time to spend in the kitchen, and only enough money to pay for essentials. Very little, if anything, that was not grown on the spot ever reached his table. Food then, apart from being a necessity, was also one of the few sources of enjoyment, distraction, and gratification. It had to be tasty, economical, reasonably quick or easy to prepare, and had generally to go around for a crowd. (If, by and large, these are national characteristics of Italian cooking, we do not want to say that all Italian cookery is peasant style. After all, where money and power flourished, so did a more sumptuous table whose dishes, when exported, became *haute cuisine.*)

As for variety, Italy is a long, thin peninsula stretching from north to south in the form of a boot. Trimmed at the top by the arc of the Alps, it is ribbed down its length by the Appenines, with the triangular island of Sicily a stone's throw from the toe. To the west of the mainland is Sardinia, the largest of the Mediterranean islands. With the generous sprinkle of smaller islands, Italy ends up with an area slightly smaller than California, but with all the geographical variations of the North American continent.

Many people simply divide Italian cuisine into northern and southern, but that is too elementary a distinction. The country has nineteen major regions, each in turn subdivided into provinces, and these into counties, most of which differ not only in topography, climate, and economy, but also in dialect, history, folklore, and ways of cooking. Moreover, through the ages foreigners (from Albanians to Zouaves) have come and stayed in one region or another of the *Garden of the Mediterranean,* thus leaving their cultural and culinary imprint. Accept all these factors, and you can begin to understand Italy's quantity and diversity of regional dishes.

Today, in spite of fast produce delivery, more money, and more widespread availability of everything throughout the country, there are still many dishes that taste best when made and eaten in a particular region. Modern ingenuity and social changes in Italy plus a recent tendency to gloss over humble origins, have created many embellished variations of the same dish. The most enjoyable sort of field research has convinced us that the old basic recipe is usually the best. These original recipes are the foundations of this book.

Some Italian dishes have crisscrossed the oceans and become rich and flamboyant. An American pizza pie, for example, is to a pizza in Naples what an apple pie is to a *torta di mele:* a wild mutation of the original. This is not our kind of cooking.

Traditional Italian cookery emphasizes not only flavor and texture but also color and contour. To regard as important the hue and form of a food may sound frivolous, but having watched a thousand tables set we feel that they are important considerations. The sense of color and shape that expresses itself throughout Italian life dominates the way a display in a store window is set up, the arranging of the glorious fresh produce at the open market, the planning of a vegetable garden, the way a meal is presented.

Italians very rarely consider a dish all by itself, but set it in the context of the meal as a whole. For them a meal has a certain definite pattern: there is a distinct first, second, and third course, with each dish congenial and complementary to the others in taste, texture, color (where possible), and of course in substance. Thus, we have listed the dishes in the same order as they would appear on a family table:

Antipasti — before the meal, appetizers
Primi piatti — first courses, which include pasta, soup, rice, *polenta,* and other traditional offerings
Secondi piatti — meat, poultry, fish, eggs
Contorni — vegetables and salads
Dolci — sweets, both fruit and pastry (usually the Sunday variety)
Svogliature — snacks, pizza

Needless to say, we've found that two cooks in the kitchen do not spoil the broth. A cooking partnership, in addition to being more entertaining for the participants, saves a lot of time. How do we divide the labor? There is no formula, really. When there are familiar recipes in a menu, we each tend to make our own old favorites. When learning any new dish, each of us naturally does the part he or she likes and does best. Everyone has a certain attraction to particular kinds of cooking techniques. After anyone has made a few dishes, it's usually obvious which details he performs most skillfully. Some cooks thrive on chopping, others on basting or frying. In our case anyway, our two distinct self-assignments in kitchen duty seem to balance out and complement each other. In short, divide the labor, and double the rewards.

Margaret and G. Franco Romagnoli
Boston, November 1, 1987

ANTIPASTI
APPETIZERS

Antipasto is literally translated as "before the meal": an appetizer. It is designed to stay hunger pains, whet the appetite, and fill the pause while the pasta water or broth is coming to a boil. Frankly it seldom shows up on the everyday Italian family table, but is mostly reserved for Sundays, feast days, and parties to make the meal a special occasion.

While the fancier Italian restaurants list all kinds of *antipasti,* the family cook makes good use of only a few. These few seem to have been born of the season's best offerings.

Some *antipasti* wear two hats, and appear also as side dishes or part of a cold meal. Like sauces, they are the cook's choice, and anything goes: think of something delightful, light and cheerful, a springboard for your palate.

Antipasto di Mare
SEAFOOD COCKTAIL

Baby clams, the smallest squid possible, shrimp, and mussels are simmered with seasonings and served with olive oil, lemon, chopped fresh parsley, and capers.

½ pound baby squid	*salt*
1 pound small shrimp	*5 peppercorns*
½ pound small cherrystone clams	*½ clove garlic*
1 pound mussels	*1½ tablespoons chopped parsley*
1 carrot	*1 tablespoon chopped capers*
1 stalk celery	*6 tablespoons olive oil*
1 onion	*juice of 1 lemon*
1 bay leaf	

Clean the squid (pages 104–105). Cut in small strips or rings, leaving the tentacles whole. Shell the shrimp, saving the shells. Scrub the clams and mussels with a stiff brush and rinse well under running water.

Put the carrot, celery, onion, bay leaf, shrimp shells, about a teaspoon of salt, and the peppercorns in a pot with 3 quarts of water. Bring to a boil, reduce the heat, cover, and simmer for 15 minutes. Add the clams and mussels, and cook for about 3 minutes or until the shells open. Remove the clams and mussels from the pot and add the shrimp. Remove the shrimp when they are coral colored, about a minute's cooking, and add the squid. Cook the squid about a minute or until the tentacles turn lavender. Strain the contents of the pot, reserving the liquid, and remove the squid pieces to join the shrimp. Take the clams and mussels from their shells.

Rub the inside of a serving bowl with the garlic. Put in the shrimp, clams, mussels, and squid. Sprinkle with the chopped parsley and capers. Dress with olive oil, lemon juice, and a tablespoon of the reserved fish stock, and toss gently.

Chill for half an hour before serving. For 6.

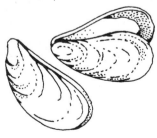

Bagna Cauda
HOT SAUCE WITH RAW VEGETABLES

Bagna Cauda, literally translated from the Piedmontese, would read "Hot Bath," or, more loosely, "Hot Dip." Neither does justice to Bagna Cauda, especially if pronounced in the harmonious tones of the Piedmont dialect. Today, Bagna Cauda is considered an antipasto, but once its social function was the same as that of the pizza in more southern climates: a good excuse, if one was ever needed, for family or friends to gather around a table and share food, fun, and gossip. On a cold wet day, add a bottle of old Barolo or one of young Grignolino and have them go around the table. Listen to the conversation sparkle and watch the cold window panes get misty.

The actual quantities and types of vegetables to be dipped are the cook's choice and must depend on what is in season. Cardoons, rarely found in our local market, are a perennial Mediterranean plant similar to celery and their stalks are used as a vegetable throughout Italy. If you can't find them just skip them. The peppers should be meaty, the celery stalks white and from the center of the bunch, and the cauliflower and the broccoli should be small and tender, as should the zucchini.

Some Piedmontese, to reduce the strong flavor of garlic, soak the minced cloves in milk for a few hours before draining and using them. Others suggest stirring in a little cream at the end of cooking in order to slightly thicken the sauce. Experience will tell you which method you prefer to follow.

SUGGESTED VEGETABLES
5 cardoons, with 1 lemon
1 red sweet pepper
1 green sweet pepper
5 celery stalks
½ small head cauliflower
½ small head broccoli
5 small carrots
5 or 6 cabbage leaves
½ small zucchini

6 radishes
2 very fresh artichokes

SAUCE
5 tablespoons unsalted butter
6 garlic cloves
12 anchovy fillets
1 cup olive oil
salt to taste

Wash the cardoons, peel off the stringiest ribs, cut these into 3-inch pieces and soak in water for an hour with the juice of the lemon.

Melt the butter over very low heat, possibly in an earthenware casserole. Mince the garlic, and sauté it in the butter for 5 minutes. Mash the anchovies into a paste and stir it into the butter. Slowly stir in the olive oil. Continue cooking over very low heat, stirring occasionally for 30 minutes. Add salt to taste.

While the sauce is simmering, prepare the rest of the vegetables. Core the peppers and cut them into thin strips. Wash the celery stalks and cut them in half lengthwise. Break the cauliflower and broccoli into bite-size flowerlets. Peel the carrots and cut them on the diagonal into ovals or into lengthwise strips. Slice the zucchini into even ovals, cutting on the diagonal. Make the radishes into roses, leaving a bit of leaf or stem to hold them by.

When the sauce is ready, transfer it from the stove to a warming device on the table. It must be kept warm while everyone dips his vegetable pieces in it. Dipping can be done either with the fingers or, perhaps an unnecessary refinement, with long forks like those used for fondue. For 6.

Carciofini all'Olio
ARTICHOKE HEARTS IN OLIVE OIL

This favorite *antipasto* is also a popular way of cooking, serving, and preserving the young artichokes that appear at the beginning of the season. They're cooked in wine, spiced with bay leaf and cloves and lemon. To prepare the artichokes see pages 226–27.

2 dozen small artichokes, fresh, or 2
    10-ounce packages of frozen ar-
    tichoke hearts, thawed
1 cup lemon juice
5 cloves
14 peppercorns
8 bay leaves
5 thin slices lemon
1½ cups dry white wine
2 tablespoons vinegar
1½ cups water (approximate)
1 cup olive oil (approximate)

Dip fresh artichoke halves in lemon juice, and put them in a medium-size saucepan. If using frozen artichokes, thaw them at room temperature and place in the saucepan.

When all the artichokes are ready, add to the pan all 5 cloves, 10 of the peppercorns, 4 of the bay leaves, the lemon slices, white wine, vinegar, and enough water so that the artichokes float. Bring to a boil, cover, reduce the heat, and boil gently for about 10 minutes, or until the artichokes' hearts are tender when stuck with a fork.

Drain thoroughly, discard the cooked spices, and put the artichokes in a jar with the remaining 4 bay leaves and 4 peppercorns. Pour in enough olive oil to cover. Let stand a few days before serving. For 6.

Carciofi alla Giudia
ARTICHOKES, JEWISH STYLE

The attribute *Giudia* means Jewish-style. It is a traditional and appreciated cuisine, especially in Rome where in the center of the old city there is a section still called the Ghetto (it has no derogatory connotations) where some of the best Italian Jewish cooking can be found today.

The whole procedure of *Carciofi alla Giudia* seems more fussy than it actually is. No matter what, once you serve and taste them, it is all worthwhile. We recommend, nonetheless, that you wear long sleeves and an apron.

1 globe artichoke per person for antipasto
2 lemons

vegetable oil for deep frying
salt to taste

Clean and trim the artichokes (see p. 00), but leave the stems attached and do not remove the chokes. Soak in cold water with the juice of the lemons for about ½ hour to make the leaves less resistant to opening up.

Drain the artichokes thoroughly. A partial opening of the leaves is wanted at this stage. You may do this by prying with your fingers or by using a lemon: hold one artichoke in your left hand and a lemon in your right hand. Place the more pointed end of the lemon down into the center of the artichoke leaves. Push down and twist the lemon back and forth, thus loosening the leaves and opening them slightly. The heat of the cooking oil will soften the leaves further to create a final wide-open flowerlike effect.

Pour vegetable oil to the depth of about 5 inches in a deep frying pot. Heat to 300° to 350°F.

Using a pair of long-handled kitchen tongs, clasp the stem of an artichoke and immerse it in the hot oil. This will provoke quite a commotion in the oil and its temperature will rise. Both will subside when the natural moisture of the artichoke has boiled away. After about 2 minutes, clasp the stem of the artichoke again with the tongs and press the head of the artichoke down on the bottom of the pot to encourage the leaves to open up like a flower's petals. Let the artichoke fry, turning it from time to time, until the stem and all the leaves are a golden brown.

To add to the crispness, when the first artichoke in the pot is golden brown, add a second, uncooked artichoke. This will make the oil temperature rise (it sounds like a paradox but it works that way), so leave the already golden artichoke to fry a few more seconds, then drain it and continue to cook the second artichoke, and proceed on to the third and fourth as the case may be.

Serve the artichokes well drained and warm, not hot. Salt to taste.

Carpaccio
RAW BEEF SLICES WITH CAPER-PARSLEY DRESSING

The origins of *carpaccio* are attributed to the Cipriani restaurant and Harry's Bar, famous Hemingway haunts in Venice. But its roots are solidly planted in the Piedmont, as we were made aware in a Turin restaurant years ago. When we asked the waiter for *carpaccio*, he looked at us reproachfully and said, "Here in Turin, what you ask for is *Insalata di Carne Cruda* (raw beef salad)." When it was served, it was exactly like *carpaccio*, but topped with slivers of white truffles and aged Parmesan cheese. It was, naturally, delicious. And if there is a lesson in this, it is that when it comes to food Italians are quite chauvinistic: my village first!

A piece of top round, kept in the freezer for about 1½ hours, becomes semifrozen, and is easily cut with a meat slicer or knife.

If using a knife, pound the hand-cut slices with a meat pounder.

10 to 12 ounces prime top round, frozen and cut paper thin against the grain (18 slices approximately)
extra virgin olive oil
3 teaspoons fresh lemon juice

6 teaspoons capers, rinsed and drained
6 teaspoons Italian parsley leaves, chopped
3 large mushrooms
freshly ground black pepper

Place 3 slices of the beef, slightly overlapping, to cover each of 6 plates. Using a pastry brush or back of a spoon, lightly coat the beef with olive oil, just enough to make the meat glisten. Sprinkle each plate with a few drops of lemon juice. Mince the capers with the parsley and sprinkle evenly, about 1½ teaspoons, on each plate. Slice the mushrooms in thin slices and place them evenly spaced around the edge of the meat. Sprinkle lightly with freshly ground pepper, to your taste. For 6.

Crescentine di Grasso
MEAT AND CHEESE-FILLED FRIED PASTRIES

FOR THE FILLING:
1 sprig rosemary, or 1 teaspoon dried
1 1/2 ounces prosciutto
1 1/2 ounces capocollo
1/2 ounce lean beef
1 egg
1 ounce Parmesan cheese, grated
pinch of freshly grated nutmeg
hint of white pepper

FOR THE PASTRY:
1 3/4 cups (9 ounces) all-purpose flour
1 teaspoon baking powder
1/2 ounce unsalted butter
1/2 cup plus 1 tablespoon cold beef broth
1 egg white, slightly beaten
frying oil, preferably vegetable

Strip the rosemary from the sprig and mince it. Mince the meats using either a very sharp knife or the food processor with the steel blade. Mix rosemary, meats, egg and cheese, nutmeg and pepper until well amalgamated and let rest.

Place the flour on a board or clean counter. Add the baking powder and make a crater in the center of the pile. Place the softened butter in the crater and mix briefly with your fingers. Gradually add the broth and knead until you have a soft, elastic dough. Or mix briefly as you would most doughs in the food processor.

Divide the dough into two manageable pieces. Cover one so that it will not dry out and roll the other into a strip about 5 inches wide and very thin, less than the thickness of a dime.

Drop the filling evenly spaced about two inches apart as if for ravioli on one sheet of dough. Dip a pastry brush in the egg white and paint the strip along its edges, down the middle and around the filling. Cover with the second strip of dough and press firmly to seal the edges. Cut as you would ravioli, but on the diagonal.

Bring the frying oil to 350° and fry several at a time until crisp and toasted on the outside. Drain on paper towels and sprinkle lightly with salt, if you wish. For 6–10.

Funghi all'Olio e Limone
MUSHROOMS WITH OIL AND LEMON

This particular way of cooking mushrooms is an easy dish to prepare ahead of time and goes very nicely with *Carciofini all'olio* and its delicately flavored olive oil.

1 pound small white mushrooms
½ cup olive oil
1 medium clove garlic

½ teaspoon salt, or to taste
¼ lemon
1 tablespoon chopped parsley

Peel and clean the mushrooms, and cut caps from stems. Slice off the very bottom of the stems where they are slightly dried out.

Put the oil in a medium-size frying pan; add the garlic. Sauté over medium heat until golden, and then discard. Add the mushrooms, raise the heat, and sauté quickly, stirring them so they don't brown. When the mushrooms start to give up their juices, add the salt. When they are tender but still firm (about 4–5 minutes), squirt them with the lemon, stir well, add the parsley, stir again, and take them off the heat.

Serve warm or room temperature in their own flavored oil. For 6.

Granzeola alla Veneziana
CRABMEAT, VENETIAN STYLE

This is a light antipasto, and very easy to prepare. The Adriatic crab used in Venice yields quite a bit more meat than those of the eastern shore of the United States, so we have adjusted the measures accordingly. However, you can easily substitute snow crabs, king crab legs, or East or West Coast crabs. When using fresh crabs, try to preserve the shell intact to serve the *granzeola* in as it is done in Venice.

1 pound cooked crabmeat
2 to 3 tablespoons Italian parsley,
    minced
juice of 1 large lemon

3 tablespoons olive oil
salt to taste
white pepper

Shred the crabmeat into a small bowl. Mix in the parsley. Add the lemon juice and olive oil and mix well. Add salt to taste, but go gently as the crabmeat is usually salted in cooking.

Add a sprinkle of white pepper. Chill thoroughly and serve on chilled plates. For 6.

Mozzarella alla Caprese
MOZZARELLA, CAPRI STYLE

The original of this recipe is *Insalata alla Caprese,* in which slices of tomato and cubes of *mozzarella* are dressed with a touch of fresh basil, a pinch of oregano, pure olive oil, and mixed, and let marinate ½ hour or so before serving.

This is a dish to be made only with garden-ripe tomatoes and fresh *mozzarella,* as the winter tomatoes leave a great deal to be desired and commercial *mozzarella* lacks the texture and flavor of freshly made *mozzarella.* The latter is found frequently in cheese stores carrying international cheeses. It is usually imported, but lately we have found it made locally at reasonable prices. The fresh *mozzarella* is egg shaped, weighing approximately six ounces.

3 fresh mozzarella (approximately 6 ounces each)
3 large tomatoes (approximately 8 ounces each)

5 tablespoons virgin olive oil
2 teaspoons fresh, chopped oregano or ½ teaspoon dried
freshly ground pepper

Slice each *mozzarella* into six slices, allowing three per person. Core and slice each tomato in eight slices. Discard the two end slices. Starting with a center slice of tomato, place it with a center slice of *mozzarella* on a plate and layer three of each diminishing size down the center of each plate. Sprinkle each serving with about 1 tablespoon of the olive oil and a pinch of the oregano, and add freshly ground pepper to your taste. For 6.

Pâté alla Veneziana
VENETIAN PÂTÉ

This is for grand celebrations. It is a 200-year-old recipe resurrected and reworked by us for the sheer pleasure of its delicate taste and texture. We have used Venetian pâté for fund-raisers for good causes, New Year's Eve galas, anniversaries along the years. It is a dish that can be dressed up by molding it in decorated aspic (see pages 242–43), or it can be served in bignè, large or small. They are easy to make, easy to fill, and very nonfussy to serve. See page 13 for the bignè recipe.

1 1/2 tablespoons olive oil
1 1/2 tablespoons unsalted butter
1 1/2 rounded tablespoons minced Italian parsley
1/4 celery stalk, minced
1 medium onion, peeled and thinly sliced
4 fresh sage leaves, or about 1/2 teaspoon dried
1/2 teaspoon salt
1/4 teaspoon freshly ground pepper
1/2 cup chicken broth (page 88)
1/2 pound boneless chicken breast, skinless and cubed

1 pound calves liver, trimmed and cubed
3/4 pound unsalted butter, softened to room temperature
1 teaspoon Dijon mustard
1 1/2 rounded teaspoons nutmeg, freshly grated
1/4 cup Italian brandy
grated rind of 1/4 large orange
1/2 cup medium cream
8 mammoth black ripe olives, pitted and quartered

Sauté in butter and oil the parsley, celery, onions, and sage until limp. Add salt, pepper, and broth and cook over low heat for 15 to 20 minutes or until most of the liquid has been cooked away. Add the chicken and liver, raise the heat, and cook for 6 minutes or until the meats are cooked and tender. Let cool.

Process the cooked, cooled meats in a food processor using the steel cutting blade, or send them through a meat grinder twice.

The pâté is now ready for its final seasonings and butter. To the processed meats, add the softened butter, mustard, nutmeg, brandy, orange rind, and cream. Process or beat until smooth, creamy, and perfectly blended. Fold in the olives.

When the pâté has been seasoned, chill in a mold or in 2 molds, lined with plastic wrap (or aspic, if you wish).

Serve with thinly sliced toasted Italian or French bread or white Melba toast, or use the pâté to fill bignè. Makes approximately 2 pounds of pâté, enough for 2 dozen guests.

11

Pâté di Fesa alla Milanese
PÂTÉ OF VEAL, ROLLED IN *PROSCIUTTO*

Having had our full share of rich or hearty country pâté, we found this a wonderful alternative. It is an old Milanese recipe, made with veal and flavorings and dotted with pistachios—a nice start to a full-course dinner. *Pâté di Fesa* can be multiplied to serve a large party, and its delicate flavor complements a variety of wines nicely. It keeps well wrapped in aluminum foil in the refrigerator for up to one week.

2 tablespoons unsalted butter
1 large carrot, cubed
1 stalk celery, cubed
1 onion peeled, cut in chunks
1 bouillon cube (if using water)
1/3 cup water or beef broth
1 1/2 pounds veal round, boned and cubed
8 tablespoons unsalted butter
1/2 cup heavy cream
1/4 cup cognac

1/4 cup grated Parmesan cheese
1 teaspoon freshly grated nutmeg
white pepper, freshly grated
1/2 teaspoon salt
2 ounces pistachios, dry roasted and shelled
12 capers (1/8 ounce), drained and minced
9 to 10 slices of prosciutto *(about 7 ounces)*

Place two tablespoons of the butter and vegetables with the water and bouillon cube (or broth) in a big sauté pan and cook gently over a low flame, turning frequently, until all the vegetables are soft, about 5 minutes.

Add the veal and continue cooking until the meat is pale in color and has given up some of its juices. Place the cooked mixture in the bowl of a food processor and process until the mixture is a very fine mince. Add the butter, cream, and cognac and process until the mixture is smooth. Add the cheese, nutmeg, pepper, salt and then process until all are incorporated. Taste for flavor and adjust to fit your palate. We usually use about 1/2 teaspoon of freshly grated white pepper for our taste. However, this is a light, delicate pâté and should not be overwhelmed with any one flavor. Stir in the nuts and capers.

Chill the entire bowl in the freezer. Spread aluminum foil to cover a cookie sheet, lay slices of *prosciutto* overlapping, the boned (or rough end) toward you. Spoon the now chilled pâté down over the near end of the *prosciutto* slices. Lift the aluminum foil gently to roll the slices and the pâté over and away from you. Keep rolling until the pâté is enclosed, you have a 2-inch-wide roll of pâté, and you have reached the ends of the *prosciutto* slices. Place the aluminum-wrapped roll in the refrigerator for 2 to 3 hours. When ready to serve, cut in 1/2-inch slices, allowing 2 to 3 per person. For 8–10 people.

Serve with toasted rounds of French or Italian bread, thin cut.

12

Bignè
BIGNÈ FOR ANTIPASTI

Bignè is the Neapolitan interpretation of the French *beignet.* Either Neapolitan or French, they appear on the American table as cream puffs.

1 1/4 cups water
5 tablespoons butter
3/4 cup all-purpose flour, sifted

pinch of salt
4 large eggs

Bring the water and butter to a boil in a saucepan over high heat, and the minute the mixture boils take the pan off the heat and add the flour and salt all at once. Stir immediately and vigorously with a wooden spoon, putting the pan back over the heat. The mixture turns into a paste right away and must be stirred continuously until it forms a ball and no longer clings to the sides or bottom of the pan. Keep on stirring a little more, until the paste sounds as if it were frying. Remove it from the heat and cool.

Add the eggs, one at a time, stirring in each completely before adding the next, keep on stirring until the soft dough is perfectly amalgamated, smooth, and rather like drop-cookie dough. Cover and let stand 15 minutes in a cool place.

Preheat the oven to 400°. Drop the batter by the tablespoonful on a buttered cookie sheet, leaving at least 2 inches between them. Bake at 400° for 20 minutes or until golden brown in color, crisp on the outside, and nearly double in size. Remove from the heat and stick with a cake tester to allow steam to escape. When cool enough to handle, break open gently and let cool further. When cool, fill with pâté. Makes 16 large, 30 small bignè.

Peperoni Arrosto
ROAST PEPPERS

These roast peppers are frequently served as a vegetable course as well as an *antipasto,* with *Funghi all'olio* and *Carciofini all'olio.* Roasting the peppers gives them an incredibly different taste. After roasting, they're sliced in strips, and bathed in lemon and olive oil.

6–8 large peppers (red, green, yellow, sweet and meaty)
2 lemons

8 tablespoons olive oil
salt to taste

To use a gas stove: turn the grates of the top burners upside down to cradle the peppers, and set the flame at medium high. Put the peppers on the grates, and keep an eye on them as they roast. As soon as one side of a pepper is blackened, turn it a bit to the next uncharred portion. Keep turning until all the outer skin is blackened and blistered.

To use an electric stove: put the peppers in the broiler, as close to the heating element as possible, and keep turning them as they blacken. We have to admit that this broiling process doesn't cook the peppers as well as the gas burners: it tends to overcook them. If, however, you use really fresh, plump peppers, the results are good. Roast until the outer skin of the peppers is completely charred.

Put the charred peppers under a cold stream of water, and peel off the black with your fingers. This makes a great mess in the sink, but the taste of the peppers will repay you for cleaning it up.

Cut off the top stems, take out the inner seeds, and slice the peppers lengthwise into ¼- to ½-inch-wide strips. Drain briefly, and put in a serving dish. Squeeze the lemons and pour their juice over the peppers. Add the olive oil and salt to taste. Baste well.

The roast peppers can be served right away, but they improve if they marinate for half an hour or so. For 6.

Prosciutto e Melone
PROSCIUTTO AND MELON

For more people than any of us can count, Italian *prosciutto,* cured ham, is the leading star in any lineup of Italian *antipasti.* Cut thin, served by itself, accompanied by crusty, fresh bread and unsalted butter, prosciutto is simply grand. Coupled with partners, recipes below, it becomes even grander while remaining the simplest appetizer to prepare. If you cut the *prosciutto* slices and melon in reasonable sizes to slip onto a cocktail pick, you'll find it is a pleasant variation for informal outdoor dining or cocktail parties.

1 large ripe cantaloupe *12 thin slices* prosciutto

Chill the melon thoroughly before opening it. Cut it in half, scoop out the seeds, and then cut each half into 6 wedges. Finally, cut the melon meat away from the rind, place the rindless wedges around a platter, alternating them with loosely rolled slices of *prosciutto,* and serve. For 6.

Prosciutto e Fichi
PROSCIUTTO AND FRESH FIGS

12 ripe figs, either the purple or the green variety *12 slices* prosciutto

Chill, then peel the figs before serving. To peel, cut off the very tip of the pointed end of the fruit. Make 4 shallow incisions in the skin as if you were going to cut the figs into quarters. Slide the knife underneath the incisions at what would be the top of a quarter, and peel back the skin, cutting it away from the fig at the very bottom. Place figs and *prosciutto* alternately around a serving platter, and that's all there is to it. For 6.

15

Prosciutto e Mozzarella
PROSCIUTTO AND *MOZZARELLA*

2–3 *fresh* mozzarella *(approximately 1½ pounds)*
9 ounces *prosciutto, thinly cut*

5 tablespoons virgin olive oil
1½ teaspoons dried oregano
freshly ground black pepper

Cut the *mozzarella* in three slices per person. Cut the *prosciutto* slices in half. Place a center-cut *mozzarella* slice on each plate. Fan a half-slice of prosciutto and place it halfway over the *mozzarella.* Follow with a second slice of *mozzarella* cov-ering the *prosciutto* and continue until all the slices are layered. Drizzle each plate with the olive oil and sprinkle with the oregano. Dust with as much freshly grated pepper as you wish. For 6.

Mozzarella in Carozza
GOLDEN FRIED *MOZZARELLA* SANDWICHES

When done, the *Mozzarella in Carozza* resembles what is frequently called French toast in America or *Pane Gajardo* in Italy. No matter the name, a great favorite of any generation.

2 dozen 2×2-inch crustless thin
 slices of Italian bread or firm
 sandwich bread
1 dozen 2×2-inch slices fresh mozzarella

flour
½ to ¾ cup milk
2 large eggs
vegetable oil for frying

With the thin slices of bread make a dozen *mozzarella* sandwiches. Press the edges of each sandwich together firmly and then press into the flour to make as much flour adhere as possible.

Dip the sandwich edges into the milk briefly to form a paste with the flour. Set aside in a deep platter to rest for 10 minutes. This should ensure that the *mozzarella* won't escape during frying.

Beat the eggs well and pour them over the sandwiches, letting the bread absorb all the egg possible. Let stand about 10 minutes.

Place four or six at a time (depending on the size of your frying pan) in hot frying oil and fry until golden brown. Remove from the oil and drain briefly on paper towel. For 6.

Pomodori al Riso
TOMATOES STUFFED WITH RICE

Without fail, these tomatoes bring back memories of summer days at the beach. Mamma would pack a lunch for us children and frequently it was rice-stuffed tomatoes, right from the oven, and rice *supplì.* Then, with that treasure carefully wrapped, we would take the shuttle train from Rome to the beach at Anzio. One hot day, anxious to get to the water, we forgot our lunch on the train. We realized our loss as soon as the train had taken off for Nettuno, the turning point a few miles down the line. We explained our misery to the stationmaster, who, aware of the gravity of the situation, gave us permission to search the train's compartments on its return stop in Anzio. And so we did. The right compartment signaled itself by the familiar aroma. But that was all that was left: the mouth-watering aroma. Sad day at the beach. However, ever since and forever, when rice-stuffed tomatoes, or *supplì* for that matter, are around, I don't let them leave my sight for a moment. GFR

For a brief description of the various rices and their uses, see page 112 in the rice section.

6 medium-size tomatoes
4 tablespoons chopped parsley
6 fresh basil leaves
½ clove garlic

½ cup medium-grain rice, preferably arborio
½ cup olive oil
½ teaspoon salt

Preheat the oven to 375°.

Wash the tomatoes, and cut off the tops about a quarter of the way down, so that you can get at the insides. Save the tops. Scoop out the seeds and the inner pulp with its juices, and strain through a sieve or vegetable mill into a small bowl. Salt the tomatoes and turn upside down to drain for 15 minutes. Chop the parsley, basil, and garlic very fine, and add to the tomato juice with the rice. Add ¼ cup of the olive oil and ½ teaspoon of the salt. Mix well.

Put this mixture into the tomato shells, filling them no more than half full. Place them in a shallow baking dish just large enough to hold them. Sprinkle with the remaining ¼ cup of the olive oil, and cover each tomato with its own top.

Bake (at 375°) for half an hour. Then reduce the heat to 350°, and baste the tomatoes with the juice from the baking dish, using a bulb baster to get the liquid into the rice without disturbing the tops too much. Bake another half an hour or so, until the rice is really tender. For 6.

17

PRIMI PIATTI
FIRST COURSES

No proper Italian meal can begin without a *primo piatto* (a first course) of either *minestra* (soup, with or without pasta) or *pasta asciutta* (pasta without soup, cooked in water, drained, and married to a sauce) or a variation of the two. This last category includes rice dishes, *timballi* (casseroles) such as the famous *lasagne, gnocchi* (dumplings), or *polenta* (northern Italy's cornmeal concoction) with a sauce.

The *primo piatto* has a definite purpose as a course: it soothes the appetite with something important, for on the traditional Italian table it is still the main part of the meal. It also sets the pace for the dishes that follow.

First courses reflect regional variations in climate, economy, and the availability of products. Colder and more prosperous than the South, the North of Italy tends to serve rich soups, dishes made with rice, and sturdy *polenta*—all in all, a rather serious, no-nonsense cookery. In the sunnier South, the *primo piatto* is zippier and, because fewer rich ingredients are available, frequently more inventive.

In choosing a first course, depend on what's in your larder or the local market, and remember to make it complementary to the rest of the meal in color, texture, taste, and consistency. A spicy second course should be preceded by a bland first, a delicate meat by a hearty *minestra,* and so on. Never forget the weather and, above all, the mood of the moment.

Pasta

Pasta in General

For simplicity's sake we divide pasta into two major categories: commercial and homemade.

A glance at a shelf in a store will show you how many, many commercially produced shapes and sizes there are. Moreover, as a pasta shape is adopted by one region or another, it may even change its name. What's *tagliatelle* in Bologna could be *fettuccine* in Rome. Every once in a while a pasta maker further compounds the confusion by coming up with his own original creation. To update the list would be both an impossible task and a rather useless exercise.

However no matter whether pasta is homemade or mass produced, its shape dictates how it will end up: either in *minestra* or as *pasta asciutta*.

The smaller shapes are generally used in soups: *quadrucci, stellette, pastina, capellini,* to name a few. They will make their appearance in the *minestre* (soups) section.

The longer and bigger shapes are generally used for *pasta asciutta.* The overall title of *pasta asciutta* (literally, dried-off pasta) means that it is drained of the liquid it's cooked in, and then is served with a sauce. Spaghetti, *rigatoni, ziti, perciatelli, vermicelli, linguine, fettuccine,* all these are only a few names on the *pasta asciutta* roster.

Most commercially packaged pasta is made with flour and water, and it is the flour you have to watch out for. Commercial pasta should be made with semolina and water. If not, it will not have the character and body it should have when cooked.

Pasta fatta in casa (homemade pasta), whether for soup or for use with sauce, is made with all-purpose unbleached flour, eggs, and a pinch of salt. (All-purpose flour contains a higher percentage of hard wheat [durum] flour, a requisite for good pasta, than does pastry flour.) Also called *pasta all'uovo* (egg pasta), it is the most delicate of all, the Queen of Pasta (the gender of *pasta* is feminine in Italian).

In Italy, there are many shops that make *pasta all'uovo* daily, and you can simply buy the amount and cut you wish, just as you might buy fresh bread at a bakery. Currently there are a lot of new shops selling fresh *pasta all'uovo* in America. Not all of them, however, make their pasta with all-purpose, unbleached flour. Some add oil. (Some use the semolina flour and the results are disappointing.) But don't despair. The knack of making pasta is not difficult to master, and you'll find it a positive pleasure to be your own supplier, especially when you consider the enormous culinary rewards you'll receive.

How to Make *Pasta all'Uovo, Fatta in Casa*
HOMEMADE EGG PASTA

I knew none of the following steps and formulae when I was served my first plate of *pasta fatta in casa.* It was Thanksgiving Day and I had been in Rome about 6 weeks. My Italian was nonexistent except for early morning sessions with the cook-carekeeper of the apartment. Dictionary in hand, I'd look up things like potatoes, meat, and a vegetable and carefully say that that would be my dinner. Rina, the cook, with a ready smile would repeat the words after me and promise it would be ready at any time I wanted it. And it was Rina who invited me for Thanksgiving. She explained slowly that her mother would like to meet the American signorina and she knew it was a feast day and would be honored if I would come. I suppose because I had given no wild parties I was thus, perhaps, due an honor. So off we went, midmorning of the day, to arrive about noon at the modest apartment where Rina's mother and some of her 13 brothers and sisters then lived, a public housing type of building for people who'd been bombed out during the war. Everything was new, including the dining-living room, jammed to its corners with as many chairs as would fit. Each chair, it being just before the feast, was draped with huge sheets of pale gold pasta, drying briefly before its cutting and cooking. I knew of pasta but had never seen it spread for the feast so to speak.

Everyone tried to talk slowly and loudly and explain the dishes, the past, the war, and who did what, and I in turn talked to them. When the mammoth platter came to the table, steaming with the pasta and a Bolognese sauce, I could hardly believe the sight. My first forkful was so delicate, yet so rich I couldn't believe it, but the conversion to life in Italy had begun. Rina's family glowed with friendship for me, representing all of the U.S., and I glowed back, ready for the next bite. MR

The only utensils you really need are a clean flat surface no smaller than 24 × 24 inches, a fork, and a perfectly cylindrical rolling pin, or a food processor paired with a pasta-rolling machine. Illustrations on pasta making appear on pages 23–25.

As for ingredients, the Italian rule of thumb is 1 (American medium) egg and a scant ¾ cup of flour per person, but remember that the average Italian portion of pasta could be considered overabundant for the American serving.

For beginners we advise starting with a small batch of pasta: let's say 2 eggs, approximately 1½ cups of flour, and a pinch of salt, for 2–3 people. This will give you not only expertise in the making of pasta but also a good idea of how many eggs and cups of flour you will eventually need for the exact number and size of portions you wish to serve.

As the number of servings grows, a process of de-escalation takes place, i.e., 6-egg batch for 8 servings, 7-egg batch for 10, 9-egg batch for 12, and so on. To make a batch that will serve 6 American portions:

3½ cups all-purpose, unbleached flour (approximate)
5 medium eggs (room temperature)
¼ teaspoon salt

This batch will make *fettuccine, linguine,* or *tonnarelli* for six, or about 150 *tortellini* or 50 *ravioli* or lasagne sheets for 1 lasagne for six. The same amount of pasta will make approximately 20 *cannelloni.*

Homemade Pasta

1. Turn your mound of flour into a crater and break the eggs into it.

2. Beat the eggs with a fork held in one hand. Use the other hand to shore up the walls of the crater.

3. It gradually becomes too difficult to work the newly created dough with a fork.

4. Put the fork aside and begin working with your hands.

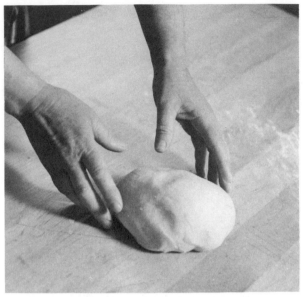

5. Knead the dough well until it is smooth and elastic to the touch and the working surface is practically clean.

6. Flour the working surface and rolling pin lightly and begin to roll the pasta out.

7. Continue rolling until the pasta is the desired thickness, about that of a dime.

8. Fold the pasta over and over itself into a flat roll about 4 inches wide.

9. Using a sharp knife, slice the roll into strips. Different widths make different pasta cuts; in this case, strips about 1/4 inch wide are cut for *fettuccine.*

10. If using a pasta machine, break off a piece of dough the size of the palm of your hand, flour it, and send it through the adjustable rollers set at their widest distance apart.

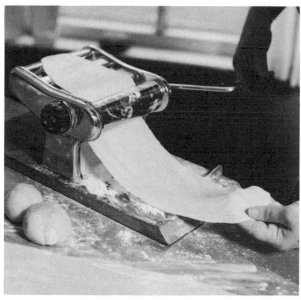

11. Send the pasta through the machine again and again, reducing the space between the rollers until the pasta has reached the desired thickness.

12. To cut *fettuccine,* dry the rolled pasta about 15 minutes, flour lightly, and send it through the wider cutting rollers.

To make by hand:

Make a mound of the flour in the center of your working area, which may be a pastry board or kitchen counter or table. Stirring with your fingers, make a hole in the top of the mound, and keep on stirring until you touch your working surface and have turned the mound into a crater with walls high and thick enough to contain the eggs, which you now break into the middle. Add the salt.

Start beating the eggs with a fork held in one hand. As the beaten eggs try to flood through the walls, your other hand should embrace the crater and should keep building up the outside all around, bottom to top, simultaneously managing to spill some flour inside. The two motions combined will make the eggs inside absorb more and more flour, and will turn the two elements into one thick paste.

When it becomes too difficult to continue with the fork, flour your hands and work the paste with your fingers, admittedly a sticky business at first. Adding more flour slowly will turn the paste into a real dough. Keep on flouring your hands and the work surface until the dough can't absorb any more flour.

By the way, if your ball of dough is too hard, flaky, and in general doesn't want to amalgamate smoothly, it means that more flour has been used than the eggs can absorb. To reestablish the balance, mix in a little water, a few drops at a time. Do it when nobody is watching because this procedure is scorned by the professionals. Nobody else will know the difference.

At this point you'll have some flour left over (the quantity depending on the size of the eggs, quality of flour, moisture of the room, and other variables), but it won't be wasted. Push it aside, and scrape the surface of the working area clean. This is also the moment to clean your hands if they're still sticky. As you get more proficient, you'll reach this point with almost clean hands.

Once you've tidied everything up, flour your hands and working surface, and begin to knead the ball of dough. Everyone develops his own technique for kneading, but the standard one is to push the ball of dough down with the open palms of your hands and roll it away from you. At the end of the roll, press hard with the heels of your hands, spreading the dough out into an oblong shape. Fold it over so that it becomes even more oblong. Then lift it, and, while bringing it back toward you, double it over on itself and slap it onto the working surface. The dough is almost a ball again, and is ready for another kneading cycle.

Keep kneading for about 10 minutes, sprinkling flour on the working surface from time to time, or until you have a ball of dough that is smooth, golden, and elastic. By this time, the working surface should be almost spotless (clean it up if it isn't), and you are ready to roll.

To roll by hand:

Break off a piece of dough the size of a tennis ball and pound it flat with your hands. Flour your rolling pin, and roll it over the dough so that the spreading action is from the center toward the edges. When the dough is visibly thinner, turn it by 90°, and roll again. Since this process tends to squeeze the moisture out of the dough, keep dusting the working surface, rolling pin, and dough with flour. Keep rolling this way until you reach the desired thickness, which we can best describe as about that of a dime.

When you have reached the thickness desired, put the sheet to rest on a clean, dry towel, and get to work on the remaining dough.

To make by machine:

You can also make pasta with the food processor, which cuts your work time in half. The food processor will do some of the kneading for you and a rolling machine can finish the job.

If you wish to make your pasta using the food processor, start with a small batch (see page 22).

Place the flour and salt in the bowl of a food processor with the steel blade and pulse on/off. Beat the eggs slightly with a fork and pour them very slowly into the bowl with the processor on. When the eggs are in, pulse on/off three or four times and then process until the flour and egg mixture forms a ball at the end of the blade (or is in the form of tiny pellets which cling together well when pinched), about 1½ minutes.

If the ball does not form and the dough does not cling, add 1 or 2 teaspoons of water slowly with the motor on and process another 30 seconds or so. When the dough clings well or forms a ball, remove it and form it into two balls of pasta.

To roll pasta by machine:

Break off a piece just smaller than the palm of your hand. Flour the piece and press it as flat as you can. Send it through the widest gap of the machine rollers 4 to 5 times, folding it in half at each pass. At first the dough will be slightly ragged but by the last pass through the gap it should have smoothed out to almost a silky texture. Now reduce the width of the gap, send the pasta through, and keep reducing the gap between the rollers and passing the pasta until you reach the thinness you need.

Tortellini uses the thinnest of pasta as does angel hair, while *fettuccine* and *linguine* are the next up on the scale and the *tonnarelli* cut for square spaghetti is as thick as it is wide.

Rolled pasta can wait spread out and covered with clean kitchen towels until all the pasta is ready to be cut.

Pasta Verde
GREEN PASTA

In recent years *pasta fatta in casa* has taken on more colors than the rainbow and a whole lot of new flavors. Most of the colors change drastically when cooked, as do the flavors used. We stick with the two principal pasta colors—pale gold and green. Pasta, after all, is to complement the sauce and vice versa, and the more the colors and herbs change the harder it is for the pasta to work with what we like to think of as an infinity of sauces.

Green pasta is just like *pasta all'uovo* but with fresh or frozen minced spinach substituted for 1 or more eggs, depending upon how many servings are made. This recipe has been developed for the food processor.

10 ounces fresh or frozen spinach
3½ cups all-purpose unbleached flour

3 medium eggs
1 teaspoon salt

To use fresh spinach, wash and remove the stems. Cook the leaves briefly in as little water as possible with the salt. Drain thoroughly, pressing the spinach against the sides of a sieve. (If you have cheesecloth handy, wrap the cooked spinach in it and squeeze dry.) Coarsely chop the spinach.

To use frozen whole or chopped spinach: cook in boiling salted water, drain and squeeze dry as above. Chop the whole spinach leaves coarsely. With the steel blade in place, put the flour in the food processor bowl. Add the spinach and process on/off until well mixed, a matter of a few seconds.

Beat the eggs slightly and add slowly to the spinach-flour mixture with the processor on. Process, pulsing on/off until the mixture has formed tiny pellets that cling together when pinched or a ball of dough has formed on the end of the blade.

Remove the mixture from the processor, knead briefly, and start rolling it out with the pasta-rolling machine as in the preceding recipe (page 27). (If making green pasta by hand, add the minced spinach to the eggs and beat together slightly before adding to the flour. Proceed as for *pasta all'uovo.*)

Whether rolling *pasta verde* by hand or by machine, bear in mind that the dough takes just a bit longer to get to the cutting stage. With a pasta-rolling machine, you will see that the green dough tends to shred more than the yellow dough on its first trip through the rollers because of the moisture in the spinach. It is by no means uniform in color throughout, but as you keep working it the green becomes solid and the pasta gets as smooth as heavy silk. Pay no attention to the look, flour the dough, fold it and, undaunted, keep on sending it through. Roll it to the desired thickness and spread on clean kitchen towels until all of it is ready to be cut. Proceed as described on page 29.

Pasta all'Uovo: How to Cut It

Fettuccine: Yellow or green, let your rolled dough rest on a clean kitchen towel. The timing depends on the climate of the kitchen but should never be so long that the edges become brittle. If cutting by hand, fold the pasta up in a flat roll about 4 inches wide. With a very sharp knife, cut the roll in ribbons (which is what the name *fettuccine* means) about ¼-inch wide. After every few cuts, stop to pick up the *fettuccine* and shake them out. Flour the towelling or counter slightly and spread the cut pasta out to dry further. *Fettuccine* may be used at once or may continue to dry. The drier the *fettuccine,* the more fragile they are and the longer they take to cook. Very dry pasta takes about 5 to 6 minutes while the very fresh cook in 2 to 4 minutes.

Linguine: This cut is the same thickness as *fettuccine* but just about half the width. Follow cutting procedure for *fettuccine.*

Tonnarelli: Proceed as for the *fettuccine* but cut the pasta in ribbons as wide as the pasta is thick, the end result being perfectly square spaghetti. Spread the cut pasta as you would for *fettuccine,* but do not let them dry completely as they will be easily broken when they go into the pot. *Tonnarelli* are also called *pasta alla chitarra,* named for an Abruzzese guitarlike contraption they used to be cut on.

When cutting any of the above by machine, it is merely a matter of changing cutters from wide, to medium, to small. Angel hair, *Capelli d'angelo* or *capellini,* is another cut of homemade pasta. It is the thinnest and most narrow of the ribbons and used principally in soups, as its delicacy gets rather lost in most sauces. When cut, angel hair dries much more quickly than other cuts and therefore becomes brittle more quickly. Thus it may be worth your while to cut just before cooking time.

Pasta Asciutta: How to Cook It

The proof of the pasta is in the eating, which means that, packaged or homemade, it has to be cooked correctly. An old Italian saying is, "The death of the pasta is by boiling it: it can go to hell or to paradise in the process." For a heavenly pasta, the rules are few and simple, and so are the tools. Essential are a pot big enough to contain at least 1 quart of water per serving of pasta (if you are cooking only 1 or 2 portions, however, you should start with at least 3 quarts of water), a long wooden fork or spoon, and a capacious colander for draining. True pasta lovers today can buy the perfect pasta/stock pot in stainless steel with its own built-in colander. This

29

allows you to drain the pasta by just lifting the colander out of the pot.

The Water: The water should be brought to a rolling boil, then salted with 1 teaspoon of salt per quart of water. Salting at this time makes the water boil more than ever. Only then is it ready to receive the pasta, which should not be dumped in all at once but in portions, to minimize the cooling of the water, and should be stirred gently to avoid sticking. The water should then be brought back to a full boil as quickly as possible. Covering the pot helps immensely at this time. Once the water is back to the full boil, uncover and stir the pasta. Purists insist this should be done with a wooden implement, as a metal one lowers the temperature and susceptible pasta suffers, but then purists wouldn't cook pasta at a high elevation either; at mountain altitudes water boils at a lower temperature.

The Cooking Time: Cooking time varies with different varieties of pasta. It ranges from 7 to 8 minutes for thin spaghetti to 12 to 15 minutes for the sturdiest *rigatoni.* Generally the time is a few minutes less than that recommended by commercial manufacturers. Homemade pasta is much more sensitive, and cooks in about 2 to 4 minutes. It also floats to the top of the water when almost done.

The main preoccupation is that, whether commercial or homemade, it cook *al dente.* Some sort of literary prize should be given to the poet who can describe *pasta al dente.* The term means that it is biteable but not raw, can be felt under the teeth but is neither crunchy nor rubbery; it means that each piece of pasta retains its individuality and texture, yet is just tender enough to please. Overcooked pasta is a mushy affair and a terrible offence to the ingenuity of generations of pasta-makers: all their creations in sizes and shapes are turned to an indifferent blob. *Al dente* then is what you must achieve in cooking, and the only way to find out when this occurs is by testing.

In Naples, homeland of *vermicelli,* legend says that the cook would extract one piece of pasta out of the boiling pot and fling it at the tiled wall: the pasta, when *al dente,* would stick to the tile for the count of three, then plop to the floor. If it didn't stick, it wasn't done yet. If it stuck longer, it was overcooked, and the cook would commit suicide. This kind of testing is not recommended.

A simple method is to fish out periodically, using the wooden implement, one piece of pasta, blow gently on it, and bite. The *al dente* stage will make itself known.

The Draining: When this critical moment has arrived, the pasta has to be drained. So, if you don't use a pot with a colander in it, have a good-size colander ready in the kitchen sink. Pour the pasta into the colander. Then put the colander over the empty pot to finish draining. This lets the last of the hot water drip into the pot, and its steam keeps the pasta warm a minute or two. For some sauces, you may need a tablespoon or two of that water at serving time. Anybody who rinses hot pasta with cold water should be condemned to eat cold pasta all of his life. (There is one exception to the above: *lasagne* or *cannelloni* pasta cuts may be put under cold water for a brief minute to aid in quick handling.)

Mixing with the Sauce: With pasta cooked and *al dente,* there is little time to waste. The pasta should be married immediately to the waiting sauce, served, and consumed. Ahh!

Pasta Asciutta: Il Sugo
SAUCES FOR *PASTA ASCIUTTA*

Even properly cooked *pasta asciutta* is nothing without a sauce. Italians call the sauce *il sugo.* The Italian-English dictionary translates *sugo* as juice, gravy, strength, vigor all combined. *Pasta asciutta* has to be married to a *sugo,* even the simplest, to become a full-bodied, satisfying entity. With the hope of being as clear as possible, we will refer to any *sugo* as a sauce, which is the most common term used in English, and get on with the game.

Some Italian sauces take hours to prepare, but many of them take only minutes. They are devised to be ready by the time the pasta is cooked. Many of them have lovely romantic names, frequently geographical, but you don't have to be a map reader or live in Italy to make the most of them. Their ingredients are generally readily available in the United States. Several standard rules apply to practically all sauces.

Use fresh herbs whenever possible, because they are always more flavorful. Probably the most frequently used herbs are basil, which combines magnificently with tomatoes, and parsley, the flat-leafed Italian variety (it has more taste than the curly type), together with its cousins celery and carrot. All herbs and other seasonings in the Italian kitchen should be used sparingly, so that no one overpowers the other. Garlic is a case in point.

As for the spices, the two most commonly used are pepper and nutmeg. Freshly ground pepper, whether white or black, is so much better than the packaged preground variety that we recommend the use of pepper mills. As for nutmeg, packaged grated nutmeg can't hold a candle to freshly grated, and we strongly urge you to use the whole nutmeg and a grater. If you can't get one, however, use packaged nutmeg but about half the amount specified in our recipes.

Use the red pepper pod stripped of its seeds to give a hot taste that can be controlled depending upon how long the pod sits in the sauce it is flavoring. Red pepper flakes tend to burn easily and get bitter, and are impossible to remove once they have done their job. Tabasco or ground cayenne are reasonably good substitutes.

Use unsalted butter whenever possible, because it has a lighter, sweeter taste. If you are using salted butter, use less salt than indicated in the recipe.

Many sauces begin with the mincing of a mixture of *odori* (literally, aromas): fragrant seasonings, celery and onion and carrot, combine with one or more herbs and a slice of salt pork. The *odori* and herbs are piled on top of the salt pork, and are sliced through into tiny pieces. Then the combination is chopped again and again, with the knife going back and forth over the pile until it is reduced to a paste. The end product is called a *battuto* (the word is the past participle of the verb *battere*, to beat, to pound). If *odori* are not treated in this way, they neither blend well nor flavor quickly. A good sharp knife and a wide cutting board are fine tools for making a *battuto.* So are the half-moon chopper *(lunetta)* and the hand-operated spring choppers that you push up and down, turning as you chop. If you are using a food processor, cut the carrot, celery and onion in chunks, the salt pork in strips and discard the thickest of the parsley stems. Put the steel blade in the bowl, add all the ingredients, and process on/off until you have the consistency you wish. You will find it necessary to scrape the sides down with a spatula but the chopping is still speeded up considerably.

Salt pork, which is called *pancetta* or *guanciale* in Italy, is the equivalent of unsmoked bacon. We have found American-made *pancetta* in Italian food stores here, but frequently it is strongly flavored with pepper, and the curing process leaves a different taste from the one we want. So we use American lean, cured salt pork (cut in ⅛-inch slices), which is very close to Italian *pancetta* in both taste and texture. It is generally soft to the touch, lightly salted, and as streaked with lean as a good piece of bacon. Most of the brands are heavily salted, so blanch the salt pork briefly before use. An alternative to salt pork is bacon. Regular thick-sliced or rindless slab bacon can be used, but it adds a smoky flavor that is not characteristic of the original sauce.

When they are in season, use really ripe fresh plum tomatoes. Their flavor and meatiness without a doubt make a superlative sauce. If fresh ones aren't available, use peeled whole canned plum tomatoes. They are produced in both California and Italy. Some, however, are canned in a very thin watery liquid instead of tomato juice, in which case drain and use the tomatoes only. As for tomato paste, handle it warily. It is a real concentrate, and can completely overpower all other flavorings.

Olive oil is another important ingredient of many sauces. It is somewhat expensive, but its flavor justifies the cost, and most sauces don't use an awful lot. Olive oil varies, however, in grade and brand. Look for pure virgin olive oil, which is delicate in flavor and light green gold in color. Its taste should be unmistakably that of olives, and should linger on the tongue briefly and then disappear. Buy small amounts of various kinds until you find the one you like. Tasted on a morsel of Italian bread, olive oil delights the palate.

Use Italian bread for tasting sauces as they simmer. It has more body and is less sweet (it should be made with wheat flour, yeast, salt, and water, and no sugar or other additives) than the average American bread. A morsel dipped in a cooking sauce should indicate the way that sauce will taste with pasta, and is a much more accurate test for the ultimate combination than a sampling of straight sauce.

In all sauces, consistency is very important. When a sauce has simmered the proper length of time, it begins to coat the spoon used to stir it.

When we suggest cooking times for sauces, we realize that stoves differ greatly. So after you have made a sauce or two that has clung to the pasta properly, make a note of your timing and stick to it.

Finally, when cooking a sauce, remember a bit of Italian advice, "A simmering sauce should not scream but murmur," which means it should bubble along gently and slowly. It should never be simply abandoned to its fate. A sauce is a living thing, and so requires attention as it murmurs on the back burner: stirring, tasting, covering, uncovering, as the case requires.

When served, many of the sauces are topped with grated cheese: *Parmigiano* or *pecorino*. *Parmigiano* (Parmesan cheese) comes grated and un-grated in the American market. A properly aged, imported, ungrated Parmesan cheese is recommended when possible. Its delicate flavor compensates for the slightly higher cost and the extra time you spend in grating it as needed. *Pecorino*, a sheep's milk cheese, is marketed in the United States under the name *Pecorino-Romano* or simply Romano cheese. It is sharper than Parmesan and some find it too sharp, in which case blend it with Parmesan to your taste.

Any sort of cheese is banned from sauces that include or are based on fish. For these and a few others where cheese would not add to the final results, the alternative is toasted bread crumbs.

We found that choosing the following sauces and pasta was like trying to catalogue "old friends": it was impossible to choose which should come first in either popularity or importance. So we decided to group them in families—taste, the use of a particular ingredient, and mood being the common denominators.

Sauces for Pasta: First Group

The first group uses butter and cheese as the principal ingredients, is marked by the absence of tomatoes, and has a mellow, soothing taste. Geographically these recipes have their roots in northern and central Italy.

Fettuccine alla Panna
FETTUCCINE IN CREAM SAUCE

This embellished modern version of the old *burro e parmigiano* is sometimes known as *fettuccine all'Alfredo.* The butter is melted with the cheese and cream in a serving bowl, and then turned into a smooth, creamy sauce without benefit of saucepan.

Years ago, during my first tour of duty in Rome, I had my first dish of *fettuccine all'Alfredo* at Alfredo alla Scrofa. With great flourish, the *maitre* served the famous dish with a golden fork and spoon, which, legend has it, were donated by Douglas Fairbanks and Mary Pickford in gratitude for perfect pasta. The pasta was further enriched by the tiniest and most perfectly cooked first-of-the-crop peas, an enrichment I shall always endorse. MR

FOR THE SAUCE:
¼ pound unsalted butter
½ cup all-purpose cream
¼ teaspoon freshly grated nutmeg
8 tablespoons grated Parmesan cheese

FOR THE PASTA:
6 quarts water
6 teaspoons salt
5-egg batch pasta all'uovo *cut into* fettuccine

Put the butter, cream, and nutmeg in a wide, shallow serving bowl or deep platter in a warm (150°) oven or, even better, on top of the pot containing the heating pasta water. When the butter has melted, stir in about ⅔ of the cheese. Keep this cream sauce warm while the *fettuccine* cooks.

When the pasta water comes to a good boil, salt it, and put in the *fettuccine* by the handful. When *al dente,* after about 3 to 4 minutes of cooking, drain it thoroughly, and put it in the bowl with the cream-butter-cheese sauce. Turn it over and over until the sauce is well distributed. Serve immediately, and sprinkle with the remaining cheese. For 6.

Rigatoni, Burro e Salsicce
RIGATONI WITH BUTTER-AND-SAUSAGE SAUCE

This is another quick sauce that practically makes itself in the serving dish while the pasta is cooking. Made with butter, sausage, cream, and cheese, it is also excellent with big shells, or any large tubular pasta of your choosing.

FOR THE SAUCE:
¼ pound unsalted butter
2 Italian sweet sausages made without fennel
½ cup medium cream
8 tablespoons grated Parmesan cheese
salt

FOR THE PASTA:
6 quarts water
6 teaspoons salt
1¼ pounds rigatoni

Put half the butter in a serving bowl, which you then either put in a warming oven or use as a cover for the pasta pot as the water comes to a boil, and let the butter melt.

Meanwhile, skin the sausages and mash them up in a small frying pan with the rest of the butter. Sauté over medium heat until cooked but not crisp. Sausages, even if all labeled Italian, come in many different sizes, weights, and especially compositions. Some are leaner, some are fatter. If the latter is the case, cook them separately, drain the extra fat, and then join them with the melted butter.

Add the sausages and their butter to that in the serving dish, stir in the cream and half of the Parmesan cheese. Once well mixed, salt to taste, and put the dish in the warming oven while the pasta cooks.

Cook and drain the pasta and put it on top of the sauce in the serving dish. Turn the pasta gently over and over until coated with sauce and sausage bits. Serve immediately and sprinkle with remaining cheese. For 6.

Fettuccine ai Funghi
FETTUCCINE WITH MUSHROOMS

An elegant way of serving pasta, this sauce uses fresh sliced mushrooms and crisp chopped parsley, whose flavors are blended with butter and heightened with grated Parmesan cheese.

FOR THE SAUCE:
¾ pound mushrooms
¼ pound unsalted butter
¼–½ teaspoon salt, or to taste
dash of pepper
3 tablespoons chopped parsley
3–4 tablespoons grated Parmesan cheese

FOR THE PASTA:
6 quarts water
6 teaspoons salt
1 5-egg batch pasta all'uovo cut into fettuccine (page 29), or 1¼ pounds egg noodles

Slice the mushrooms, stems and all, into thin wedges, and sauté them in half the butter over medium heat. After about 5 minutes, or when the mushrooms start to give up their juice, add ¼ to ½ teaspoon of salt, and pepper. Sprinkle with the chopped parsley, and cook another 2 or 3 minutes, or until the mushrooms are tender. Remove from heat, but keep warm.

Cook and drain the pasta thoroughly, and put it on a serving platter. Dot with the rest of the butter. Toss lightly. Pour the mushrooms with their sauce over the pasta. Toss again and serve with Parmesan cheese. For 6.

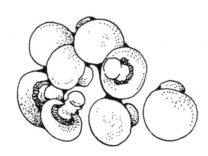

Tonnarelli alla Burina
TONNARELLI, PEASANT STYLE

In the Roman dialect *burino* is an adjective used to describe a person from the country, with peasant manners, uncouth. In times not so remote to escape my memory, a real, live *burino* existed in my life. A farmer from the Abruzzi, to round out his meager income, he would make periodic visits to our house to sell all sorts of goodies: country butter, fresh eggs, farm cheese, wild mushrooms, vegetables . . . all the best of the seasonal farm produce. Mamma would choose, buy, and put in an order for his next visit. Many times he would leave with our family's dismissed clothes, still "good for the farm"—Mamma's Brownie points toward the quality of his next delivery.

That was before World War II. During the war, with food in the city either scarce or nonexistent, he kept making his supply trips to Rome, still a *burino,* but a black-marketing one. He drove to town in a fast car and wore the latest fashions, and we became just another name in his long list of clients. He became fabulously wealthy, though he still had not much couth, and after the war turned into a movie producer. Years later I had the chance to work as cinematographer on some of his productions. I was very careful not to remind him of his previous life as a *burino:* I loved my work.

Now, can you blame me if I think of *Tonnarelli alla Burina* as a dish full of farm country flavors, but also rich and theatrical? GFR

Tonnarelli are also called *pasta alla chitarra* because of the ancient contraption strung like a *chitarra* (guitar) that was once used to cut the thin noodles that look like square spaghetti. Here, *tonnarelli* are served in a sauce made of mushrooms, peas, salt pork, cheese, and cream.

FOR THE SAUCE:
½ cup all-purpose cream
6 tablespoons grated Parmesan cheese
¼ pound unsalted butter
2 slices (2½ ounces) blanched lean salt pork (or 3 to 4 slices prosciutto)

1 cup fresh mushrooms
1 cup peas (fresh or frozen)

FOR THE PASTA:
6 quarts water
6 teaspoons salt
5-egg batch pasta all'uovo (or 1¼ pounds egg noodles)

Put the pasta water on to boil, and place your serving dish on the pot as a cover. Pour the cream into the dish, add 4 tablespoons of the cheese and half of the butter. (If you like a really rich, thick sauce, use heavy cream.) Stir gently with a fork to get the cheese spread around, and let the dish sit over the warming water until the butter has melted and blended with the cheese to form a creamy sauce.

Put the other half of the butter into a big frying pan and melt it over medium heat. Dice the salt pork, and add it to the butter, cooking it until it has become translucent. The pork should add just the right amount of saltiness to the dish. (If you want to be really fancy, substitute *prosciutto* for the salt pork, but stir it in after you have tossed the pasta.)

Cut the mushrooms into thin slices. If you use fresh peas, add them to the frying pan, and cook 5 minutes. Then add the mushrooms, and cook another 5 minutes, or until both are tender. If you use frozen peas, add both mushrooms and peas together, and cook 5 minutes, or until both are tender.

If you make your own pasta, cut it into *tonnarelli* (see page 29).

Cook and drain the pasta, and pour it over the cream sauce in the serving dish. With a fork and spoon, toss the pasta well, distributing the cream sauce. Then add the mixture of salt pork, peas, and mushrooms, turn some more, and finally add the remaining 2 tablespoons of Parmesan cheese. If you wish, add even more cheese. For 6.

Pasta, Burro e Parmigiano
PASTA WITH BUTTER AND PARMESAN CHEESE

Here we have pasta served with the simplest of all sauces: unsalted butter and Parmesan cheese. If made with homemade *fettuccine*, this dish becomes a work of art, most delicate and pleasing to the palate.

FOR THE SAUCE:
¼ pound unsalted butter
6 tablespoons grated Parmesan
    cheese

FOR THE PASTA:
6 quarts water
6 teaspoons salt
5-egg batch pasta all'uovo *cut into*
    fettuccine *(or 1¼ pounds egg*
    noodles or spaghetti)

Heat the serving dish with the butter in it, either by using it as a cover on the pasta pot until you are ready to cook the pasta, or by placing it in a warm (150°) oven. In either case, let the butter melt in the dish as it warms.

When the water boils, add the salt and put in the pasta. Transfer the warm serving dish to a warm oven, if it isn't already there. Let the pasta cook at a good boil, stirring frequently until it is *al dente*, about 4 minutes.

Then drain the pasta thoroughly, and pour it on the sauce in the warm serving dish. Using a serving fork and spoon, turn the pasta over and over until it is all buttery, adding the grated Parmesan cheese as you do so until everything is nicely coated. Serve immediately on hot plates. For 6.

Sauces for Pasta: Second Group

The recipes for this second group of sauces are country cousins of the first. Again, they include no tomatoes, but the sauces are zippier. Butter has been replaced by olive oil and cured, lean salt pork, or nothing at all. They used to be (and still are, to a lesser extent) the favorites of young blades who, on the spur of the moment and generally late at night, had to have a *spaghettata*—a blend of midnight snack and spaghetti feast and convivial exchange of late news. These sauces generally come from central Italy and the beginning of the south.

Aglio, Olio, Peperoncino
SPAGHETTI WITH GARLIC, OIL, AND RED PEPPERS

This is a hot sauce, best served with spaghetti, *spaghettini*, or *linguine*. It's a game of contrasts: the bite of pepper and the flavor of the garlic versus the fresh taste and color of parsley. The amounts of garlic and red pepper, or either one of the two, can be varied to suit individual tastes. The ones we use are middle-of-the-road.

Instead of cheese, which traditionally is never used with *Aglio, Olio, Peperoncino*, a neat addition is that of toasted bread crumbs: put 6 tablespoons of unseasoned bread crumbs in a saucepan with 2 teaspoons of olive oil. Cook and stir over a medium heat until the bread crumbs are evenly toasted.

This sauce is also great as a base. Try making a double or triple batch and use it in cooking vegetables, shrimps, and other seafood, making your own sauce for pasta.

FOR THE SAUCE:
3 cloves garlic
3 red pepper pods, seeded
1/3 cup olive oil
2 tablespoons chopped parsley

FOR THE PASTA:
6 quarts water
6 teaspoons salt
1 1/4 pounds spaghetti

Sauté the pepper pods and garlic in the olive oil in a small frying pan over medium heat. When the garlic is golden and the pepper dark brown, remove them from the oil and turn off the heat.

Cook and drain the pasta thoroughly and put it on a warm serving platter or in a warm bowl.

Sprinkle with the parsley. Bring the flavored olive oil to a high heat and pour it over the pasta. Turn and mix, so that all the pasta is covered with the oil and the parsley is well distributed. Serve immediately. For 6.

Spaghetti alla Carbonara
SPAGHETTI, CHARCOAL MAKERS' STYLE

This sauce also has a base of lean salt pork and lashings of freshly ground pepper, but the added enrichment of beaten eggs gives it an altogether different flavor from the preceding recipe. It's almost a meal in itself.

In the U.S. there are so many versions of this dish that the only resemblance to the original is the name. It is said to come from the simplicity afforded the charcoal makers in making it at their camps in the mountain forests. Moreover, the abundant freshly ground black pepper would hide any charcoal dust that strayed to the plate. But I prefer to think that the restaurant at Tor Carbone once owned by Signori Micarelli was the one that launched the *Carbonara* and made it a Roman favorite. Before moving to Tor Carbone, once a location famous for its truck gardens at the outskirts of Rome, and now totally built over by the expanded city, the Micarelli had their restaurant in the center of town, near to Palazzo Chigi, the then Ministry of Foreign Affairs. The restaurant was a favorite haunt of the Ministry high bureaucrats, a fact that helped it a lot during strict wartime food rationing, with some extra—and illicit—supplies. All this would not have involved me too much if Signori Micarelli had not happened to be favorite friends of my favorite uncle, which made me their favorite honorary nephew. My house was a good four miles from the restaurant, and it is without shame that I admit that almost every evening in the blacked-out city I took the long round trip to collect one or two small *sfilatini* (a 3-ounce loaf of bread), very fresh and very illegal. But those were the days of my adolescence, of unsatisfiable appetite and of very scarce food. That was the best bread, legal or not, that I ever ate in my whole life, and my gratitude to the Micarelli is undying. To show it, the least I can do is to declare them the real creators of *Spaghetti alla Carbonara*. GFR

FOR THE SAUCE:
4 slices lean salt pork
3 tablespoons olive oil
freshly ground black pepper
3 large (4 medium) eggs
grated Parmesan cheese (optional)

FOR THE PASTA:
6 quarts water
6 teaspoons salt
1 ¼ pounds spaghetti

Dice the lean salt pork slices and sauté them in the oil until the pork is translucent. One allowance we make to ourselves is to cook the salt pork in very little oil over a low heat, and then drain it from the oil and resulting fat, as is normally done with bacon. Then we reheat the cooked salt pork in 3 tablespoons of olive oil just before mixing it with the pasta. Add pepper (several good twists of the pepper mill).

Crack the eggs onto an unheated serving platter. Beat them until foamy, and add pepper (again, several twists of the mill).

Cook the pasta and drain it the minute it is *al dente*, reserving some of the water in case you need it later. Put the drained pasta on the beaten eggs, and toss well until the heat of the spaghetti has cooked the eggs and they have coated the pasta. (If your pasta has cooled off too much, it won't cook the eggs. If your eggs aren't big enough, the dish will be a bit dry. You can remedy the latter by adding a tablespoon or so of the hot pasta water or olive oil.)

Add the lean salt pork together with its flavored olive oil. Mix again, and serve with more pepper to taste. The dish may or may not be sprinkled with the Parmesan cheese—it is a matter of individual taste. For 6.

Spaghetti al Guanciale e Pecorino
SPAGHETTI WITH LEAN SALT PORK AND ROMANO CHEESE

In this recipe, so simple it can be made on the spur of the moment, freshly ground pepper combines with salt pork (and it must be lean) and *pecorino* to make a year-round favorite.

FOR THE SAUCE:
1/4 *pound lean salt pork, sliced, diced, and blanched*
1/2 *cup olive oil*
1 *tablespoon coarsely ground pepper*
3–4 *tablespoons grated* pecorino *(Romano cheese)*

FOR THE PASTA:
6 *quarts water*
6 *teaspoons salt*
1 1/4 *pounds spaghetti*

Sauté the diced salt pork in the olive oil in a small frying pan over medium heat until it is translucent.

Cook and drain the pasta thoroughly and put it on a warm serving platter. Pour the pork bits and oil over the pasta, add the pepper, and toss thoroughly. Sprinkle with the cheese and serve. For 6.

Rigatoni Ricchi al Prezzemolo
RICH *RIGATONI* WITH PARSLEY

Out there in video-land there is a TV crew of about 15 people all told who were "turned on" to *Rigatoni Ricchi* while taping with us. A simple sauce with a sophisticated taste, like so many of the Italian kitchen, it reached repeated use instantly. Phone calls were exchanged about how the sauce alone had "made" a party or been "the highlight of the evening."

FOR THE SAUCE:
1/4–1/2 cup *garlic-oil-hot-pepper sauce, approximate (see recipe, page 39)*
4 *anchovy fillets*
4 *ounces* mozzarella, *chopped*
4 *ounces chopped parsley*

3–4 *tablespoons toasted bread crumbs*

FOR THE PASTA:
6 *quarts water*
6 *teaspoons salt*
1 1/4 *pounds* rigatoni

Bring the pasta water to a boil, add the salt, and put the pasta in to cook. Heat the garlic-oil-pepper sauce in a sauté pan. Add the anchovies, mashing them up with a fork.

Stir and cook the sauce until the anchovies have melted. When your pasta is cooked, drain it well and put it in a serving bowl. Add the garlic-oil-pepper sauce. Add the *mozzarella* and toss well. Add the parsley and toss again. Serve with toasted bread crumbs. For 6.

Sauces for Pasta: Third Group

Here comes the tomato in this third group of sauces, which we call the summer sauces. Many use tomatoes and all use the vegetables when they are at their best, in season. Some are variations on a theme, the differences among them perhaps being more apparent in the eating than in the reading.

Salsa di Pomodoro
BASIC TOMATO SAUCE

When you feel like cooking up a large amount of this sauce, do it and freeze it in containers sized for your average use. There will be many a night or day when thawing a bit of basic tomato sauce will make the start of a meal easy, quick, even touched with nostalgia if you are a tomato freak and have once used fresh plum tomatoes from your own garden.

One note of advice: always let the pan with the flavored oil cool down a minute or two before adding tomatoes or tomato sauce. This will avoid instant and furious splattering all over you and your stove.

Another bit of advice: when using canned tomatoes, use the whole plum tomatoes from Italy or California put up in their own juices, not in purée and not crushed.

1 small carrot, peeled
1 celery stalk, washed
1 small onion, peeled
3 sprigs parsley
3 fresh basil leaves
3 tablespoons olive oil

3 cups (1½ pounds) peeled plum
  tomatoes, fresh or canned
1 teaspoon salt, or to taste
¼ teaspoon sugar (optional, de-
  pending on tomatoes' acidity)

Mince the carrot, celery, onion, parsley, and basil by hand; or process on/off a few times.

Sauté the mince in the olive oil until golden in a saucepan or a pressure cooker. Add the tomatoes and salt, stir, and cover. If using a conventional pan, bring to a boil, lower the heat, and simmer 30 minutes, stirring occasionally. Taste and adjust seasonings as necessary.

If using a pressure cooker, bring up to 15 pounds pressure and cook 5 minutes. Stir and taste the sauce. Adjust seasonings as necessary and simmer for about 10 minutes, uncovered, to reach sauce consistency, thick enough to coat a spoon. For 4–6.

Maccheroni co'a Pommarola 'n Coppa
MACARONI WITH NEAPOLITAN SAUCE

The title of this recipe is Neapolitan dialect for macaroni with a scoop of tomato sauce on top. Possibly Naples's most beloved tomato sauce, it is really something special when made in season with very ripe fresh plum tomatoes.

FOR THE SAUCE:
5 fresh basil leaves
1 clove garlic
1 onion
4 tablespoons olive oil
3 cups (1½ pounds) plum tomatoes, fresh or canned
1½ teaspoons salt

pepper, to taste
6 tablespoons grated Parmesan cheese

FOR THE PASTA:
6 quarts water
6 teaspoons salt
1¼ pounds macaroni

Mince the basil, garlic, and onion practically to a paste. Sauté gently in the olive oil until golden. Chop tomatoes (whether fresh or canned) coarsely. Add them to olive oil. Cook until the natural juices have boiled down to a good thick sauce consistency. Pass through a food mill and keep warm. Add the salt and freshly ground pepper (5–6 twists of the pepper mill).

Cook and drain the pasta thoroughly and serve in individual plates with a scoop of sauce on top. Sprinkle with the Parmesan cheese. For 6.

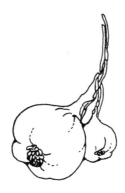

Vermicelli alla Marinara
THIN SPAGHETTI, SAILORS' STYLE

Plum tomatoes are the name of the game in this meatless Neapolitan tomato sauce lightly flavored with garlic, oregano, and red pepper. It is called Sailors' Style, perhaps because it is as common in Naples as the sailors of the famous gulf.

FOR THE SAUCE:
¼ cup olive oil
1 clove garlic, peeled
1 pod red pepper, seeded
3 cups plum tomatoes
½ teaspoon oregano
1 tablespoon chopped parsley
1 teaspoon salt, or to taste

4–6 tablespoons grated Parmesan cheese (optional)

FOR THE PASTA:
6 quarts water
6 teaspoons salt
1¼ pounds thin spaghetti (spaghettini, or vermicelli)

Heat the olive oil in a small frying pan over medium heat along with the garlic and red pepper. When the garlic is golden and the pepper deep brown, remove them: they've done their flavoring job. Cool the pan and then add the tomatoes, crushing them slightly as you stir them in. Add the oregano and bring the combination back to a boil, reduce the heat to a simmer, and cook about 20 minutes, or until the sauce has thickened. Add the parsley.

Cook and drain the pasta and put it on a serving platter. Cover with sauce and gently turn the pasta over and over. Sprinkle with cheese if you wish and serve at once. For 6.

Pasta al Burro, Pomodoro e Basilico
PASTA WITH BUTTER-TOMATO-AND-BASIL SAUCE

This perfect summer dish is made with garden-fresh ingredients. The sauce is classic with macaroni *(mostaccioli, ziti, rigatoni)*, and rather special and more delicate with homemade *fettuccine.*

FOR THE SAUCE:
1/4 *pound unsalted butter*
3 *cups (1½ pounds) fresh plum tomatoes*
6 *fresh basil leaves*
1½ *teaspoons salt*
6 *tablespoons Parmesan cheese*

FOR THE PASTA:
6 *quarts water*
6 *teaspoons salt*
1 *batch 5-egg green pasta cut into fettuccine, or 1½ pounds egg noodles*

Melt the butter in a big frying pan over medium heat. Remove from heat. Add the tomatoes.

If you use fresh plum tomatoes, peel them and cut into chunks before adding to the butter. If you use canned tomatoes, crush them gently with a wooden spoon as you stir them in.

Break the basil leaves into the pan, add the salt, raise the heat, and when the whole combination starts to boil, lower the heat to a simmer. Let it bubble along about 20 minutes, or until the juice has cooked away a bit and the color darkened. Stir occasionally during the simmering process. If the sauce hasn't simmered enough, it will sink to the bottom of the dish instead of coating the pasta when mixed.

Cook and drain the pasta, and turn it out on a deep platter or wide, shallow bowl, cover with sauce and sprinkle with the Parmesan cheese. Turn the pasta with a serving fork and a spoon to get the sauce to coat the pasta. Serve immediately. For 6.

Vermicelli alla Puttanesca
VERMICELLI, STREETWALKERS' STYLE

This is a Neapolitan dish served especially in *trattorie,* small family restaurants, of the port area. The saucy title may show that even if the Neapolitan ladies of the evening have a limited sense of morality, perhaps they make up for it in good eating habits. There are many versions of this sauce and here is the one most favored by the clientele at the Romagnolis' Table in Boston.

FOR THE SAUCE:
1 garlic clove
½ cup olive oil
6 canned anchovy fillets
3 tablespoons capers
24 pitted Sicilian black olives (packed in brine, not dried)
¼ cup chopped fresh parsley
1 cup chopped fresh peeled plum tomatoes

freshly ground pepper
3 tablespoons toasted bread crumbs

FOR THE PASTA:
6 quarts water
6 teaspoons salt
1¼ pounds vermicelli

Sauté the garlic in the olive oil until golden and then discard the clove. While the pasta water is coming to a boil, finely chop together the anchovies, capers, olives, and parsley, and add to the flavored olive oil. Add the chopped tomatoes and bring to a gentle boil and cook only as long as it takes to cook the pasta, about 8 to 10 minutes. Remove from heat. Drain the cooked pasta, put it into a hot serving bowl, dress with sauce, and sprinkle with the bread crumbs. Toss and serve immediately. For 6.

Bucatini all'Amatriciana
MACARONI IN THE STYLE OF AMATRICE

This way of serving thin macaroni in a fairly robust sauce originated in the little mountain town of Amatrice in central Italy and features tomatoes and lean salt pork. The town rests just on the border between Latium (Lazio), of which Rome is the capital, and the Abruzzi region whose capital is l'Aquila. Through the centuries, for geopolitical reasons, Amatrice was sometimes on one side and sometimes on the other of the border. The gastronomic result is that both Rome and l'Aquila make *Amatriciana* their specialty and nobody loses.

In the United States *bucatini* are also called *perciatelli.* Another version of the *Amatriciana* sauce is made with the addition of 1 medium-size onion, thinly sliced, and ⅓ cup dry white wine.

Add the onion to the oil and red pepper and cook until the onion is limp. Add the diced salt pork and cook until it is translucent. Then add the wine, stir, and cook until the wine has evaporated. Proceed as in the version of this sauce which follows. GFR

FOR THE SAUCE:
4 tablespoons olive oil
1 red pepper pod, seeded
4 slices lean salt pork
3 cups plum tomatoes
1 teaspoon salt

6 tablespoons grated Pecorino-
Romano cheese

FOR THE PASTA:
6 quarts water
6 teaspoons salt
1¼ pounds thin macaroni

Put the water on to boil for the *bucatini.*

Pour the olive oil into a large frying pan over medium heat, and add the pepper pod to the oil. Dice the lean salt pork, add it to the pepper and oil, and continue cooking over medium heat.

Remove the pepper when it has turned a dark brown (it should have seasoned the oil enough by this time, but if you like a really hot sauce, let the pepper linger longer). Continue cooking the salt pork until its fat is translucent and its lean a pale pink.

Add the tomatoes, crushing them as they go in. Bring the sauce to a boil and then lower the heat to a simmer. Keep it at a simmer about 20 minutes, or until the liquid has reduced, the color darkened, and the consistency has thickened.

Taste for salt; if the salt pork has done its job, 1 teaspoon should be enough.

While the sauce is simmering, cook the macaroni until *al dente*, stirring from time to time. Drain pasta, and put it in a deep platter, cover with sauce, and turn gently. Serve and let each person choose his own amount of cheese. For 6.

Penne all'Arrabbiata
MACARONI IN HOT TOMATO SAUCE

The literal translation of the name is "angry" *penne*. *Penne* are short macaroni that are sometimes labeled *mostaccioli* in the United States. This sauce, which isn't angry at all, just pleasantly hot, is spiced with red pepper and garlic.

FOR THE SAUCE:
¼ cup olive oil
3 cloves garlic
3 red pepper pods, seeded
3 cups plum tomatoes
4 tablespoons Romano cheese
2 tablespoons (approximate)
    chopped Italian parsley

FOR THE PASTA:
6 quarts water
6 teaspoons salt
1¼ pounds macaroni

Heat the olive oil in a flameproof casserole big enough to hold the cooked pasta. Add the garlic and pepper pods. When the garlic is golden and the pepper pods are a deep brown, discard them and turn off the heat. Add the tomatoes, crushing them as you stir them in. Raise the heat to a boil and then reduce to a simmer. Simmer the sauce for about 20 minutes, or until the tomato juice has reduced, the color has darkened, and the sauce generally thickened.

Cook and drain the pasta, and put it into the casserole with the sauce. Add the cheese. Increase the heat and turn the pasta over and over until it is coated with piping hot sauce. Sprinkle with chopped parsley and serve immediately. For 6.

Linguine Smeraldo
LINGUINE WITH EMERALD SAUCE

During the winter, when fresh basil is just a memory and we've used up our reserves of *pesto,* we use the *smeraldo* sauce to replace it.

FOR THE SAUCE:
2 cups packed parsley, with some stems
2 garlic cloves
2 ounces almond slivers
6 anchovy fillets
1 tablespoon lemon juice
1 cup olive oil
1–1½ teaspoons Tabasco (or to taste)
salt

3 tablespoons grated Parmesan cheese
1 teaspoon unsalted butter, optional

FOR THE PASTA:
6 quarts water
6 teaspoons salt
1 5-egg batch pasta all'uovo cut into linguine, or 1¼ pounds commercial linguine

Wash the parsley and discard the largest of the stems. Put the almonds and garlic in the bowl of the food processor with the steel blade in place. Process almonds and garlic to a paste and then add the anchovies, parsley, lemon juice, olive oil, and Tabasco. Process until the mixture has the consistency of thick cream. Taste and add a drop of Tabasco and a pinch of salt, as needed. If by any chance the mixture is too thick, add a bit more olive oil and pulse on/off. Finally add the Parmesan cheese.

Serve as you would *pesto:* on hot, well-drained pasta with a tablespoon of pasta water or with a teaspoon of unsalted butter. For 6.

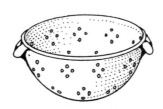

Vermicelli alla Bella Gina
BELLA GINA'S *VERMICELLI* WITH TRUFFLES AND PEAS

Here is what we consider an incredibly delicious sauce. True, truffles are a rare item, but you can order them fresh from major produce importers. Hence we recommend the best ingredients, either homemade egg pasta or top-quality commercial *vermicelli,* the tiniest fresh or frozen peas, and a piece of good Parmesan cheese to be grated at the last minute so as not to lose any of its flavor.

If you cannot find fresh truffles, we humbly suggest you skip this sauce until you can find them.

We prefer the white truffles from the Piedmont to all the other truffles, but accept the fresh black ones happily when available.

FOR THE SAUCE:
*1 10-ounce package frozen tiny peas,
    or 1 pound fresh*
6 tablespoons unsalted butter
*½ teaspoon freshly ground white
    pepper*
2 or 3 fresh truffles, sliced paper thin

*½ cup freshly grated Parmesan
    cheese*

FOR THE PASTA:
6 quarts water
6 teaspoons salt
1¼ pounds vermicelli

Cook the frozen peas a minute in boiling salted water. If using fresh peas, be sure they are tiny also, and extend the cooking time to about 4 minutes or until just tender.

Melt the butter in a medium-size saucepan over low heat. Add the pepper and peas. Continue cooking over low flame about 5 minutes to flavor the butter.

Cook the *vermicelli* and drain thoroughly, and put it on a serving platter. Add the pea-butter sauce, toss gently. Add fresh truffles and serve with the Parmesan cheese. For 6.

Spaghetti al Limone
SPAGHETTI WITH LEMON SAUCE

The name may evoke a pungent taste, but the dish is a most delicate one with the fragrance of lemon. The original recipe uses a shot of *grappa,* the fiery drink of the Alps. We have substituted vodka because of its availability on the market and also to obtain an even more delicate flavor. If you can find a good grappa in your area, go ahead and be daring.

FOR THE SAUCE:
grated zest of 2 lemons
2 cups medium cream
⅓ cup vodka or grappa
¼ teaspoon freshly grated nutmeg
juice of 1 lemon

FOR THE PASTA:
6 quarts water
6 teaspoons salt
1¼ pounds spaghetti, or 1 5-egg batch pasta all'uovo *cut into* tonnarelli

Put the pasta to cook in boiling salted water.

Grate the zest of the lemon, being careful not to grate any of the white part of the peel.

In a large skillet over very low heat put the cream and the zest of lemon and let them steep for 5 minutes. Add the vodka and stir in the nutmeg.

Drain the pasta when it is barely *al dente* and add to the sauce in the skillet. Raise the heat to medium and stir and toss the pasta until it has absorbed most of the liquid and the sauce is thick and creamy. Add the lemon juice, toss again, and serve. For 6.

Fettuccine alle Noci
FETTUCCINE WITH WALNUT SAUCE

FOR THE SAUCE:
2½ cups light cream
1 cup walnut meats, coarsely chopped
1 teaspoon of dried sage leaves, crushed, or 6 fresh sage leaves, cut in strips
pinch of white pepper
3 tablespoons unsalted butter
3 slices (3 ounces) prosciutto, *cut in julienne strips*

3 to 6 tablespoons grated Parmesan cheese or to taste

FOR THE PASTA:
6 quarts water
6 teaspoons salt
1 5-egg batch pasta all'uovo *cut into* fettuccine, *or 1¼ pounds egg noodles*

Put the cream, nuts, sage, and pepper in a saucepan at the same time as you put the pasta in boiling salted water. Bring the cream to a boil, lower the heat to medium and simmer, do not boil, until the pasta is cooked. Drain the pasta thoroughly and add it to the saucepan. Add the butter and the *prosciutto* strips and toss over medium heat until the pasta is well mixed with the sauce. Serve with grated Parmesan cheese. For 6.

Fettuccine alla Modenese
FETTUCCINE IN THE STYLE OF MODENA

This is another old recipe, which called the *fettuccine tagliatelle,* as appropriate for Modena. In adapting it for our restaurant use, we have reduced the amount of cream and butter a bit and, with a bit of license, call this *Fettuccine alla Romagnoli.* My father came from Modena, as well as a whole host of Romagnolis. And they all cling to the grand traditions of the city that vies with Bologna as the gastronomic capital of all Italy. Modena is a rich city, famous as an agricultural center with its farmers' wheeling and dealing in the public marketplace; for its production of cured meats and good wine, its university, a superlative gothic cathedral, as well as its rather comfortable (but not stuffy) way of life. GFR

FOR THE SAUCE:
8 tablespoons unsalted butter
salt to taste
6 tablespoons frozen peas
6 tablespoons sweet red, green, or yellow peppers, diced
1/4 pound fresh, medium-size mushrooms, sliced
2 cups medium cream
1/2 pound plum tomatoes, peeled, diced
4 ounces prosciutto *(slices, cut a bit thicker than for* antipasto*), cut in 1/4-inch dice*
6 tablespoons butter
1/2 cup Parmesan cheese, grated (approximate)

FOR THE PASTA:
6 quarts water
6 teaspoons salt
1 5-egg batch pasta all'uovo *cut into* fettuccine, or 1 1/4 pounds egg noodles

Melt the butter in a large sauté pan. Add the peas, sweet peppers cut in julienne strips, and mushrooms, and sauté briefly so that the flavors are drawn out but not long enough for them to lose their distinct textures and consistency. Add the cream and continue to cook over medium heat until the sauce is reduced by about 1/4. Cook the pasta *al dente* in the salted water and drain thoroughly. Add the tomatoes, *prosciutto,* and cooked pasta to the sauce; toss. Add the Parmesan cheese and the last of the butter and toss again. Serve immediately. For 6.

Vermicelli alla Siracusana
VERMICELLI IN THE STYLE OF SYRACUSE

Simply translating the name of this pasta dish doesn't tell you much at all, but a cook of Syracuse in Sicily would need no further description of this sauce made of eggplant, sweet yellow peppers, and plum tomatoes, flavored with herbs and cooked only long enough to tenderize and not so long as to lose color. The sauce is most frequently paired with *vermicelli*, very thin spaghetti, but if you're not a traditionalist, it's good with *tonnarelli* and spaghetti.

FOR THE SAUCE:
1 medium eggplant
1 large sweet yellow pepper
½ cup olive oil
1 garlic clove
2 cups peeled plum tomatoes, cut in chunks (28-ounce can plus a bit of the juice)
12 Sicilian black olives (packed in brine, not dried)

3 or 4 fresh basil leaves
1 tablespoon capers
salt to taste
3 or 4 tablespoons Romano cheese, grated or to taste

FOR THE PASTA:
6 quarts water
6 teaspoons salt
1¼ pounds vermicelli

Cut the eggplant in half and prepare as on page 234. After scraping off the salt, cut into small cubes. Roast the pepper (page 14). Remove its charred skin, core it, and cut it into thin strips.

Heat the olive oil in a big frying pan over medium heat. Add the garlic and sauté until golden, then discard it. Add the cubed eggplant and cook for 5 minutes, or until the eggplant is a bit limp and golden. Add the tomatoes, raise the heat to a boil, and then lower to a simmer.

Chop the olives coarsely with the basil and capers. (If using salted capers, wash them thoroughly.) Add these flavorings to the tomato sauce and continue simmering for 15 minutes. Taste for salt (the olives and the capers have added some) and add more if necessary. Add roast peppers just before you take the sauce off the heat.

Cook and drain the pasta and put in warm serving bowl. Add the sauce, toss gently, sprinkle with the cheese, and serve. For 6.

Fettuccine con Bieta e Funghi
FETTUCCINE WITH SWISS CHARD AND MUSHROOMS

FOR THE SAUCE:
1 pound Swiss chard
¼ pound fresh mushrooms
6 tablespoons unsalted butter
salt to taste
3 tablespoons olive oil
6 tablespoons grated Parmesan cheese

FOR THE PASTA:
6 quarts water
6 teaspoons salt
1 5-egg batch pasta all'uovo, *cut into fettucine, or 1¼ pounds egg noodles*

Wash the chard thoroughly; cut the leaves from the stems. Bring a big pot of water to boil, salt it, put in the stems, and when the water has returned to a boil add the leaves. When the stems are tender, drain the chard, pressing it down in the colander with a plate. When it's cool enough to handle, squeeze out any remaining water with your hands. Chop the cooked chard well.

Wash the mushrooms and cut them into thin slices. Melt the butter in a big frying pan and sauté the mushrooms 5 minutes or until just limp. Add salt, the chard, and the olive oil, and stir well. Continue cooking about 3 minutes, or until the chard is heated through. Taste for salt and add some if necessary.

Cook and drain the pasta and put it into a shallow, wide, warm serving dish. Dress with the mushrooms and chard, sprinkle with the Parmesan cheese, toss well, and serve. For 6.

Tonnarelli con Le Zucchine
TONNARELLI WITH ZUCCHINI

FOR THE SAUCE:
3 tablespoons unsalted butter
3 tablespoons olive oil
1–2 zucchini (9 to 12 ounces)
3–6 tablespoons Parmesan cheese, grated

FOR THE PASTA:
6 quarts water
6 teaspoons salt
1 5-egg batch pasta all'uovo *cut into tonnarelli, or 1¼ pounds spaghetti*

Heat the butter and oil in a saucepan. Cut the zucchini into long thin julienne strips. (Most food processors do a fine job of this and the strips are the size of the pasta.) Add them to the saucepan. Add the salt and cook and stir a minute until the zucchini are barely limp.

Cook the pasta in the boiling salted water until *al dente*, drain well, and place on a warm serving platter. Add the zucchini and toss well. Serve with the Parmesan cheese. For 6.

Fettuccine con Spinaci e Funghi
FETTUCCINE WITH SPINACH AND MUSHROOMS

When the chard is out of season, look for spinach and make this version of the preceding sauce.

FOR THE SAUCE:
1 pound fresh spinach, washed
6 ounces mushrooms, sliced
1 large or 2 small garlic cloves, minced
6 tablespoons unsalted butter
½ teaspoon salt or to taste
freshly ground black pepper to taste

3 to 6 tablespoons Parmesan cheese

FOR THE PASTA:
6 quarts water
6 teaspoons salt
1 5-egg batch pasta all'uovo cut into fettuccine, or 1¼ pounds egg noodles

Cut off and discard spinach stems. Cut the leaves into wide strips and sauté them with the mushrooms and garlic in the butter in a large sauté pan. Turn the spinach leaves over and over until they are wilted and the mushrooms have released their juices. Add salt and pepper to taste and remove from the heat.

Cook the pasta in abundant boiling salted water until *al dente.* Drain and place in the sauté pan with the sauce. Toss quickly over high heat and serve with Parmesan cheese. For 6.

Penne con Le Punte d'Asparagi
PENNE WITH ASPARAGUS AND TOMATO SAUCE

FOR THE SAUCE:
1½ pounds fresh asparagus
½ cup olive oil
1 teaspoon salt, or to taste
2 cups (1 pound) peeled and mashed plum tomatoes, fresh when in season
freshly ground pepper

3–6 tablespoons Parmesan cheese, grated

FOR THE PASTA:
6 quarts water
6 teaspoons salt
1¼ pounds penne

Break off and discard the root end of the asparagus and cut the edible part into bite-size pieces, putting tips in one pile and stems in another. Wash and drain each thoroughly.

Put the asparagus stem pieces and the olive oil in a big frying pan over medium heat and sauté for 2 minutes. Add the salt, stir, and add the mashed plum tomatoes. Cook uncovered over medium heat 15 minutes. Add the asparagus tips and cook another 3–4 minutes or until the tips are cooked but still a bit crisp. Add pepper to taste.

Cook and drain the pasta, and put on a warm deep platter. Add the asparagus sauce, toss gently, and serve with Parmesan cheese to your taste. For 6.

Sauces for Pasta: Fourth Group

With this fourth group of sauces, you are definitely south and so close to the sea you can taste it. These are the sea-going cousins of the third group, and fish is the defining flavor.

Linguine al Granchio
LINGUINE WITH CRABMEAT IN TOMATO-CREAM SAUCE

Basic tomato sauce and cream, paired with seafood and vodka to produce a special effect.

FOR THE SAUCE:
1½ cups basic tomato sauce (page
    43), or tomato and basil sauce
    (page 46)
3 tablespoons chopped parsley
6 tablespoons cream
dash of Tabasco sauce
1½ ounces vodka

6 ounces crabmeat, fresh cooked,
    flaked

FOR THE PASTA:
6 quarts water
6 teaspoons water
1¼ pounds linguine

Put the pasta on to cook. Heat the tomato sauce in a large sauté pan. Add the chopped parsley and the cream and simmer about 3 minutes. Add the Tabasco and the vodka and cook until the alcohol has evaporated.

Cook and thoroughly drain the pasta and add it to the sauce. Toss well. Place on 6 hot pasta plates. Dress each plate with flaked crabmeat proportionately. Serve with additional chopped parsley to your taste. For 6.

Spaghetti alle Cozze
SPAGHETTI WITH MUSSELS

FOR THE SAUCE:
3 pounds mussels
1 medium onion
1 garlic clove
3 tablespoons chopped fresh parsley
4 fresh basil leaves
4 tablespoons olive oil
1 tablespoon unsalted butter

6 peeled plum tomatoes, chopped
½ cup dry red wine
½ teaspoon salt, or to taste

FOR THE PASTA:
6 quarts water
6 teaspoons salt
1¼ pounds spaghetti

Clean the mussels with a stiff brush and pull out the "beards." Discard any mussels that do not close up at touch. Put enough water to cover the bottom of a pot big enough to hold the mussels. Bring to a boil over high heat, add the mussels, cover, and cook about 5 minutes, or until the mussels have been steamed open. Put aside to cool.

Chop together the onion, garlic, parsley, and basil, and sauté them in the olive oil and butter until the leaves have darkened and the bits of onion are golden. Add the chopped tomatoes and wine, stir, bring to a boil, and then lower the heat and simmer for about 15 minutes.

While the sauce is simmering, take the mussels out of their shells, holding them over the pot in order to save all their juice. Strain the juice through a fine sieve lined with cheesecloth. Chop all but one dozen of the mussels coarsely. Once the sauce has boiled down and is quite reduced, add the mussels and ½ cup of the strained juice. Stir and simmer slowly for another 5 to 10 minutes, or until the sauce is reasonably thick again. Taste for salt.

Cook and drain the spaghetti. Pour the sauce on top, toss, and decorate each plate with the reserved mussels before serving. For 6.

Spaghetti alla Pirata
PIRATE'S SPAGHETTI

A summer dish, when the catch of *frutti di mare*, fruits of the sea, is most abundant and varied. The act of piracy happens only in the fish market in getting a variety of the smallest and best of shellfish. Also, pirates being hot-blooded, the name of this pasta is justified by its definitely "hot" character. As for the variety, you can add to the sauce any of your favorite fruits of the sea or the best the market has to offer.

FOR THE SAUCE:
1 pound fresh mussels
1 pound fresh littleneck clams
2 to 3 small squid
*½ pound small shrimp, peeled and
  deveined*
½ cup olive oil
2 cloves garlic, crushed and peeled
2 hot red pepper pods
3 cups fresh plum tomatoes, peeled

salt to taste
2 to 3 drops Tabasco, optional
3 tablespoons chopped parsley

FOR THE PASTA:
6 quarts water
6 teaspoons salt
*1¼ pounds spaghetti or 1 5-egg
  batch pasta all'uovo, cut into .
  tonnarelli*

Scrub clean the shellfish. Clean the squid (pages 104–105) and cut into small rings. Put 4 tablespoons of oil in a soup pot large enough to contain the mussels and the littlenecks, add the crushed garlic and the seeded pepper pods. Sauté until the garlic is golden. Add the mussels and clams, cover the pot, and cook-steam, stirring occasionally, until the shells open. Let cool and remove the mollusks from the shells, letting the juices fall into the pot. Leave a few mussels and clams unshelled for decoration, if you wish.

Heat the remaining oil in a large skillet. Add the liquid and shrimp and sauté until the squid turns lavender and the shrimp has turned coral (about 1 to 2 minutes). Strain the liquid from the soup pot through a cheesecloth-lined strainer into the skillet. Chop the tomatoes coarsely and add to the skillet. Bring the sauce to a boil and reduce the heat and let it cook gently for 10 minutes. Taste for salt and add some if need be. At this point, if you wish an even hotter sauce, add the Tabasco.

Cook the pasta *al dente*, drain well, and add to the skillet. Add the chopped parsley and toss again over the heat. Put on a warmed serving platter (pirates would serve directly from the skillet), decorate with the reserved clams and mussels, and serve. For 6.

Linguine con Salsa Margherita
LINGUINE WITH BRANDY AND SEAFOOD SAUCE

In our experience in the United States, it has been difficult to find the very smallest of baby clams suitable for an extremely delicate sauce. Hence, and don't any purist throw up his or her hands in horror, we use the canned tiny baby clams. They are available in many stores, gourmet and everyday. Drained and used as freshly opened clams, they make a very acceptable substitute. Large, minced quohogs won't do.

FOR THE SAUCE:
½ cup olive oil
3 garlic cloves
1 dozen fresh mussels, scrubbed and debarbed
1 hot red pepper pod, seeded, or 2 dashes Tabasco
1 dozen shrimps, peeled
6 large mushrooms, sliced
4 tablespoons brandy
2 cups tomato sauce (see page 43)

6 tablespoons whole baby clams, canned, drained
4 tablespoons heavy cream
3 tablespoons chopped parsley

FOR THE PASTA:
6 quarts water
6 teaspoons salt
1¼ pounds linguine, or 1 5-egg batch pasta all'uovo, cut into linguine

Put 2 tablespoons olive oil and 1 tablespoon of water in a large sauté pan with a good cover. Add 1 of the garlic cloves and the mussels. Place over high heat, covered, and cook for 1 minute or 2 or until the mussels have opened.

Remove from heat and let cool a minute. Remove the mussels from their shells, letting the juice fall back into the sauté pan. Reserve both mussels and juices.

Mince the remaining garlic and put it in a second pan with the rest of the olive oil. Add the red pepper pod and sauté until the garlic is golden and the pepper pod dark brown. Remove and discard the pepper. Add the shrimps and mushrooms to the pan and sauté 1 minute or until the shrimp is coral.

Add the brandy and let cook until it has evaporated. Strain the juices from the mussel pan through cheesecloth into the shrimp. Add the mussels, tomato sauce (Tabasco, if using it), and baby clams. Add the cream. Cook and stir 30 seconds or until heated through. Remove from heat.

Cook the *linguine al dente* in boiling salted water. Drain thoroughly and place on 6 hot pasta plates. Add the sauce proportionately. Garnish with a sprinkling of chopped parsley and serve. For 6.

Fettuccine al Caviale
FETTUCCINE WITH CAVIAR AND CREAM SAUCE

Lump-fish black caviar is the least expensive and available, as is the red salmon roe, in most supermarkets. American golden caviar has made culinary headlines these last few years and is superb, available in specialty shops in many, many cities. Beluga imported caviar is for the affluent and, quite frankly, those whose palate requires the very best hesitate to serve caviar with anything at all. However, we find that the red caviar, paired with green homemade *linguine,* treats the palate and the eye quite nicely, thank you.

FOR THE SAUCE:
2 cups sour cream
¾ cup sweet light cream
6 ounces caviar (red salmon roe,
black lump fish, American
golden, or imported sturgeon
caviar)
3–6 tablespoons chopped parsley

FOR THE PASTA:
6 quarts water
6 teaspoons salt
1 5-egg batch pasta all'uovo *cut into*
fettuccine or linguine

Put the two creams in a bowl and mix gently until blended. Add half the caviar and fold it in. Cook the pasta *al dente*, drain it, and add it to the cream. Toss well and place on a hot serving plate. Sprinkle with parsley and place the last of the caviar here and there on the pasta. Serve immediately. For 6.

Linguine al Caviale e Aragosta
LINGUINE WITH CAVIAR AND LOBSTER

For lily gilders only: an enrichment of riches—Caviar and Lobster Sauce.

FOR THE SAUCE:
8 tablespoons butter (approximate)
8 ounces cooked lobster meat
*½ cup sour cream (6 heaping table-
    spoons)*
3 ounces caviar of your choice
*3 heaping tablespoons parsley,
    coarsely chopped*

FOR THE PASTA:
6 quarts water
6 teaspoons salt
1 5-egg batch pasta all'uovo, *cut into*
    linguine *or* fettuccine

Melt the butter in a small saucepan, lower the heat, and add the lobster meat. Let simmer while the pasta cooks.

Drain the pasta when *al dente* and place it on a hot serving plate. Add the butter and lobster and toss gently. Serve in individual plates, topping each serving with a heaping tablespoon of sour cream, ½ ounce of caviar, and a sprinkling of chopped parsley. Let each diner toss his own pasta. For 6.

Vermicelli alle Vongole
VERMICELLI WITH CLAM AND TOMATO SAUCE

Thin spaghetti appears this time in a delicate sauce of baby clams and tomatoes. *Vongole,* the small clams of the Mediterranean, are distant cousins of cherrystone clams, but their taste and texture more closely resemble canned baby clams. In short, the smaller the clams, the closer to the original taste your sauce will be.

FOR THE SAUCE:
*2 pounds fresh small cherrystone
    clams, or 1 10-ounce can baby
    clams*
4 tablespoons olive oil
1 garlic clove
2 cups peeled plum tomatoes
1 teaspoon salt
freshly ground pepper to taste
1 tablespoon chopped fresh parsley

FOR THE PASTA:
6 quarts water
6 teaspoons salt
1¼ pounds vermicelli

If you use cherrystone clams: wash them thoroughly and sauté them in a wide frying pan with 1 tablespoon of the oil over high heat. Stir the clams around until they open their shells. Take them from the heat and cool slightly. Remove the meat from the shells. Filter the clam juice and oil in the pan through a very fine sieve and set aside. Chop the clams coarsely.

Brown the garlic in a saucepan with the remaining 3 tablespoons of oil, and remove it when well browned. Add the clams and sauté them quickly. Add the tomatoes, clam juice, salt, and pepper (2 or 3 twists of the mill), and boil gently without a cover for 15 minutes, or until the juices have evaporated a bit, the color darkened, and the sauce thickened. Add the parsley. Cook another minute and serve.

If you use canned clams: sauté the garlic in the 4 tablespoons of oil and discard it when well browned. Drain the clams, saving the juice they're packed in. Add the tomatoes, 5 tablespoons of the clam juice, salt, and pepper (2 or 3 twists of the mill). Cook uncovered for 15 minutes or until nearly sauce consistency. Add the clams and cook gently for another 5 minutes. Add the parsley and cook another minute.

Cook and drain the pasta thoroughly, put it on a serving platter, and cover with sauce. Toss gently and serve. For 6.

Vermicelli alle Vongole in Bianco
VERMICELLI WITH CLAM SAUCE

FOR THE SAUCE:
2 pounds fresh small cherrystone clams, or 1 10-ounce can baby clams
4 tablespoons olive oil
1 garlic clove
¼ cup dry white wine
1 teaspoon salt

freshly ground pepper to taste
1 tablespoon chopped parsley

FOR THE PASTA:
6 quarts water
6 teaspoons salt
1¼ pounds vermicelli

Prepare the clams as in the preceding recipe.

Flavor the olive oil with the garlic over medium heat, discarding the garlic when golden. Add the cleaned and chopped clams, their juice, and the dry white wine. Cook over medium high heat for 2 to 3 minutes, or until the wine has evaporated. Add the salt, pepper (2 or 3 twists of the mill), and chopped parsley, and simmer for 5 minutes.

Cook and drain the pasta thoroughly, put it on a serving platter, and add the clams in the white sauce. Toss gently and serve. Please, no cheese, but you can sprinkle some toasted bread crumbs for added texture.

Sauces for Pasta: Fifth Group

The sauces in the fifth group are few, three in number, but without these three, rather like wonderful old friends, the Italian cuisine would be poor indeed. They are all meat sauces, a bit more elaborate than most of the others in that they take some planning. Each could well figure on the gastronomic coat-of-arms of its native city: *regaglie* for Rome, *ragù* for Bologna and *pesto* for Genoa.

Ideally, both the Roman and Bolognese sauces should be cooked in Italian terra-cotta pots on top of the stove, as should any long-cooking sauce, but we've found that the American-made equivalent of terra-cotta just can't take the direct heat. So we recommend enameled cast iron or very heavy stainless steel. Also, for beauty's sake alone, we aim for the prettiest heavy casserole possible when a pasta dish is to be served from the pot in which its sauce is cooked.

Rigatoni con Le Regaglie
RIGATONI WITH GIBLETS

Regaglie is the all-inclusive word for the chicken's giblets: heart, liver, gizzard. This much loved Roman dish puts *regaglie* to marvelous use in a sauce of tomatoes, onions, and mushrooms, with *rigatoni,* the big macaroni. At first reading, the recipe looks like a real production, but if done in four steps, and if you have the pots (4 of them), it shouldn't take any more time than is necessary to bring the pasta water to a boil and cook the *rigatoni.*

FOR THE SAUCE:
3 tablespoons olive oil
1 medium onion
½ stalk celery
½ small carrot
2 cups plum tomatoes
salt and pepper, to taste
1–1½ cups chicken livers, hearts, gizzards (the equivalent of the giblets from 5 average chickens, or 1 pound mixed)

½ pound fresh mushrooms
¼ pound unsalted butter
⅓ cup grated Parmesan cheese

FOR THE PASTA:
6 quarts water
6 teaspoons salt
1¼ pounds rigatoni

First step and first pot: put the pasta water on to boil.

Second step: put the olive oil in a heavy stove-to-table casserole. Mince the onion, celery, and carrot. Sauté them until golden in the olive oil over medium heat. Then add the plum tomatoes, breaking them up as you stir them in, salt (approximately 1 teaspoon), and pepper (2 or 3 twists of the mill). Bring to a boil and then reduce the heat, simmering the sauce gently about 15 minutes, or until it has cooked down a bit, its color darkened, its flavors blended.

Third step: The preparation of the *regaglie.* In a small pot (your third) boil the gizzards in salted water to cover for 5 minutes. Then skin them and chop them to bits (less than ¼ inch) with the livers and hearts. Cut the mushrooms into thin slices. Melt the butter in a sauté pan (your fourth and last pan), and sauté the *regaglie* and mushrooms quickly (about 5 minutes) over medium heat.

Cook and drain the pasta and put it into the pot with the tomato sauce, which is still simmering. Stir well and add the cheese. When that's well distributed, stir in the now cooked giblet-mushroom mixture with its butter. Raise the heat and stir again until the bits are well distributed throughout and the cheese has melted. Serve immediately. For 6.

65

Ragù I, o Sugo di Carne alla Bolognese
BOLOGNESE MEAT SAUCE I

And here it is, the classic meat sauce from Bologna. Even if the name has a French echo, the beef, pork, veal, chicken livers, tomatoes, and dry red wine form a chorus with the unmistakable accent of Emilia-Romagna. Nearly all the regions of Italy have their own variations of the theme, such as the use of dry white wine instead of red. This master sauce is served on all sorts of commercial pasta and rice, but it is traditional with homemade *fettuccine* and *lasagne.*

Considering its diversity, *ragù* is ideal for making ahead of time, and in large batches it can be stored 3 or 4 days in the refrigerator, or it can be frozen in well-sealed plastic containers.

1 slice lean salt pork
3 small onions
3 small carrots
3 stalks celery with leaves
olive oil
necks, hearts, livers, gizzards from 3 chickens
1 pound lean ground beef

1 pound mixed ground beef, veal, pork
1 cup dry red wine
4–5 teaspoons salt, or to taste
freshly ground pepper
8 cups plum tomatoes
1 small can tomato paste, plus same measure hot water

Chop the salt pork, onions, carrots, and celery over and over until they're nearly a paste. Sauté gently until golden in a big heavy pot, the bottom of which you cover with olive oil. Chop finely the chicken livers and hearts, skin and chop the gizzards, and regrind the meats if they aren't already twice ground. When the carrot, onion, celery, and salt pork are golden and limp, put in all the meats and the chicken necks, and brown thoroughly. Work the meats over with a wooden spoon, breaking up any possible lumps to insure a smooth sauce, and when the meats are well browned, add the wine and let it evaporate. Add the salt and a good

grind of pepper, and then the tomatoes, tomato paste, and water. Bring to a boil, cover, and lower heat. Simmer for 2 hours.

Remove the chicken necks, taste the *ragù* for salt, adding some if necessary. Simmer another hour without cover to reduce liquid.

If the *ragù*, because of the quality of the meats, turns out to be fattier than it should be, you can skim off the fat at the end of cooking or chill the *ragù* and then easily slip off the congealed fat. The less fat in your sauce, the better your pasta dish. For 18 servings of pasta or for *lasagne* for 12.

66

Ragù II
BOLOGNESE MEAT SAUCE II

This recipe for 6 generous servings of the traditional Bolognese meat sauce is cooked in exactly the same way as the big one. The difference is that, unexpectedly, the ingredients for the smaller batch are not exactly ⅓ those required for the recipe serving 3 times as many people. When used with *pasta all'uovo* cut either in *fettuccine* or *tonnarelli*, it makes as superb a *primo piatto* as *lasagne*.

Many people, especially in the Emilia-Romagna region, add a bit of rich cream after the sauce has cooked. When in Rome, we use a dry white wine instead of a dry red.

If you wish, this sauce as well as the larger one can be made in a pressure cooker: sauté the salt pork and flavorings in the pressure cooker until limp. Add all the meats and brown them. Add the wine and let it evaporate. Add the tomatoes, tomato paste, and water. Cover the pressure cooker and, following the manufacturer's instructions, cook as you would a stew, about 40 minutes. When the pressure falls, open the cooker, stir, taste, and adjust seasonings.

FOR THE SAUCE:
1 slice lean salt pork
½ small carrot
1 small onion
1 stalk celery with leaves
¼ cup olive oil (or enough to cover the pot bottom)
1 chicken neck, gizzard, heart, liver
1 pound twice-ground beef or mixed veal, pork, beef
½ cup dry red wine
4 cups plum tomatoes

½ cup water
1 tablespoon tomato paste
2 teaspoons salt, or to taste
3–4 tablespoons grated Parmesan cheese

FOR THE PASTA:
6 quarts water
6 teaspoons salt
1 5-egg batch pasta all'uovo or 1¼ pounds egg noodles

Cook exactly as *Ragù* I.

If using homemade pasta, see page 29 for cutting and drying.

Cook and drain the pasta and serve with *ragù* and a generous sprinkling of Parmesan cheese. For 6.

Pesto
PESTO

Pesto, a pounded basil-nut-garlic sauce, is perhaps Genoa's best-known contribution to pasta. *Pesto* means pounded, and in this case a mortar and pestle are used to crush a combination of nuts and fresh basil with cheese until, when mixed with olive oil, the juices become a sauce.

Pesto is frequently used with *linguini* and also in *minestrone* or other hearty soups, the flavors of which can stand up to such a heady addition. *Pesto* is good, also, with boiled meats and poached fish.

FOR THE SAUCE:
2 cups loosely packed fresh basil leaves
5 sprigs parsley leaves
2 medium cloves garlic
1 teaspoon salt
2/3 cup pine nuts (3 ounces approximate)
1 tablespoon grated Parmesan cheese

1 tablespoon grated Romano cheese
3/4 to 1 cup olive oil
6 tablespoons unsalted butter

FOR THE PASTA:
6 quarts water
6 teaspoons salt
1 1/4 pounds linguini

Mix together the basil, parsley, garlic, and salt, and chop them to fine bits. Crush the pine nuts with a rolling pin or meat pounder, and add them to the garlic and basil. Chop some more, and then put everything into a large mortar. Pound and grind the mixture with a pestle until a good thick paste is formed. Add the cheeses and grind some more until the paste is homogeneous. Add the olive oil a tablespoon at a time, working with the pestle until the paste has absorbed as much of the oil as it can. Depending on how moist the cheeses and the basil leaves are, you may need to use a little more or a little less oil to reach a thick sauce consistency. This *pesto* may be made with more or less garlic, depending on taste, but the proportions above produce a flavor in which the basil and garlic and pine nuts share equally.

Cook and drain the pasta (reserving a small amount of the water) and put it on a warmed serving dish or 6 individual warmed dishes. Add 1 teaspoon butter per person to the pasta and toss lightly. Then add 1 heaping tablespoon *pesto* per person and toss again. If the *pesto* has been chilled and is stiffened, you may add a tablespoon of the reserved hot pasta water to your pasta and toss again. For 6.

Blender Pesto: Coarsely chop the basil and garlic together; add the salt and put the mixture into a blender. Add half the olive oil and blend briefly at low speed until the herbs are minced. Add the cheese and pine nuts and blend at medium speed until everything is well amalgamated but not puréed. Stop blending two or three times and scrape the mince from the sides of the blender.

Scrape the mixture into a small bowl. Beat in by hand as much of the remaining oil as needed to make a thick sauce. For 6–8 servings.

Food-Processor Pesto: Place everything but the olive oil and pine nuts in the food processor bowl with the steel knife in place. Process on/off briefly until all the ingredients form a very fine mince. Slowly add the pine nuts and olive oil through the tube, continuing to process as you do so. Scrape the sides of the bowl with a rubber spatula once or twice, and stop processing when you have the consistency of a thick sauce. For approximately 6–8 servings.

To conserve *pesto,* put it in a jar with a tight lid, but before you seal it make sure a thin film of olive oil has formed on top of the herb-nut mince. If it hasn't, add a few drops of oil. Keep refrigerated until time to use and then bring it to room temperature. Do not heat in a saucepan, as the color becomes rather unattractive and the flavor dissipates a bit and changes. *Pesto* may be frozen if you make it without the cheese, adding the cheese to thawed *pesto* before serving.

Lasagne, Timballi, Pasta con Ripieni, Eccetera
LASAGNA, FILLED PASTA, AND ASSOCIATES

Geographically speaking, this tribe of first courses comes from all over Italy. Although somewhat more elaborate to prepare than other first courses, these recipes frequently can be made well in advance, so that the effort involved isn't all that demanding. The results are definitely worth a little work.

As for filled pasta—homemade pasta cut in different shapes and enclosing a filling of meat and/or cheese—we have selected a few of the most familiar. A complete list of such creations would prove one thing: that when confronted by a piece of homemade pasta, Italian cooks can't resist the temptation to invent a filling, a shape, and a name. The differences are regional or so subtle (contemplate, for example, *ravioli: agnolotti, bauletti, marubini; tortellini: cappelletti, anolini, agnolini . . .*) that we had to stop short in compiling our list and retreat, famished, to the kitchen. The following recipes are just an introduction to the unending, wonderful possibilities of filled pasta.

Filled Pasta

1. To make *cappelletti*, cut the pasta into 2″×2″ squares, put a dab of filling in the center of each square, fold over the diagonal, and press the edges together tightly to seal.

2. Wrap the stuffed pasta triangle around your finger, one corner over the other, and press to make them stick together. If they don't stick, moisten the corners where they overlap each other and press again.

3. If making *agnolotti* or *ravioli*, position the filling in even rows on one sheet of pasta so that each dab is the center of a 2″ × 2″ square. Cover with another sheet of pasta, and with your fingers press the two together around each mound of filling. Cut between the mounds with a pastry cutter.

Lasagne, Paglia e Fieno
YELLOW AND GREEN LASAGNA

Lasagne, Paglia e Fieno (Straw-and-Hay) is made with two kinds of egg pasta, one straw yellow and the other hay green. The pasta is layered with Bolognese meat sauce, white sauce, *mozzarella,* and Parmesan cheese. A recipe for a real feast, this one serves 12 to 14 easily. Naturally, *lasagne* can be made using only one color of pasta: a 5-egg batch of *pasta all'uovo,* or a 3-egg batch of *pasta verde* for *Lasagne Verdi.*

This is one of those dishes that is great for two cooks. But if you are making *lasagne* by yourself, with a bit of planning you can make the *ragù* a day ahead, the pasta on the morning of the day needed, and the *besciamella* (white sauce) just before layering; it all goes together simply.

Lasagne, once layered, can sit in the refrigerator before baking 5 or 6 hours without damage; but then it does take a bit more than 30 minutes to heat it through and get all the cheese melted. So allot your time accordingly. If there is any *lasagne* left after the feast, transfer it to a smaller casserole and reheat the next day. It won't have lost its character.

FOR THE FILLING:
1 recipe Ragù I (page 66)
1 recipe Besciamella *(page 73)*
2 pounds whole-milk mozzarella, *shredded*
½ cup grated Parmesan cheese

FOR THE PASTA:
1 recipe pasta all'uovo
2¼ cups all-purpose flour (approximate)

3 eggs
pinch of salt
1 recipe pasta verde
2¼ cups all-purpose flour
2 eggs
5 ounces spinach, fresh or frozen
½ teaspoon salt
6 quarts water
6 teaspoons salt

After the *ragù* is done, the *besciamella* is cooling, the cheese is grated and shredded, and the pasta is rolled, you are ready to begin assembling your *lasagne.*

Preheat the oven to 350°.

Cut both types of pasta into 6 × 4-inch rectangles about the size of a postcard or just a bit bigger. Bring the 6 quarts of water to a boil, add the 6 teaspoons salt. Drop in the rectangles one by one,

to a total of no more than 10 at a time, take the *lasagne* out the minute they're *al dente,* which takes about 3 or 4 minutes. Rinse in cold water and spread out on dish towels. Don't stack the pieces because they tend to stick together. Keep on cooking the pasta pieces in batches of about 10 until all of it is cooked.

Ladle a thin layer of *ragù* into the bottom of a large ovenproof casserole (14 × 10 × 3 inches is a good size). Cover with pieces of yellow pasta, a layer of sauce, and 5 or 6 generous tablespoons of *besciamella.* (If you wish to be Roman, instead of *besciamella* use *ricotta,* 2 pounds of it.) Sprinkle with *mozzarella.*

Repeat the layering, alternating yellow and green pasta until the casserole is filled. Finish with a layer of grated *mozzarella,* sprinkle with Parmesan cheese, and bake for half an hour (at 350°), or until all the cheese has melted. Cool about 15 minutes before cutting, so that the sauce, cheese, and *besciamella* cling together and the *lasagne* can be cut into slices without falling apart. For 12.

Besciamella
WHITE SAUCE

Here is the basic white sauce used for layering *lasagne,* covering *cannelloni,* and making casseroles in general. This recipe makes enough for a large (12 to 14 servings) *lasagne,* and is of medium consistency, a factor controlled by using more or less flour as you wish.

¼ pound unsalted butter
¾ cup all-purpose flour, unbleached
4 cups milk

½ teaspoon nutmeg, freshly grated
½ teaspoon salt
¼ teaspoon white pepper, freshly grated

Melt the butter in a heavy 2-quart saucepan over low heat.

Add the flour to the melted butter all at once. Continue to cook, stirring until blended.

Bring the milk to scalding and add it all at once to the flour, stirring all the while. Continue to stir and cook over a medium heat for at least 4 minutes or until smooth and thickened and does not taste of uncooked flour. Remove from heat and add the seasonings. Taste for flavor and adjust as necessary. Makes 4½ cups.

To keep for a while before using, cover with plastic wrap pressed down on the surface.

Lasagne di Magro
LASAGNA WITH SEAFOOD

Like all the other dishes using *di magro* in the title, this is a meatless dish originally developed for use during the Lenten fast days prescribed by the Catholic Church. It may include other types of fish than we have used here, the market being the deciding factor.

This can be prepared in stages, as the Bolognese *lasagne,* or if you wish you may layer individual *lasagne* in gratin dishes.

When using *besciamella* for fish *lasagne,* add 2 tablespoons chopped fresh parsley.

FOR THE FILLING:
1 recipe besciamella *(page 73)*
1 recipe fish broth *(page 105)*
1 pound fresh fillet of sole
1 pound fresh small shrimp
1 pound fresh salmon
8 tablespoons unsalted butter
3 anchovy fillets
12 ounces fresh mushrooms, sliced
1 ounce dried mushrooms, soaked in
   warm water

⅛ teaspoon white pepper, freshly
   ground
½ cup unflavored bread crumbs
¼ cup grated Parmesan cheese

FOR THE PASTA:
6 quarts water
6 teaspoons salt
1 3-egg batch pasta verde, *cut in rectangles about the size of a postcard*

Make the *besciamella* and set it aside to cool with plastic wrap pressed down on the top.

Make the pasta, cut it into the 6 × 4-inch rectangles, cook them 3 to 4 minutes, and spread out on kitchen towels.

In 4 cups of fish broth, poach the three kinds of fish, one after the other until almost but not quite cooked through completely. The best pan for this is a large and deep frying or sauté pan. As the fish are cooked, spread out on a platter. The sole fillets do not have to be cut. The salmon should be cut into less-than-bite-size pieces.

Melt 3 tablespoons of the butter in a saucepan. Add the anchovies and stir. Add the fresh mushrooms and cook about 4 minutes. While the fresh mushrooms are cooking, remove the dried mushrooms from their water, cut in pieces about the size of the fresh mushrooms, and add them to the saucepan. When the anchovies have more or less melted and the mushrooms have given up their liquids, add pepper, stir, and remove from heat.

Butter a lasagna pan and dust it with bread crumbs. Place pasta overlapping slightly to cover the pan bottom. Spread the sole fillets, reserving one, over the pasta and dot with about half the shrimps. Using a pastry bag, make about 4 strips of rosettes of *besciamella* or ribbons over the length of the pan. Cover with pasta.

Make a second layer, using half the mushroom mixture, more *besciamella* rosettes or ribbons, and cover with another layer of pasta.

Sprinkle with ¾ of the salmon bits. Add the *besciamella* and cover with pasta.

Make the final layer of fish, using the last of the sole and salmon, and dot with the remaining shrimp. Make the *besciamella* ribbons or rosettes and cover with pasta. Tuck the ends of the pasta and the sides down with the help of a knife or spatula.

Make a topping of the last of the mushrooms. Dot with the last of the *besciamella* and sprinkle with the bread crumbs.

Melt the remaining 5 tablespoons of butter and dribble back and forth over the top. Sprinkle with the Parmesan cheese.

Bake at 350° for ½ hour and then let rest for 15 minutes before cutting. For 10–12.

Lasagne al Sugo di Funghi
LASAGNA WITH MUSHROOM SAUCE

This meatless version of the classic *lasagne* is very light, very delicate, and very special. To make it even more so, add some dried *porcini* mushrooms or, when available, some fresh wild mushrooms. The mushroom sauce by itself can be used with *fettuccine*.

FOR THE SAUCE:
15 sprigs parsley
1 garlic clove
1 5-inch sprig fresh rosemary, or 1
*   teaspoon dried*
6 tablespoons unsalted butter
3 tablespoons olive oil
3 cups peeled plum tomatoes
½ cup tomato purée
½ cup water
1 pound big mushrooms

1½ teaspoons salt
¾ cup grated Parmesan cheese

WHITE SAUCE:
1 recipe Besciamella *(page 73)*

FOR THE PASTA:
1 4-egg batch pasta all'uovo, *cut for*
*   lasagne*
6 quarts water
6 teaspoons salt

Make the egg pasta, cut it into 6″ × 4″ rectangles and dry briefly on clean dish towels or floured cookie sheets.

Make the *besciamella* and let it cool.

Chop the parsley, garlic, and rosemary thoroughly, and sauté in butter and olive oil until limp, about 5 minutes.

Chop the tomatoes coarsely and add to the flavored olive oil. Add the tomato purée and water, bring to a boil, lower the heat, and simmer while you prepare the mushrooms.

Clean and slice the mushrooms into ¼-inch-thick slices. Add them to the simmering tomatoes. Sprinkle with the salt, stir, cover, and continue cooking about 15 minutes. Taste for salt and add some more if necessary. The sauce at this time should have condensed somewhat, coat the spoon, and be dark in color.

While the sauce is simmering, bring a pot of at least 4 quarts of water to a boil, salt it (1 teaspoon to each quart), and cook the *lasagne* a few at a time. Using a strainer, remove the *lasagne* when they have floated to the top and are *al dente* (this takes about 3 to 4 minutes). Drain them in a colander as all the remaining pasta cooks. Rinse in cold water and spread out on dish towels.

While you preheat the oven to 350°, the assembling process may begin. Coat the bottom of a *lasagne* baking dish (14″ × 10″ × 3″) with a very thin layer of mushroom sauce, 2 or 3 tablespoons. Cover with a layer of *lasagne.* Add another thin layer of sauce, then form a layer of *besciamella* by evenly spacing the tablespoonsful of the white sauce about 2 inches apart. Sprinkle with some Parmesan cheese. Add another layer of pasta. Continue until all the ingredients are used up, aiming to finish with a layer of Parmesan. Tuck the pasta in all around the edges.

Bake (at 350°) for about 30 minutes. Cool for 15 minutes before cutting. For 8.

Agnolotti
PASTA CIRCLES, FILLED

Agnolotti, circles of pasta filled with meat, cheese, and spinach, seasoned with nutmeg, take a bit of time and practice to make, but are a lovely opener for any meal. Since the meat in the filling, as in most fillings for pasta, should be cooked before it is sent through the meat grinder, this is an appetizing way to use a bit of leftovers from an earlier meal.

FOR THE FILLING:
2–3 slices pork loin (or beef or veal), cooked or uncooked
5 ounces (½ package) frozen chopped spinach
½ teaspoon salt
1 large egg
1 teaspoon freshly grated nutmeg
8 tablespoons grated Parmesan cheese

freshly ground white pepper
3–4 tablespoons unsalted butter

FOR THE PASTA:
1 3-egg batch pasta all'uovo
5 quarts water
5 teaspoons salt

If you are using uncooked meat, cut off any extra fat, melt a tablespoon of butter in a small frying pan, and sauté quickly over medium heat until done on both sides. Do not overcook.

When cooked, cut the meat in halves or thirds for easy handling, and put it through a grinder, using the smallest grind, or process in a food processor. Cook the spinach in boiling salted water, drain it thoroughly, and put it through the grinder or processor. Place the meat-spinach mixture in a medium-size bowl, add the egg, and stir to mix everything well. Add the nutmeg, 3 tablespoons of cheese, and 2–3 twists of the pepper mill. If you haven't got white peppercorns, a pinch of black will do. Stir the mixture again and set it aside to fill pasta circles for 6 servings, about 15 to a serving.

The pasta for *agnolotti* is made in the same fashion as any homemade pasta, but because it must stick together, it is just a little more moist than usual, and it must be filled and sealed before it dries out at all.

So, when you have rolled out 2 big sheets of pasta (or 3 to 4 pairs of matching strips with the pasta machine), cover all the pasta sheets but one with plastic wrap or a dampened, very well wrung-out dish towel. On the uncovered pasta, drop little dabs of filling in even rows, positioning the filling so that each dab is the center of a potential circle 2 inches in diameter. Cover this sheet of pasta with another, and with your fingers press the two together around each bit of filling. (If the edges are not well pressed together, cooking water can seep in and make a very watery and unsatisfactory *agnolotto*.) If by any chance the pasta has dried too much before cutting, the pasta won't stick together with pressing. So, dampen (with a wet finger) around the mounds of filling before putting on the top sheet of pasta.

Using a 2-inch cookie cutter, cut between the

2-inch circles so that the mounds of filling are the center of each circle and the circles themselves become individual pillows. Put the cut *agnolotti* on a flour-dusted cookie sheet until time to cook. They may dry an hour or so before cooking. Or they may be refrigerated a few hours until use. Or you may freeze them and then cook them days later without thawing them.

Bring the water to a boil, salt it, and put in the *agnolotti* a few at a time. They float to the top immediately and crowd for position, so keep the pot at a low boil but covered, and cook for about 8–10 minutes, or until the pasta pillows are tender at the edges. Remove them with a slotted spoon and drain thoroughly.

Serve immediately with butter and the remaining 5 tablespoons of Parmesan cheese, or with tomato sauce (page 43) or *Ragù* II (page 66). For 6.

Ravioli

A filling that is most popular uses *ricotta* and spinach and no meat, and we call the resulting pasta *ravioli.*

FOR THE FILLING:
1 pound fresh ricotta
1 large egg
¼ cup grated Parmesan cheese
freshly grated nutmeg
½ teaspoon salt

5 ounces cooked, chopped spinach,
  squeezed dry

FOR THE PASTA:
1 3-egg batch pasta all'uovo
5 quarts water
5 teaspoons salt

Mix all the ingredients together well. Place about a teaspoon of the mixture on a pasta sheet. Drop more teaspoonsful of the mixture about 1½ inches apart until you have used it all up.

Cover the pasta sheet with a second sheet and then cut in squares, enclosing the little piles of ricotta with a pastry cutter, or use a *ravioli* form. Check all the cut *ravioli* to make sure their edges are sealed. Cook in slowly boiling salted water until the pasta is *al dente.* Serve with just butter and more Parmesan cheese or with tomato and basil sauce (see page 46). For 6.

Tortellini alla Panna
TORTELLINI IN CREAM

Homemade pasta, cut in squares, filled with a mixture of meat, poultry, and *mortadella,* is folded to look like little hats, called *cappelletti* or *tortellini.*

Delicious when cooked and served in broth, *tortellini* are positively superb when served in a cream-and-cheese sauce. Here are directions for both the filling and the pasta for about 100 *tortellini,* enough to serve 6–8 persons worthy of such a treat.

FOR THE SAUCE:
1 recipe cream sauce (page 34)

FOR THE FILLING:
4 tablespoons white meat of turkey
    (or chicken)
2 slices mortadella
4 tablespoons ground veal
4 tablespoons ground pork
2 tablespoons unsalted butter
1 tablespoon finely chopped parsley
3   tablespoons grated Parmesan
    cheese

1 teaspoon freshly grated nutmeg
½ teaspoon salt
freshly ground white pepper
1 egg

FOR THE PASTA:
1 3-egg batch pasta all'uovo

TO COOK THE PASTA:
3 quarts broth

The filling: Cut a small slice of turkey (or chicken) breast, and chop it into ¼-inch bits. Chop up the *mortadella* also, discarding any pieces of peppercorn. Melt the butter in a saucepan over medium heat, and add all the meats and chopped parsley, stirring everything around as it cooks quickly (2–3 minutes). When the poultry meat has whitened, and the veal and pork have cooked to a toasty color, scoop them out and grind them twice in a meat grinder so that they are smooth and pasty.

Put the meat mixture in a bowl, and add the cheese, nutmeg (if using preground from a can, be sure it is still fragrant and use only ½ teaspoon), salt, 3–4 twists of the pepper mill, and egg. Mix well.

Remember that in this recipe it's cook's

choice: if you don't have turkey, substitute chicken; you can use beef instead of veal; you can use white meat of poultry and *mortadella;* but the combination of all the meats is pretty special, and we recommend it.

The pasta: make your *pasta all'uovo* and roll it first as thin as for *fettuccine,* and then continue rolling until it's almost paper thin.

At this point you will want to work quickly because this pasta must be folded before it dries out and becomes fragile. Naturally the more helping hands, the better the work goes, and once stuffed, *tortellini* can sit for hours. So once you've rolled your pasta, cut it into 2-inch squares. Put a tiny dab of filling on a square of pasta. Fold on the diagonal, pressing along the edges to seal. If the dough

79

doesn't seal with pressure, dampen the inner edge with a drop of water on your fingertip and press again.

Now you have a stuffed triangle. Take the two corners of the base and wrap them around the tip of your finger. Press the corners together so that they stick. If they don't, moisten the corners where they overlap each other and press again. Fold the third corner, which sticks up, back on itself, and there is your first *tortellini*. Keep on filling, sealing, pressing, and turning, until all the squares have turned into what looks like little hats.

To cook *tortellini*, bring the broth to a boil and put in all the little hats by the handful, bring the broth back to a boil and cook gently for about 10–15 minutes, or until the pasta is tender.

The sauce: meanwhile make the cream sauce by putting the butter to melt with the cream on a platter in a warm oven. When the butter has melted, add the Parmesan cheese and stir. Keep the sauce warm until the *tortellini* are cooked. Drain them thoroughly, saving the broth for future use, and put them on the warm platter with the cream sauce. Turn them over and over gently until they are well coated with sauce. Serve immediately. For 6.

Tortellini Gratinati
BAKED *TORTELLINI*

1 batch tortellini *(page 79) or 1 pound approximately*

4 tablespoons unsalted butter

1 tablespoon all-purpose flour, unbleached

2 cups milk, scalded

1½ teaspoons nutmeg, freshly grated

¼–½ teaspoon salt, or to taste

¼ teaspoon white pepper, freshly grated

3½ ounces Fontina (to be measured), coarsely grated

2 tablespoons grated Parmesan cheese

1 ounce prosciutto, *cut in strips from thin slices*

While the *tortellini* cook in boiling salted water, melt the butter in a heavy saucepan over low heat. Add the flour all at once and whisk rapidly until blended. Add the milk all at once, stirring constantly, and continue to cook and stir until the flour mixture has blended into the milk and the sauce has thickened and no longer tastes of uncooked flour (about 4 minutes).

Stir in the seasonings and about ¾ of the Fontina.

Pour the sauce over the now cooked and drained *tortellini*. Mix well and put in 6 gratin dishes. Place the strips of *prosciutto* over the *tortellini* and add the last of the Fontina and the Parmesan.

Place the dishes in a moderately hot (350°) oven until the cheese on top has melted and become toasted. For 6.

Tortellini in Pasta Sfogliata
TORTELLINI IN PUFF PASTRY SHELLS

12 pastry shells, baked
1 batch tortellini *(page 79) or 1 pound approximately*
3 tablespoons unsalted butter
1½ cups tomato and basil sauce (page 46)

½ cup cream
3 tablespoons Parmesan cheese
¼ teaspoon freshly grated nutmeg, or to taste

Place the pastry shells in a warm oven until the sauce is ready.

Cook the *tortellini* in boiling salted water, drain thoroughly, and return them to their warm cooking pan in a warm place. Add ½ tablespoon of butter to the *tortellini* and stir gently to keep them from sticking to each other.

Put the tomato sauce in a blender or food proccssor and blcnd or proccss until smooth.

Bring the cream to scalding and whisk in the cheese. Keep on the heat until the cheese is melted and the cream thickened. Add the nutmeg. Pour the tomato sauce into the cream. Keep on heat briefly and add the butter.

Stir in the *tortellini* and then ladle them into the pastry shells. Cover the shells with their caps and add a few *tortellini* and sauce around the shell. For 6.

Cannelloni e Spinaci
CANNELLONI WITH *RICOTTA* AND SPINACH

FOR THE FILLING:

1 pound ricotta

1 egg

4 tablespoons grated Parmesan cheese

½ teaspoon nutmeg, freshly grated

½ teaspoon salt

10-ounce package chopped frozen spinach, cooked and drained

FOR THE SAUCE:

1 recipe tomato sauce (page 43)

3 tablespoons unsalted butter

4–5 tablespoons grated Parmesan cheese

FOR THE PASTA:

1 3-egg batch pasta all'uovo

5 quarts water

5 teaspoons salt

Prepare the pasta and cut into 4- × 5-inch rectangles. Cook them and cool and dry on a clean dish towel.

Prepare the tomato sauce.

Preheat oven to 350°.

Mix together the *ricotta,* egg, Parmesan cheese, nutmeg, salt, and spinach. Spread 2–3 tablespoons of the filling down the center of each rectangle and roll up, letting one side overlap slightly making 12 to 18 *cannelloni.*

Butter an ovenproof casserole large enough to accommodate the rolls, and put a thin layer of tomato sauce on the bottom. Cover with filled pasta rolls, fold side down. Put 1 tablespoon of tomato sauce (more if you wish) on each *cannellone.* Dot with butter and sprinkle with Parmesan cheese. Bake (at 350°) for about 15 minutes and serve. For 6.

Rotolo di Pasta alla Fiorentina
PASTA ROLL, FLORENTINE STYLE

1 4-egg batch pasta all'uovo

1½ pounds fresh ricotta

1½ pounds fresh spinach (approximate) or 2½ 10-ounce packages frozen leaf spinach

¼ pound mushrooms, thinly sliced

¼ pound mozzarella, grated

½ cup Parmesan cheese (2½ ounces approximate)

2 eggs

¼ pound prosciutto, sliced

3 cups tomato and basil sauce (page 46)

Make the pasta and roll it out until it is the thickness of *lasagne* sheets. Cut it into a large rectangle, about 10 by 14 inches. Cook 3 to 4 minutes, remove from water and place the pasta on a large piece of double cheesecloth on the counter.

Put the *ricotta* in a large bowl. If using fresh spinach, cut off and discard the stems. Cook the spinach in a minimum of boiling salted water. Drain well and chop fine. Add the spinach, mushrooms, *mozzarella,* Parmesan cheese, and eggs to

82

the *ricotta* and mix carefully. Add salt and pepper to taste.

Leaving a 1-inch margin all around, cover the pasta sheet with the cheese mixture and then with *prosciutto* slices. Using the cheesecloth to nudge the pasta and its filling along, roll the pasta slowly up like a jelly roll, beginning with one of the short sides. Tie the cheesecloth at both ends of the roll. Place the roll in a fish poacher or a roasting pan with a rack. Cover with boiling salted water. Bring to a gentle boil and poach for 30 minutes. Remove the roll from the water, let it drain and cool a few minutes, and then unroll it carefully onto a serving platter. Slice into 1-inch slices. Dress with a tablespoon of hot tomato and basil sauce. For 6.

If using a microwave oven, the cooking procedure is as follows: roll up the filled pasta. With a very sharp knife cut it carefully in 12 slices. Place 2 slices of roll in each of 6 gratin dishes. Add the tomato and basil sauce. Cover with plastic wrap and cook 1½ minutes. For 6.

Timballo di Fettuccine
FETTUCCINE CASSEROLE

FOR THE FILLING:
6 ounces unsalted butter
5 eggs
1 pound ricotta
8 ounces Parmesan cheese
2 cups besciamella *(page 73)*
¾ pound mortadella, *cut in ribbons like* fettuccine
½ pound mozzarella, *cut in ribbons like* fettuccine
¾ cup unseasoned bread crumbs

3 cups tomato and basil sauce (page 46) (optional)

FOR THE PASTA:
1 2-egg batch pasta all'uovo, *cut into* fettucine, *or 10 oz. egg noodles*
1 1-egg batch pasta verde, *cut into* fettucine
6 quarts water
6 teaspoons salt

In the salted boiling water, partially cook the pasta, drain it well, and place in a large bowl. Add all but a bit of butter (to use to butter the spring form pan) and toss well.

Put four of the eggs in a large bowl and beat well. Add the *ricotta* and mix well. Add 6 ounces of the Parmesan cheese and the *besciamella* and mix again. Finally, combine the pasta, the cheese mixture, the *mortadella,* and the *mozzarella,* and mix until all the ingredients are well distributed.

Preheat the oven to 375°.

With the remaining butter, butter a 9-inch spring form pan. Sprinkle with bread crumbs. Twist and turn the pan to make as many bread crumbs adhere as possible. Reserve those that don't. Fill the pan with the *fettuccine* mixture. Sprinkle with the last of the Parmesan cheese and the reserved bread crumbs. Beat the last egg and drizzle it back and forth over the top of the pan. Bake 40 minutes at 375° or until the top is toasted and the mixture is hot through. Let cool 15 minutes. Remove from pan to a platter and cut in wedges. Serve as is or with a dressing of tomato and basil sauce. For 10 ample portions.

Cannelloni alla Toscana
CANNELLONI, TUSCAN STYLE

Cannelloni are another of the incredibly mouth-watering combinations of egg pasta cut in rectangles and rolled up with a delicate filling, this time of meat, chicken livers, eggs, and spinach. They are then smothered with *besciamella,* and baked in an oven.

FOR THE FILLING:
½ pound ground beef
½ pound chicken livers
½ package frozen spinach (or 5 ounces fresh)
7–8 tablespoons unsalted butter
1 teaspoon salt
½ cup dry white wine
4 eggs
¾ cup grated Parmesan cheese

FOR THE PASTA:
5 quarts water
5 teaspoons salt
1 3-egg batch pasta all'uovo

½ recipe besciamella *(page 73)*

Roll out the pasta as you would for *lasagne,* cut it into rectangles 4 × 5 inches, and cook to the *al dente* stage. Remove from boiling water and spread out on dish towels.

For the filling, you can use already cooked beef or veal if you wish, or fresh, lean chopped meat. Put it through the meat grinder with the chicken livers. If you use fresh spinach, remove the stems and discard them. Briefly cook fresh or frozen spinach in boiling water with ½ teaspoon of salt, drain thoroughly, and squeeze out as much water as possible. Send through the meat grinder with the livers and beef for a second grinding.

Melt 3 tablespoons butter in a frying pan over medium heat. Add the meats and spinach, cook and stir quickly for 3 minutes. Add the white wine and cook until it evaporates. Add ½ teaspoon of salt and cool a minute or so. Scoop out the meat and spinach mixture (leaving the melted butter in the pan), and mix well with the eggs and half the Parmesan cheese.

Put 2 or 3 spoonsful of filling on each pasta rectangle and roll up, letting one side overlap slightly. Keep on filling and rolling until all the rectangles are used making 12 to 18 *cannelloni.*

Preheat the oven to 350°.

Prepare half a recipe of *besciamella* and cool slightly.

Butter a shallow casserole (better yet, individual casseroles with room for 2 or 3 *cannelloni*), put in the *cannelloni* seam side down; spoon over them the reserved butter and juices from the frying pan, cover with *besciamella,* dot with butter, and sprinkle with the remaining cheese. Bake (at 350°) until the cheese has melted and turned golden and the *cannelloni* are hot all the way through, about 20 minutes. For 6.

Insalata di Pasta
PASTA SALAD

1 1/2 pounds rotini or penne
3 ounces black olives, pitted
1 sweet red pepper, cored and diced
1 sweet green pepper, cored and diced
1 small cucumber, seeded and diced
1/2 medium onion, minced
3 stalks celery, peeled if necessary, finely sliced
1 1/2 cups mayonnaise (pages 216–17) plus 3/4 cup to serve apart

1 pound medium shrimp
2 tablespoons wine vinegar
1 bay leaf
half a lemon
3 or 4 peppercorns
salad greens, 3 to 4 nice leaves per person
6 tomatoes (optional)
parsley sprigs (optional)

Cook the pasta in boiling salted water. Drain well, rinse under cold water, and place in a large bowl. Add the prepared vegetables and the mayonnaise or other dressing and mix well.

Cook the shrimp in boiling salted water to which you have added the vinegar, bay leaf, lemon, and peppercorns. Drain thoroughly, rinse in cold water, and pat dry with paper towels. Place salad leaves on each of 6 plates. Add the pasta salad. Garnish with 3 to 4 shrimp. If you wish, make roses of the tomatoes and add them along with parsley sprigs for further garnish. Serve with extra dressing. For 6.

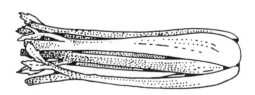

Minestre
SOUPS

Depending on your mood, the weather, and the market, *minestre* (soups in general) make a great alternative to pasta as a first course. Like pasta, *minestre* can appear in many shapes and tastes.

There are the *minestrine,* the light soups like *pastina in brodo* (little pasta shapes in broth), that are designed for light dinners or to precede hearty second courses. These are usually made with a fairly delicate broth combined with a variety of pasta or rice.

Then there are the ordinary, everyday soups that usually hide under the generic term *minestre.* They are made with a broth base also, meat or chicken or vegetable, and frequently combine rice or pasta with a vegetable, such as *riso e indivia* (rice and endive soup).

Finally, there are the big vegetable soups that are called *minestroni* (big soups) or *zuppe.* They can be filling enough to make a dent in the healthiest appetite and reduce the cook's work for the remaining courses. One famous example is Milan's *minestrone,* with its infinite variety of fresh and dried vegetables.

In and around these three basic types of soup—perhaps above and beyond them—is the extra special soup, a Sunday soup whose makings take a little extra time to prepare. Under this heading, we put the broth honored with little stuffed pasta shapes such as *cappelletti* or *tortellini.*

Italy's many fish soups—*zuppe di pesce*—also fall in this extra special category. A proper *zuppa di pesce* is so glorious it can stand alone, followed only by a salad, to make a perfect meal.

Brodo di Carne
BEEF BROTH

Plain beef broth takes about 10 minutes to organize and 2 hours to simmer. It can be made with fresh beef brisket, the small end of a bottom round roast, or soup cuts. If made in quantity, broth freezes well in plastic containers. It can be kept in the refrigerator for 3 or 4 days. The King of *Brodo* (it's masculine in Italian) is that which comes with a *bollito misto* (page 133).

When making broth for rice or *pastina in brodo,* we usually estimate 2 cups per person, plus a little more for the pot. The amounts of broth specified in any one recipe reflect this estimate. If you have big soup lovers at the table, you may want to be more generous.

1–1 1/2 pounds beef
3 teaspoons salt
1 1/2 celery stalks with leaves
2 carrots
1 medium onion
2–3 plum tomatoes (or 1/2 table-
*   spoon tomato paste)*

1 1/2 pounds beef bones
1 bay leaf
1 teaspoon dried tarragon or 1 sprig
*   fresh*
2 egg whites (optional)

Put the beef and all the other ingredients, except the tarragon and egg whites, in cold water to cover (3 quarts should be enough; if not, add a bit more). Bring to a boil slowly, uncovered, over low heat. When the liquid first boils, scoop off any froth that forms, lower the heat, add the tarragon, cover the pot, and simmer for about 2 hours. The meat should be tender, the broth a light, clear brown and flavorful.

Strain the broth, saving the meat for future use and throwing out the now overcooked vegetables and the bones. If the broth is fatty, you may want to chill it and then remove the congealed fat, or just take it off immediately with a spoon or bulb baster.

If you want a really clear broth, beat the 2 egg whites lightly, bring the defatted broth to a boil, and mix in the egg whites, beating with a wire whisk. Boil for about 3 minutes, or until the particles have been absorbed by the cooked egg whites. Turn off the heat, and when the broth has settled, scoop off the now speckled egg whites with a slotted spoon and pour the broth through a sieve lined with 2 layers of cheesecloth. For 6 to 8.

Brodo di Pollo
CHICKEN BROTH

Chicken broth, like beef broth, is used in making many soups as well as for rice and *risotti* and basting meats as they cook, and in making aspic.

If you wish to use the fowl or chicken for salad or as an addition to soup, we think it's best to remove choice parts after they have simmered an hour; bone the pieces, putting the bones back to simmer, and cut the meat as you wish.

1 3-pound fowl or chicken	*3 teaspoons salt*
1 stalk celery with leaves	*5 peppercorns*
1 onion	*1 soup bone*
1 carrot	*3 quarts cold water*
3–4 plum tomatoes	*2 egg whites (optional)*

Put everything into a big pot over a low heat, add the water, and bring it to a boil slowly. Once the pot boils, scoop off the froth that forms, cover, reduce the heat, and simmer for at least 2 hours. Strain, using a colander or sieve lined with 2 layers of cheesecloth to catch the bits of vegetable and bone marrow. Skim off excess fat with bulb baster, or chill thoroughly and remove congealed fat from the top with a spoon.

If you want a very clear broth, use beaten egg whites for clarifying as described in the preceding recipe for beef broth. For 6 to 8.

Tortellini in Brodo
TORTELLINI IN BROTH

You can find *tortellini* hand or machinemade in pasta shops or in Italian specialty stores and most supermarkets. If you make your own, you will get the delicate taste of the traditional *tortellini* (see page 79 for directions).

3 quarts broth
1 batch tortellini (1 pound approximate)

4–6 tablespoons grated Parmesan cheese

Bring the broth to a boil, put in the *tortellini* by the handful, bring the broth back to a gentle boil, and cook for 10 to 15 minutes, or until the pasta is tender. (Frozen *tortellini* take a bit more time and can be cooked without thawing.) Serve in soup plates with the broth and a generous sprinkling of the Parmesan cheese. For 6.

Mariola all Calabrese
OMELET BITS IN BROTH

This broth-base soup with the pretty name comes from Calabria. It is filled with small cut shapes of thin herb-seasoned omelets.

4 large eggs
6 tablespoons fine bread crumbs
salt and pepper to taste
1/4 teaspoon marjoram

1 teaspoon chopped parsley
1 1/4 quarts chicken broth
3 tablespoons grated Parmesan cheese

Beat the eggs thoroughly. Sift the bread crumbs and add them, along with the salt, pepper, marjoram, and parsley, to the beaten eggs.

Melt a bit of butter in an omelet pan or heavy frying pan over a medium high heat and pour in just enough egg mixture to make a thin omelet. As soon as it's solid on the underside, turn it, and as soon as the second side is cooked, remove it to a plate. Keep on making thin omelets until you have used up everything.

When the omelets are cool, cut them into about 1/2-inch squares or use aspic cutters to cut pretty shapes.

Bring the broth to a boil, drop in the omelet shapes, and serve after the broth has come back to a boil. Sprinkle with the Parmesan cheese. For 6.

Stracciatella alla Romana
BROTH WITH BEATEN EGG

Stracciatella is translated literally as "torn to rags," because when eggs, flavored with cheese and nutmeg, are beaten and dropped into boiling broth, they shred as they cook. Raggedy is certainly the way they look. Classic *stracciatella* is made with a combination of chicken and beef broths as fat-free as possible.

There are, however, a number of versions of this soup, and the second most commonly found uses bread crumbs instead of flour, but we find the results less delightful. For an even lighter soup, leave out the flour entirely.

In the Marche region, the grated rind of a half a lemon is added to the eggs, replacing the nutmeg for a very pleasant accent.

3 eggs
1 tablespoon flour (optional)
6 tablespoons grated Parmesan cheese

dash of nutmeg or grated lemon rind
2 quarts chicken-beef broth

Beat the eggs well, adding the flour if you are using it and half the Parmesan cheese and a dash of nutmeg as you beat. Bring the broth to a boil, add the beaten eggs, stirring constantly with a wire whisk for half a minute or so to make sure all the eggs have been cooked by the broth. Remove from the heat, pour into a soup tureen, and if the eggs tend to cling together again, whisk once more. Serve with a sprinkle of the remaining cheese on each dish. For 6.

Pastina in Brodo
PASTA BITS IN BROTH

Probably the simplest of all broth soups, this dish leaves a lot of leeway to the cook. The broth can be homemade beef or chicken broth, or it can be made with 12 cups of water and 12 bouillon cubes (8 chicken and 4 beef is a good combination).

The pasta shapes are cook's choice. If you use *tubettini,* small shells or bows, the amount indicated, 2 cups, is good. If you use noodle flakes, 1 cup is sufficient. Either way, it's ½ pound of pasta. In Italy, when the larder lacks *pastina,* ½ pound of spaghetti or *linguine* is wrapped up in a clean dish towel and crushed into tiny bits, thus producing instant *pastina.*

12 cups of broth
2 cups small pasta

3–4 tablespoons grated Parmesan cheese

Preparing *pastina in brodo* is about like cooking any pasta: bring the broth to a good boil, add the *pastina,* and bring the pot back to a boil. Cook uncovered until the pasta is done. Ladle out into individual soup plates, sprinkle with the Parmesan cheese, and serve. For 6.

To make for 1 person, follow this rule of thumb: about 2 heaping tablespoons of *pastina* per 2½ cups of broth.

Quadrucci e Piselli
PASTA SQUARES AND PEAS IN BROTH

Tiny pasta squares *(quadrucci)* and new peas in chicken broth make this a delicate Roman *minestra.* If made with homemade pasta and the smallest of new peas, this soup is fit for a banquet.

Making a *battuto,* the mincing of favorite herbs with or without salt pork, is a basic procedure for soups, sauces, roasts, and fillings. (See page 32.)

If making your own pasta, roll it out as for *fettuccine* (see page 29). Cut 10 or 12 strips the width of *fettuccine,* move them apart from the roll of pasta, and cut them again at ¼-inch intervals, at right angles to the first cut, thus making tiny squares. Keep on cutting, first the long, folded strips and then the squares. Spread out to dry on a dish towel until time to use, up to 5 or 6 hours if you wish, or weeks if dried thoroughly.

Quadrucci are available in stores, either under their proper name or as noodle flakes.

FOR THE BATTUTO:
1 stalk celery
½ carrot
1 onion
1 slice lean salt pork (1 ounce approximate)

FOR THE SOUP:
3 tablespoons unsalted butter

10-ounce package frozen tiny peas or 1 pound fresh
2½ quarts hot chicken broth
2-egg batch pasta all'uovo or ½ pound noodle flakes
3–4 tablespoons grated Parmesan cheese

Pile the celery, carrot, and onion on the strip of salt pork and chop the whole thing to a paste *(battuto).* Melt the butter in a big soup pot, add the *battuto,* and cook over medium heat until golden and limp. Add the peas and cook for 2 or 3 minutes. Add the hot broth and bring to a boil for 8 minutes. Then add the pasta squares and continue boiling until the pasta is cooked. Homemade pasta takes about 5 minutes, commercial pasta about 8. Stir the soup, which is now medium thick, and sprinkle in the Parmesan cheese so that it melts without lumping. Cook 1 minute more and serve. For 6.

Risi e Bisi
VENETIAN RICE AND PEA SOUP

Risi e bisi is Venetian dialect for rice and pea soup so thick you can almost eat it with a fork, a sensational as well as a substantial first course.

1 small onion
3 tablespoons chopped parsley
3 tablespoons olive oil
3 tablespoons unsalted butter
2 slices prosciutto, *cut in ¼-inch cubes (2½ ounces)*

10-ounce package frozen peas or 1 pound fresh
1 quart chicken broth
1 cup rice, medium grain*, or Italian arborio
grated Parmesan cheese

Mince the onion and parsley together. Put the oil and butter in a big, heavy pot over medium heat and add the minced onion and parsley. Sauté until the onion is translucent and limp. Add the peas and *prosciutto.* Sauté until everything is coated with butter and oil. Add the broth and bring to a boil and then add the rice. Reduce the heat and simmer about 15 minutes, stirring frequently, or until the rice is tender. The soup is now very thick. If you prefer a thinner (and less traditional) soup, add a cup or two of hot broth at this time.

Serve with a sprinkle of Parmesan cheese on each portion. For 6.

*See discussion of rice on page 112.

Riso e Indivia
RICE AND ENDIVE SOUP

1 bunch curly endive
1 clove garlic
½ cup olive oil
1 tablespoon tomato paste or 2 plum tomatoes

2½ quarts hot water
2 teaspoons salt
1 cup long-grain rice
grated Parmesan cheese

Break the endive apart and wash thoroughly. Shake as dry as possible and chop fine. Sauté the garlic in olive oil in a big soup pot over medium heat. When the garlic is golden, not browned, discard it and add the tomato paste. Stir and cook until blended. Add the chopped endive and cook 2 or 3 minutes, until wilted. Raise the heat, add the water, salt, and rice, and bring to a boil. Then lower the heat and cook gently, stirring occasionally, about 12–14 minutes, or until rice is done. Serve with a sprinkling of Parmesan cheese. For 6.

There is a nice variation for this one: substitute hot chicken broth for the hot water, and eliminate the garlic and tomato from the flavored olive oil. Just heat the olive oil, add the endive, and cook 2 or 3 minutes. Add hot broth and rice and bring to a boil. Continue cooking 12–14 minutes as above and serve. For 6.

Riso e Indivia al Pomodoro
RICE, ENDIVE, TOMATO SOUP

Fresh tomatoes make the real variation in this rice and endive soup, which is also flavored lightly with the classic *battuto* of onion, herbs, and pork.

FOR THE BATTUTO:
1 slice lean salt pork (1 1/4 ounces
    approximate)
1/2 onion
1/2 stalk celery
1 small carrot
4 sprigs parsley
2 tablespoons olive oil

FOR THE SOUP:
10 fresh, ripe plum tomatoes
1 bunch curly endive
salt to taste
1 quart hot water
1 cup long-grain rice
grated Parmesan cheese (optional)

With a knife or food processor make a *battuto* by mincing the lean salt pork with the onion, celery, carrot, and parsley. Sauté mixture until golden in the oil in a soup pot over medium heat. Once the bits are golden, turn off the heat.

Plunge the tomatoes into boiling water for about 3 minutes, drain them, and when cool enough to handle, peel them. Cut them open and remove the seeds. To save all the juice possible, do this over a plate, letting the juice and seeds fall in the plate to be strained into the soup pot after the chunks of tomato go in.

Add the cut-up tomatoes to the soup pot, turn the heat to medium high, and cook and stir for about 10 minutes.

Wash and chop the endive and add it to the pot, which is still on medium high heat, and cook for 3 or 4 minutes. Taste for salt (the pork adds some), and add some if necessary. Add the hot water, bring back to a boil, add the rice, and continue cooking until the rice is done (about 12–14 minutes). Serve hot. Optional: add a sprinkle of cheese to each dish. For 6.

Riso e Fagioli
RICE AND BEAN SOUP

Rice and bean soup is another member of the same large family of winter *minestre* that combines a vegetable and its broth with either pasta or rice to make what some of our friends call Italian soul food.

2 cups cooked kidney or shell beans
    or a 20-ounce can drained and
    rinsed
½ cup olive oil
1 clove garlic (optional)
1 onion
1 stalk celery

1 tablespoon chopped parsley
3 plum tomatoes (or 1 tablespoon
    tomato paste)
2½ quarts hot water
1 cup medium-grain rice
3–4 tablespoons grated Parmesan
    cheese

If using dried beans: put ½ pound in water to cover, bring to a boil, cook 2 minutes, turn off the heat, and let stand an hour. Then bring back to a boil, reduce heat, and simmer until the beans are tender.

Put the oil in a generous soup pot, sauté the garlic until golden (if you want to use it), and discard it. Mince the onion, celery, and parsley together, and cook them in the olive oil until the onion is translucent. Add the tomatoes and cook on a low heat for 10 minutes. Add the beans together with the hot water. Raise the heat and cook 2 or 3 minutes to flavor the beans. Crush a few beans against the side of the pot with a wooden spoon to make the soup thicker. Add the rice, stir, and boil gently for approximately 15 minutes, or until the rice is plump and cooked. Serve with a sprinkle of Parmesan cheese. For 6.

Minestrone alla Milanese
VEGETABLE SOUP, MILANESE STYLE

This is the big soup made with a garden of fresh vegetables, a *battuto* of seasoned herbs and vegetables, and a dried vegetable or two. The various ingredients go into the pot according to their cooking times: the ones that take the longest go first, e.g., fresh shell beans, when you are lucky enough to find them in season. The dried vegetables used to be a staple in *minestrone,* and they were soaked for hours prior to cooking time, but today's cook can easily resort to canned kidney or shell beans or chickpeas. Both yesterday's and today's cooks vary the vegetables according to the seasonal market, so feel free to add leeks, fresh tomatoes, purple cabbage, small green beans, etc., when you find them.

Naturally, there are many versions of this *minestrone.* We have adopted the one most commonly used whose ingredients are readily available on the American market year-round. The very, very original Milanese version also included thin strips of pork rind cooked with the *battuto.* Today's cooks reach for the same effect by doubling the original amount of salt pork in the *battuto.*

Minestrone is served hot in winter with a slice of toasted (even better, fried) Italian bread in the bottom of the soup plate and a sprinkling of Parmesan cheese on top. Serve at room temperature in summer.

The Genoese add 2–3 tablespoons of *pesto* (pages 68–69) to *minestrone.* As for the cheese on top, a good Genoese will add half Parmesan and half *pecorino.*

FOR THE BATTUTO:
1 stalk celery with leaves
1 onion
1 carrot
2 slices lean salt pork (2½ ounces approximate)
1 sage leaf
3 tablespoons olive oil or enough to cover the bottom of the pot

FOR THE SOUP:
2½ quarts hot water
3 teaspoons salt
2 stalks celery

2 carrots
3 potatoes
¼ cauliflower
2 medium zucchini
¼ head escarole
¼ head curly endive
¼ small cabbage
1 cup fresh spinach leaves
½ small onion
1 cup green peas
3 plum tomatoes
1 cup rice (or small macaroni)
½ cup canned chick-peas, strained and rinsed

*½ cup canned kidney, cranberry, or
shell beans, strained and rinsed*

*6 slices Italian bread
3–4 tablespoons grated Parmesan
cheese*

You begin a *minestrone* with a *battuto:* this time
you chop to a paste the three seasoning vegetables
along with the lean salt pork and the herb, sage.
Chop all these coarsely, and then keep chopping
(using either a knife or half-moon chopper or a
food processor with a steel blade) until everything
is reduced to a paste. When the *battuto* is ready,
sauté it in the olive oil in a big soup pot. Once the
battuto is golden, the *minestrone* is on its way.

Add to the pot the hot water and the salt; raise
the heat to high. Slice the celery, carrots, and 2 of
the potatoes into ¼-inch bits. Break the cauliflower into small pieces, preserving as much as possible the individual flowerlets. Put these 4 vegetables to boil in the flavored water for 10 minutes
while you prepare the other vegetables. Slice the
third potato with a potato peeler into paper-thin
slices and add them to the pot. Chop the zucchini
in half, then quarters, and then slice these into
½-inch bits. Break the escarole, endive, cabbage,
and spinach into ½-inch pieces. Slice the onion
into slivers. Add these, the peas, and the tomatoes
to the boiling pot, lower the heat, and let bubble
along for about 15 minutes. If you wish, add 1 cup
of rice at this time, to make a northern variation,
or a cup of small macaroni to make a southern
version.

At the end of 15 minutes, or when all the
vegetables are done, mash half of the cooked beans
and half of the chick-peas, and stir them into the
pot together with the remaining whole beans. Cook
for another 5 to 15 minutes, depending on how
thick you wish your soup. The real *minestrone* has
a nice thick consistency, although some prefer it
thinner. For 6 to 8.

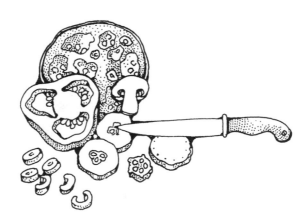

Minestrone alla Calabrese
VEGETABLE SOUP, CALABRIAN STYLE

A southern Italian variation of *minestrone*, Calabrian vegetable soup uses a variety of summer vegetables and seasons them with sweet yellow peppers.

FOR THE BATTUTO:
4 slices lean salt pork (approximately 5 ounces)
2 tablespoons chopped parsley
1 stalk celery
1 small carrot
½ clove garlic
4 fresh basil leaves
4 tablespoons olive oil

FOR THE SOUP:
1½–2 quarts hot water
1 teaspoon salt
1 pound mixed summer vegetables:
   peas, green beans, ripe plum tomatoes, zucchini, spinach, carrots, celery, potato
1 large yellow sweet pepper
½ cup rice
grated Parmesan cheese

Make a *battuto* by chopping the salt pork, parsley, celery, carrot, garlic, and basil until everything is reduced to a paste.

Heat the oil in a big soup pot, add the *battuto*, and sauté over medium heat until golden. Add the hot water and salt, and bring to a boil.

Meanwhile, chop the summer vegetables into pieces no bigger than ½ inch. If using a potato, slice it as finely as possible (with a mandoline slicer, a peeler, or a food processor). Add all the chopped vegetables when the water reaches a boil and simmer for about 15 minutes.

If the soup seems terribly thick at this point, add a cup or so of hot water. Taste for salt and add some more if necessary.

Core a yellow sweet pepper and cut into long, very thin strips. Add to the simmering soup.

When the carrot bits (or the vegetable that takes longest to cook) are tender, add the rice and boil gently another 15 minutes, or until the rice is done.

Serve with a good sprinkling of Parmesan cheese. For 6 to 8.

Pasta e Fagioli
PASTA AND BEAN SOUP

Nearly every region in Italy has its own version of this soup. It's made with shell or kidney beans and small macaroni (*tubetti*, elbows, squares, or broken-up spaghetti or *linguine*, as you wish). When made with fresh beans in the summer, it adds a whole new dimension to the first course.

If using fresh beans: when they are in season, buy shell beans, which are the ones with the pink and white speckled pods, frequently called cranberry beans; 1½ pounds give you enough for this soup, and the flavor is so delicious you will wish for fresh *fagioli* year-round.

If using dried beans: see page 95 for directions.

If using canned shell beans: be sure to get the ones put up without sugar. One 20-ounce can makes about 2 cups. Drain and rinse the beans.

FOR THE BATTUTO:
2 slices lean salt pork (2½ ounces approximate)
1 small onion
1 medium clove garlic
1 stalk celery

FOR THE SOUP:
3 tablespoons olive oil

3–4 plum tomatoes (or 1 tablespoon tomato paste)
2 quarts hot water
2 teaspoons salt
2 cups shell or cranberry beans, fresh or canned
2 cups small pasta
3–4 tablespoons grated Romano or Parmesan cheese

Make the *battuto.* Put the slices of salt pork on a chopping board. Top them with the onion, garlic, and celery and chop, then mince until the pile has turned to a paste.

Put the *battuto* in a big soup pot with the olive oil over medium heat. Sauté until golden, then add the tomatoes (or tomato paste) and cook again for about 3 minutes, or until the tomatoes have blended a bit and softened. Add the hot water, salt, and beans and bring to a good boil.

Once the water, salt, and beans are boiling, reduce the heat and cook until the beans are tender (if fresh) or heated through (if canned). Then crush a few beans against the side of the pot, add the pasta, and continue cooking until it is well done. By this time the soup is really so thick you may want to add a little more water. Taste for salt and add some if necessary. Serve with a sprinkling of the Romano or Parmesan cheese. For 6.

Pasta e Ceci
PASTA AND CHICK-PEA SOUP

For me the two words, *Pasta e Ceci,* are easily interchangeable with "Nonno and Friday." Every Friday that I can remember Nonno Nicola, my maternal grandfather, would come to lunch at our house. The menu invariably was pasta e ceci, baccalá alla Romana, green salad, and fruit. Nonno, invariably, would jokingly question our maid-cook if she had used any salt pork for the soup. (It was considered a venial sin then to consume any meats on Friday.) My mother invariably would suggest that Nonno came to lunch more to eye the maid than to visit us. The maid, a handsome, ruddy girl from the North, invariably would answer jokingly that God or the Pope or whoever was in charge had more important things to worry about than her using a few grams of pork. The idea of the High-Ups being busy was of some consolation to me: perhaps they would overlook some of my minor sins. Nonno Nicola was less lenient. After the meal he would question us children about our behavior at home and our grades at school. He would weigh the answers and then come up with the rewards: one shiny lira for my older brother, one shiny lira for my younger sister and, grumpily, one half lira for me. As part of the ritual, later, he would entrust me with some money and send me for the Errand: to buy his favorite cigars. Mission accomplished, he would tell me grumpily to keep the change, invariably a half lira. GFR

Pasta e Ceci is a hearty soup, flavored with rosemary, salt pork, and garlic.

In a not too remote past in Italy, grocery stores had a set of bins containing the different types of loose pasta, and shoppers would buy only what was necessary for the day. The grocer would collect the broken pieces of pasta at the bottom of the bins and mix them all together. The bits were then sold at great discount as *rimanenze* or remainders. In Rome the *rimanenze,* aside from the saving involved, were also appreciated for the special texture they gave to soups. Even today some die-hard Roman traditionalists (or gourmet?) make their own *rimanenze* by crushing to bits different shapes of pasta. You can use *tubettini,* small elbows, or a combination of the two, or you can break up spaghetti or *linguine* in 1- or 2-inch lengths.

2 slices lean salt pork (2½ ounces approximate)
½ cup olive oil
4 whole garlic cloves
2–3 plum tomatoes, or 1 tablespoon tomato paste

1 sprig fresh rosemary, or 2 teaspoons dried
3 cups cooked chick-peas or 1½ 20-ounce cans, drained and rinsed
2 quarts hot water
salt to taste

*½ pound small macaroni or broken-
up long pasta*

grated cheese (optional)

If using dried chick-peas: put 2 cups in 4 quarts of cold water with a scant ¼ teaspoon of baking soda. Soak overnight. The chick-peas will have absorbed some of the water, so add more water enough to cover the peas well and bring to a boil. Then reduce the heat and simmer slowly 2 or 3 hours, until cooked through. Proceed as with canned chick-peas, using the cooking liquid and adding enough hot water to make 2 quarts altogether.

Chop the lean salt pork to a paste. Sauté it in the olive oil in a big soup pot over medium heat. Cook until translucent. Add the garlic, tomatoes, rosemary, and 2 cups of chick-peas. Mash the re-

maining peas and add them. Pour in the hot water and bring to a gentle boil for 10 minutes.

Raise the heat and taste to see if the liquid is salty enough. Add some salt, if needed, and put in the pasta when the pot has come to a good boil. Once the pot is boiling again, lower the heat and cook slowly, stirring from time to time, until the pasta is tender.

When you serve *Pasta e Ceci,* look out for those 4 garlic cloves and discard them. Some people like this soup with a sprinkling of Parmesan or Romano cheese, but many prefer it just as it is. For 6.

Zuppa Santa
POTATO, LEEK, AND CREAM SOUP

4 California all-purpose potatoes,
  peeled and cubed (1¾ pounds)
4 big leeks, white part only (½
  pound)
1 teaspoon salt or to taste

2 tablespoons unsalted butter
½ cup heavy cream
½ teaspoon white pepper
2 tablespoons chopped chives, fresh
  or freeze dried

Put the potatoes and the leeks in a pot with 4 cups boiling water. Add salt. Bring the pot back to a boil, cover, lower heat, and simmer ½ hour or until both vegetables are well done.

Put the vegetables in a food processor and process them with the steel blade until they are puréed. Add the cooking liquid, the butter, and the cream. Pulse on/off. Taste for salt, adjust as necessary, and add the pepper. Sprinkle with chives and serve (hot in the winter, cold in the summer). For 4.

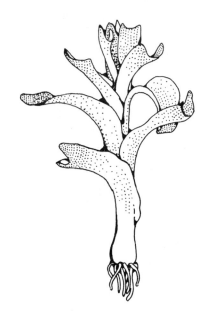

Zuppe di Pesce
FISH SOUPS

Perhaps because most Italians live close to the sea (or a well-stocked mountain lake), they understand more than others the value of its gifts: fish is highly honored on the Italian table.

Almost every sea village, if not every fisherman, boasts its own special way to concoct a *zuppa di pesce*, but by and large they all follow the same basic rules.

Remember that even if it is called fish soup, the dish is more fish than soup.

Use as many different kinds of fish as possible, including rock fish and eel.

Choose fish for varying flavors, texture, and color.

Use the fish, once cleaned and scaled, in its entirety: heads, tails, bones all go in. Remember that Italian parsimony has produced yet another proverb, *"Tutto fa brodo,"* or literally, everything makes soup. In the case of fish, everything *is* the soup. Be thereby warned that the most finicky should stay away from fish soup, or if they must, they may remove the fish heads and tails, and cook them separately, but not in the sight of a real lover of *zuppa di pesce*.

Use the largest available pot so that the fish will fit in it in the least number of layers, with the liquid used just barely covering the fish.

Be sure that the pot has a cover, so that the fish can cook by combined poaching and steaming, a very gentle process.

Be careful that the fish, whole or in chunks, is cooked but not so much as to fall apart. When adding the fish to the pot, start with the firm-fleshed kind and finish with the most tender.

When all the rules are followed, you can be assured of a feast, a celebration of the bounty of the sea. *Zuppa di pesce* should be approached with uninhibited joy, enthusiasm, and a healthy disregard for etiquette, so a large napkin and a finger bowl are recommended.

As for the preparation of the fish involved, most of it is simple and well known on this side of the ocean. But since squid seems to be less familiar on the American table, basic suggestions on how to clean it are below.

How to Clean Squid

 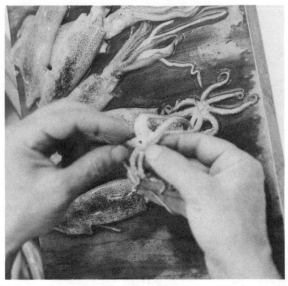

1. Cut the tentacles from the head just below the eyes.

2. Discard the mouth, which is hidden in the center of the tentacles.

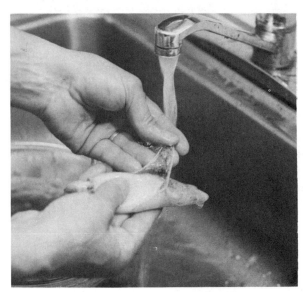 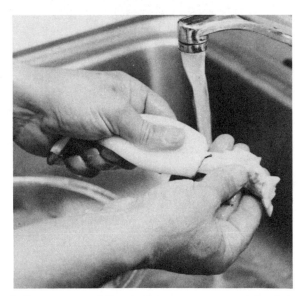

3. Hold the body of the squid under running water and peel off the thin outer skin.

4. Squeeze out the insides as you would a tube of paste, pulling the head off at the final squeeze.

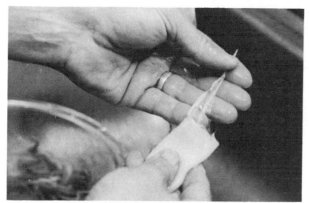

5. Pull out the transparent center bone.

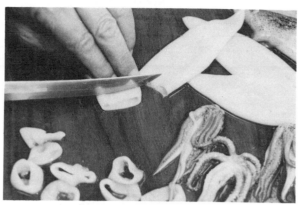

6. Slice the body into rings. If the tentacles are bigger than a mouthful, cut them in half or quarters accordingly.

Brodo di Pesce
FISH BROTH

Fish broth freezes well and is a boon to the fish-loving cook when frozen in containers the size of which suits the number of guests you usually cook for. It makes *zuppa di pesce* for two a cinch: Heat up 3–4 cups of fish broth, add 6 shrimp, 12 mussels, 2 small squid cut up, and 2 chunks of any meaty fish such as monkfish or cod. As the fish is cooking, a matter of about 5 minutes, golden fry in olive oil two pieces of Italian bread. Place one in each of 2 soup dishes. Add the cooked soup and its fish pieces. Sprinkle with chopped parsley and begin. For 2.

1/2 cup olive oil
2 garlic cloves
2 red pepper pods, seeded
2 cups peeled plum tomatoes
2 celery stalks
2 carrots, peeled
2 bay leaves

1 medium-size onion, quartered
2 cups dry white wine
2 1/2–3 pounds heads, racks, cheeks,
    and tails of various fish
2 1/2 quarts water to cover
Salt to taste

Heat the olive oil with the garlic and the pepper pods and sauté until the flavorings are golden and brown respectively. Discard the flavorings. Add the tomatoes, celery, carrots, bay leaves, and onion. Sauté until the onion is limp. Add the wine and cook until it has evaporated. Add the fish and cold water. Bring the pot to a boil, lower the heat, cover, and simmer for about 1 hour. Taste for flavor and add salt to your taste. This makes about 3 quarts of broth for use in fish soups and *risotti* and in poaching fish.

Zuppa del Venerdí Santo
LOBSTER SOUP FOR GOOD FRIDAY

The name is from history when, legend has it, Princes of the Church were allowed the luxury of enjoying a meal on the Church's saddest day of the year. The process, however, is not historical, just practical for those who make and freeze a good fish stock.

2 quarts fish broth
1 pound medium shrimp, peeled and deveined
1½ pounds cooked lobster meat, preferably in large chunks

6 large or 12 small slices Italian bread
1–2 tablespoons parsley, chopped

Bring the fish broth to a boil. Add the shrimp and cook about 2 minutes or until the shrimp are a good coral color and cooked through. Add the lobster meat and keep on a low heat for about 1 minute or until the lobster is heated through.

Golden fry in olive oil the pieces of Italian bread and place them in the soup bowls. Add the soup, being careful to dole out the pieces of fish fairly, sprinkle with parsley, and serve. For 6.

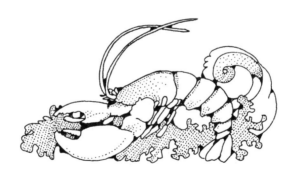

Cacciucco
TUSCAN FISH SOUP

A somewhat elaborate *zuppa di pesce* from Livorno, Tuscany, this soup starts with a *battuto* of seasoning vegetables and lots of fresh plum tomatoes; dry red wine is used instead of the usual dry white; and lobster or jumbo shrimp complete the varied list of fish included.

FOR THE SOUP:
3 garlic cloves
1 red pepper pod, seeded
½ cup olive oil
1 carrot
1 stalk celery
4 sprigs parsley
1 onion
1 cup red wine
1½ pounds fresh plum tomatoes
1½ teaspoons salt
freshly ground pepper
2 cups water

FOR THE FISH:
3–4 small squid
¾ pound medium shrimp
1 small sea bass
1 red snapper
*fillet of fresh halibut or slice of had-
    dock*
*2–3 small fish such as mullet, porgy,
    rose fish*
1 small lobster or 6 jumbo shrimp
6 slices Italian bread
1 clove garlic

Clean and cut the squid (pages 104–105). Clean and shell the shrimp, reserving the shells. Clean and scale the larger fish, cut off and reserve the heads. Clean the small fish, but keep them whole.

Put garlic cloves, red pepper, and olive oil in a large saucepan over medium heat. Add a *battuto* of the carrot, celery, parsley, and onion and sauté it until golden. Add the cut-up squid and cook for 1 minute, then remove and reserve. Add the wine, and when it is almost evaporated, add the fresh tomatoes, peeled and cut into chunks. Add the salt and a few grinds of pepper and bring to a boil. Then lower the heat to a simmer and cook for 10 minutes.

Add to the sauce the shrimp shells, the reserved fish heads, and the small fish. Add 2 cups of water, bring to a boil, and cook over medium heat for 20 minutes or until the small fish are really falling apart.

Turn the heat off and with a wooden spoon stir and mash the fish, then put the whole mixture through a coarse sieve into a big, top-of-the-stove casserole. Put in the large fish cut into chunks, and the shrimp. Bring to a boil and add the lobster cut into chunks (or the jumbo shrimp, whole and unshelled). The soup should be thick by this time and should just barely cover the fish. If not, add a bit of boiling hot water to do so. Lower the heat to a simmer and cook until the fish flakes but is not overcooked. Put the squid back in.

Toast the Italian bread and rub both sides of the slices gently with a clove of garlic. Put a slice in the bottom of each soup plate and cover with various pieces of fish and a ladle or two of soup.

Serve immediately, and relax and enjoy one of the most delicious of *zuppe di pesce.* For 6–8.

Zuppa di Pesce alla Romana
ROMAN FISH SOUP

Anzio, a fishing town forty miles south of Rome, and Civitavecchia, a port sixty miles to the north, quarrel over which of the two is the creator of this soup. Rome, halfway between, has appropriated the *zuppa*'s name and has gotten away with it.

FOR THE SOUP:
1/4 cup olive oil
1 clove garlic
1 red pepper pod, seeded
1 cup dry white wine
1 cup plum tomatoes
1 teaspoon tomato paste
2–3 teaspoons salt

FOR THE FISH:
1/2 pound small squid
1/2 pound mussels
1/2 pound medium shrimp
1 whiting
1 small red snapper or rose fish
1 slice halibut
1 porgy or scup

Clean the squid (pages 104–105) and mussels. Clean and scale the fish yourself or have it done at the market, but be sure to leave the heads and tails on.

Heat the olive oil in a big soup pot over medium heat. Add the garlic and the pepper pod. When the garlic is golden and the pepper a deep brown, discard them. Add the wine and cook until it has almost evaporated. Cut the tomatoes into chunks and add them with their juice and the tomato paste to the pot. Bring to a boil and cool 10–15 minutes. Cut the rest of the fish into good-size chunks and add them to the pot with just enough water to cover. Bring to a boil, reduce the heat to low, and add the shrimp and the mussels along with the salt. Cover the pot and continue cooking 10 minutes, or until the fish barely flakes, the mussels open, and the shrimp are tender. Add the squid. Cook for 1 minute, or until their color has changed to pink and lavender. Taste for salt and add as needed.

Scoop the fish out with a slotted spoon and serve in individual soup plates, giving everyone a little bit of everything. Pour a ladle or two of soup over the fish.

Zuppa di pesce can be served with a slice of fried or toasted bread in the bottom of each plate, but the real fisherman's way is to dunk hot, crusty bread in the soup.

If the idea of fish heads in your soup disturbs you, there is an alternative way to go about this recipe: cut off the heads and tails and put them in a second pot. Add a stalk of celery, 1/2 onion, a small carrot, a bay leaf, water to cover, and a teaspoon of salt. Bring to a boil, reduce the heat, and cook for half an hour. Strain and set aside for use in the final *zuppa.* When all the fish are in the pot, add the fish stock instead of water to cover. For 6 to 8.

Zuppa di Pesce alla Siciliana
SICILIAN FISH SOUP

Sicilian fish soup is flavored with herbs, black olives, wine, and olive oil, and is cooked in a casserole in the oven. This recipe calls for 3½ to 4 pounds (after cleaning) of fresh fish. The weight uncleaned runs to about 5½ to 6 pounds. Your choice is determined by the season and the market, but you should aim for 6–7 varieties.

FOR THE SOUP:
1 onion
¼ cup chopped parsley
1 cup Sicilian or Greek black olives
1 clove garlic
5 peppercorns
½ red pepper pod, or dash of Tabasco (optional)
1 bay leaf
½ cup olive oil
3 teaspoons salt
1½ cups very dry white wine

FOR THE FISH:
1 or 2 small porgies
1 whiting
1 flounder
1 cod fillet
½ pound shrimp
½ pound squid
1 pound mussels

6 slices Italian bread

Preheat oven to 350°.

Clean the fish, but leave the heads and tails on. Cut into chunks and put in the bottom of a big (6–8-quart) ovenproof casserole with a good cover. Leave the shells on the shrimp and put them on top of the fish. Clean and cut the squid (pages 104–105) and distribute all the pieces over the shrimp. Scrub the mussels and put them on top of all the other fish.

Cut the onion into fine slivers and sprinkle it over the fish along with the chopped parsley and black olives. Add the garlic, peppercorns, red pepper or Tabasco if you wish, and sink the bay leaf in the middle of everything. Pour on the olive oil and tip the casserole gently back and forth to let the oil coat the fish. Sprinkle with the salt and the wine.

Cut a round of brown wrapping paper just a little bit bigger than the casserole, and place it between the cover and the casserole to seal in the vapors while cooking. Bake for half an hour.

While the casserole bakes, deep-fry bread slices in the olive oil or toast them to a golden brown. Serve in the bottom of soup dishes with *zuppa di pesce* ladled over them. For 6 to 8.

Zuppa di Pesce d'Ortona
FISH SOUP FROM ORTONA

FOR THE SOUP:

4 tablespoons olive oil
1 dried red pepper pod, seeded
2 cups peeled plum tomatoes, cut in chunks
1 sweet pepper, roasted and cut in strips (page 14)
¼ teaspoon oregano
½ teaspoon salt, or to taste
freshly ground pepper
¾ cup dry white wine
1 packet Italian saffron (.005 ounce)

FOR THE FISH:

1 merluzzo (small cod, ¾ pound, approximate)
1 small red snapper (½ pound, approximate)
½ pound halibut steak
½ pound shrimp
2 pounds mussels, cleaned
1 pound squid, cleaned and cut in rings (pages 104–105)
2 tablespoons chopped parsley
4 to 6 slices fried or toasted Italian bread

Put the olive oil in the bottom of a big, heavy soup pot and sauté the pepper pod in it until dark brown. Discard the pepper and let the oil cool a moment before adding the plum tomatoes. Then raise the heat until the tomatoes start to boil. Lower the heat and simmer for 10 minutes, or until the tomatoes have blended nicely with the oil and the liquid has reduced a bit.

Add the roast pepper strips, the oregano, salt, and pepper. Bring the pot to a boil, add the wine, and continue cooking until the wine has evaporated. Cover the pot, lower the heat, and cook for 5 minutes.

In the meantime, chop off the heads and tails of the cod and red snapper, shell the shrimp, and put the fish heads, tails, and shells in a second pot in water to cover with 1 teaspoon salt. Bring to a boil, cover, lower the heat, and simmer for 15 minutes.

Cut the cod in half and add it to the first pot. Strain the broth from the fish heads and add it to the first pot. When the pot boils, add the red snapper. When the pot boils again, dissolve the saffron in a tablespoon of hot water and add to the soup, then add the halibut, return the pot to a boil, lower the heat, and simmer about 5 minutes. The timing here is important: the minute the red snapper and the halibut are tender, add the shrimp. As soon as the shrimp are tender, add the mussels and squid and cover the pot. Cook about 3 minutes longer, or until the mussels have opened up.

Sprinkle with the chopped parsley. Serve with the toasted or fried Italian bread. For 4 to 6.

Zuppa Di Cozze
MUSSEL SOUP

"Mussel soup" is only a literal translation that in no way can indicate the delicate and exciting flavor of the dish. For those lucky enough to find fresh, clean mussels, it is a treat any day of the week.

4 pounds fresh mussels
5 tablespoons olive oil
1 clove garlic
2 red pepper pods, seeded
1 cup plum tomatoes, (or 3 table-
    spoons tomato paste diluted in
    ½ cup warm water)

½ cup dry white wine
1 teaspoon salt
4 tablespoons chopped parsley
Italian bread

Scrub the mussels well and rinse carefully under running water.

Put the olive oil in a big soup pot and add the garlic and red pepper pods. Sauté over medium heat. Discard the garlic and pepper when golden and brown and add the tomatoes and wine. Cook for 4 minutes, raise the heat, and add the mussels. Stir them around a bit, add the salt, cover, and cook for about 5 minutes, or until all the shells have opened. If by any chance there are any unopened mussels, discard them. Add the parsley, stir, and serve in big soup plates (with an extra for discarded shells) with slices of hot Italian bread to dip in the soup. On the other hand, you may want to fry the bread in olive oil and serve a slice at the bottom of each soup plate. For 6.

Riso
RICE

Rice, as a separate first course for the typical Italian luncheon or dinner, is handled as carefully, specially, and diversely as any *pasta asciutta.* Cooked with saucelike flavorings or cooked separately and served with a sauce, good *risotto* was once strictly a northern dish. Today it appears all over the country.

In Italy, rice comes labeled according to usage, either for *minestre* or *risotto,* and it takes anywhere from 15 to 45 minutes to cook. American rice, as far as we know, isn't labeled for soup *per se,* but rice called fancy or long grain does well in both salads and soups. Medium-grain rice more closely resembles the Italian *arborio* or *valone,* that which is used most frequently for *risotti.* Chemically it is just the same. Cooked medium-grain American rice is slightly less "creamy" in its appearance and just a shade less firm. However, it fits well with the recipes we use that were originally for *arborio,* and thus we have adopted it for our *risotti* when we cannot find or have run out of Italian medium-grain *arborio.* Like pasta, a good rice, properly cooked, holds its shape and becomes tender but firm. Recent imports bearing names of distributors new to us seem to cook as quickly as most American rice, and thus we have adjusted our recipes accordingly.

The American instant rice, the parboiled-before-you-touch-it variety, fails to lend itself to either Italian *risotti* or *minestre,* and hence we do not recommend it.

As for the sauces, they have been developed according to the specialties in the province where they originated. Venice is famous for its fish with rice, Milan for *risotto* slowly cooked in broth, Sicily for rice with tuna and tomatoes, Bologna for rice with Bolognese meat sauce. In some dishes the sauce and the rice are cooked together. In others they are combined after each has been cooked separately. Some are simple, some are a little more complicated. All are happy alternatives to *pasta asciutta* or *minestra.* For easy reference, their sequence here is rice with butter, then meat, then vegetables, and finally rice with fish.

There are several schools of thought about the final consistency of *risotto.* Some say it should be thick, so that when served the *risotto* remains in a mound on the plate. Others prefer it *all'onda,* so that when served it is still thin enough to make "waves" on the plate. It is a matter of personal taste. You can have your preferred consistency by adding—or not—more broth or butter at the end of cooking. Some cooks we know add a touch of cream, and we sometimes add a tablespoon of grated *mozzarella* to increase the creaminess when using American medium-grain rice.

Risotto alla Milanese
RICE, MILANESE STYLE

Cooked in broth, flavored with saffron and Parmesan cheese, this is a stunning way to treat rice.

As for the broth, use 3 cups (with a fourth handy) of chicken broth mixed with 1 cup of beef broth. If you make your own chicken broth, put in 2 beef bones to enrich the flavor.

The Italian saffron used is powdered, while Spanish saffron comes in little threads. These threads should be broken up in 2 tablespoons of warm broth so that their color begins to run before they are added to the rice.

1 very finely chopped onion
¼ pound unsalted butter
1 tablespoon beef marrow, from a shin bone, optional
2 cups Italian arborio or medium-grain American rice

6–7 cups clear, hot chicken-beef broth, approximate
⅛ teaspoon saffron, or 1 packet in 2 tablespoons warm water
6 tablespoons grated Parmesan cheese

Using a wide, capacious pot (a 6-quart, two-handled, stainless steel Dutch oven, for example), melt the butter over medium heat and sauté the minced onion until golden and translucent. Scoop out a tablespoon of marrow from a soup bone and add it to the pot, breaking it up as it starts to melt. Beef marrow adds a roundness and richness to *risotto*. In the final analysis, only a Milanese brought up on *risotto* would know the presence or absence of the marrow. Add the rice and cook until it crackles. Add enough broth to cover, about ½ cup.

Keep the rice on medium heat, stirring constantly. As the broth is absorbed, add more, about ½ cup at a time. When the rice has absorbed all 4 cups of broth, taste for tenderness. If it is still hard, add an additional ½–1 cup of broth. Keep on cooking and stirring until tender but not mushy. Stir in the saffron. When the rice is evenly colored and flavored by the saffron, stir in 4 tablespoons of the grated Parmesan cheese. This is such a grand dish it deserves freshly grated Parmesan. Serve in 6 individual portions, and sprinkle with the remaining cheese. For 6.

Risotto al Salto

An off-shoot of *Risotto alla Milanese, Risotto al salto* is another great favorite with the Milanese. Like *supplí,* the dish is a preplanned leftover, but for the true rice lover, it is frequently made from scratch.

For one serving, melt 1 tablespoon of unsalted butter in an 8-inch well-seasoned sauté pan (a nonstick pan is ideal) and when it is hot, add 1 ½ cups of cold *risotto.* With a spatula or the back of a spoon, flatten the *risotto* to cover the bottom of the pan. Cook over moderate heat, shaking the pan to prevent sticking, until a light golden crust has developed. Turn the rice over and crisp the other side. Starting with *risotto* at room temperature, the whole process should not take more than 10 minutes. To make more than one portion, use a larger, well-seasoned skillet or omelet pan, and 1 ½ cups of *risotto* per serving. Cut into wedges and serve.

Risotto ai Funghi
RICE WITH MUSHROOMS

This handsome variation of *Risotto alla Milanese* uses either dried Italian (not Chinese) mushrooms or fresh ones, as well as all the ingredients of the parent recipe. Prepare the *risotto* as on page 113 and while it is cooking add the mushrooms prepared as below.

1 ounce dried mushrooms, or 7 ounces fresh

2 tablespoons unsalted butter (for use with fresh mushrooms only)

If using dried mushrooms: soak them 10 to 15 minutes in lukewarm water until limp. (If soaked too long, they lose flavor and aroma.) Drain them and check that any residual sand has washed away. Squeeze out any remaining water gently with a paper towel. Dice the mushrooms and add to the rice a few minutes after it has begun to cook.

If using fresh mushrooms: clean and slice the mushrooms and sauté them in the unsalted butter. As soon as the mushrooms start giving up their juices add them—butter, juices, and all—to the already cooking *risotto.* For 6.

Risotto con Asparagi
RISOTTO WITH ASPARAGUS

When asparagus is out of season or if you prefer another vegetable, feel free. Chopped fresh spinach, zucchini cut into tiny cubes, artichokes cut into thin wedges, fresh or frozen peas, baby green beans all can be sautéed briefly in a bit of butter and added to almost cooked (about 5 minutes away from being done) rice. A mixture of early vegetables *(Primavera)* plus a bit of grated Parmesan cheese is another pleasant way to present rice.

2 pounds fresh asparagus
1 large onion
5 tablespoons unsalted butter
3 tablespoons olive oil
2 cups Italian arborio *or medium-grain American rice*

5 cups hot water
3 teaspoons salt
1 packet Italian saffron (.005 ounce)
*   optional*
4 tablespoons Parmesan cheese, or
*   to taste*

Break the root ends off the asparagus stalks where they snap easily and discard. Wash the asparagus thoroughly and cut it into 1-inch pieces.

Finely chop the onion or slice it into thin slivers.

Melt 3 tablespoons of the butter in the olive oil in a big pot over low heat. Add the onion and cook until limp and translucent. Add the asparagus, stir, and cook 2–3 minutes.

Add the rice, 4 cups of the hot water, and the salt. Stir well, bring to a boil, cover, lower the heat,

and cook for 14 minutes. If you are using saffron, moisten it with 2 tablespoons of the warm water and stir it into the rice.

Keep checking to see that the rice doesn't dry out too much and stir it occasionally. Add some or all of the last cup of hot water as necessary.

When the rice is tender, stir in the remaining 2 tablespoons of butter and the Parmesan cheese. Mix well and serve immediately. Serve extra cheese to sprinkle on according to individual taste. For 6 to 8.

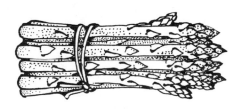

Risotto con Pomodori Freschi e Basilico
RISOTTO WITH TOMATOES AND BASIL

This *risotto* captures the flavor of ripe summer tomatoes and fresh basil. Of course you can make it at other times of the year, substituting canned tomatoes for the sun-ripened and dried basil for the fresh, but it is worth a trip to a farmer's market in season to get the most out of the dish.

1 medium onion, minced
4 tablespoons unsalted butter
1½ pounds fresh plum tomatoes
1 teaspoon salt, or to taste
freshly ground pepper to taste
15 fresh basil leaves, chopped coarsely

2 cups Italian arborio or American medium-grain rice
4 cups chicken broth, hot
2 ounces mozzarella cheese, grated
4 to 5 sprigs parsley, chopped

Sauté the minced onion in the butter in a saucepan until limp.

Cut the tomatoes into chunks and push them through a sieve or a food mill, or process them on/off briefly with the steel blade. Add the tomatoes to the onion.

Add salt, pepper, basil leaves, and rice.

Stir and cook until the rice crackles.

Add the broth, cover the pan, bring to a boil, and then lower heat slightly. Cook until the rice is tender, about 15 minutes.

When the rice is cooked, stir in the *mozzarella* and sprinkle with the parsley. Transfer to a hot serving dish and serve immediately. For 6.

Risotto al Ragù
RICE WITH BOLOGNESE MEAT SAUCE

Many consider this *risotto* to be as delicious as *pasta al ragù,* and, if you have the *ragù* ready, it goes together just as fast.

2 cups Italian arborio *or American*
    medium-grain rice
4 tablespoons unsalted butter
4 cups water

2 teaspoons salt
1–1½ cups ragù *(p.67)*
4 tablespoons grated Parmesan
    cheese

Put the rice and half the butter in a big pot with a good cover. Sauté until rice grains crackle and are coated with butter. Add water and salt, bring to a boil uncovered, lower the heat, stir well, and cover. Simmer approximately 10 minutes, or until nearly done and almost all the water has been absorbed.

Add the *ragù* and the rest of the butter. Continue cooking uncovered over a low heat until the rice is tender, about 3 or 4 minutes. Stir in half the cheese and serve in 6 individual plates. Sprinkle with the rest of the cheese. For 6.

Risotto all'Aragosta
RISOTTO WITH LOBSTER

1½–2-pounds lobster, boiled
5 tablespoons unsalted butter
1 celery stalk, minced
1 onion, peeled and minced
1 garlic clove, peeled and minced
2 cups Italian arborio *or American*
    medium-grain rice

1 packet Italian powdered saffron
1 teaspoon salt
5 tablespoons dry sherry
4½ cups chicken broth, hot
2–3 tablespoons parsley, chopped

In boiling the lobster, be sure the water is abundant (at lease 6 quarts) and as salty as sea water (1 tablespoon salt per quart). Do not overboil: 12 minutes after the pot comes back to a boil is enough for 1¼–1½ pounds of lobster.

Let the lobster cool enough to handle easily. Remove the meat from the shell. Slice the tail in neat rounds and reserve. Cut up the rest of the meat in ¼–½-inch pieces. Reserve roe if you wish.

Melt the butter in a saucepan. Add the minced flavorings and sauté until limp. Add the rice, saff-ron, and salt. Continue cooking until the rice crackles. Add the sherry and cook until it has evaporated.

Add the hot broth and the cut-up lobster meat and roe. Cover the pan, lower the heat, and cook for about 15 minutes.

When the rice is tender, stir it, put the mixture in a hot serving dish, and dress with the reserved lobster tail pieces and the chopped parsley. Serve immediately. For 6.

Risotto alla Siciliana
RISOTTO, SICILIAN STYLE

This is a dish whose special style emerges from an uncanny medley of flavorings: vegetable, herb, spice, fruit, and wine.

FOR THE SAUCE:
3 salted anchovy fillets, or 6 canned
4 tablespoons olive oil
1 large onion
2 tablespoons wine vinegar
½ cup dry white wine
juice of 1 ½ lemons
1 teaspoon mustard
1 teaspoon salt
freshly ground pepper

4 peeled plum tomatoes, chopped
1 teaspoon dried marjoram leaves
¾ cup Sicilian black olives, pitted
        (packed in brine, not dried)

FOR THE RICE:
2 cups Italian arborio or American
        medium-grain rice
4–4½ cups hot water
2 teaspoons salt

If using salted anchovies, rinse and skin under running water, open up, and remove the tail and the back bone. If using canned, drain them. Cook in the olive oil in a saucepan over low heat until the anchovies have disintegrated.

Slice the onion into thin slivers and add to the flavored olive oil. Sauté until limp and then add the vinegar. When the vinegar has evaporated, add the wine, lemon juice, mustard, ½ teaspoon of the salt, and pepper (2 or 3 twists of the mill). Stir and add the tomatoes, the remaining ½ teaspoon of salt, and the marjoram, and simmer for 10 minutes.

Put the rice into a heavy pot with 4 cups of the water and the salt. Bring to a boil, stir, cover, lower the heat, and cook for 14 minutes, or until *al dente.* Stir occasionally during cooking, and add a bit more water if necessary. When the rice is cooked, dress it with the sauce. Decorate with the black olives and serve. For 6 to 8.

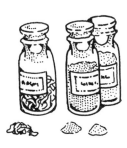

Riso con Calamari
RICE WITH SQUID

The squid in this rice dish are enhanced by tomatoes and dry white wine. The squid may be fresh or frozen. The frozen ones usually come in 3-pound boxes. Defrost at room temperature 3 or 4 hours, and proceed as with fresh squid. Incidentally, the smaller the squid, the better the taste and texture.

1 3-pound box frozen squid, or 3
*   pounds fresh*
4 tablespoons olive oil
2 cloves garlic
2 red pepper pods, seeded
1 cup dry white wine
4 cups plum tomatoes

salt, to taste
4–4 1/2 cups water
2 teaspoons salt
2 teaspoons unsalted butter
2 cups Italian arborio or American
*   medium-grain rice*

Clean the squid (pages 104–105) and slice the body into little rings. If the tentacles are bigger than a mouthful, cut into halves or quarters.

Warm the oil in a heavy Dutch-oven–type pot that has a cover, add the garlic and pepper pods, and sauté over medium heat until the garlic is golden and the pods dark brown. Remove the flavorings and put in the cut-up squid. Cook for 1 to 2 minutes, or until the squid has changed color to pink and lavender. Add the dry white wine and continue cooking until the wine has evaporated. Cut the tomatoes into bite-size chunks, and add them, juice and all, to the squid. Bring the pan to a boil, reduce the heat, cover, and simmer about 45 minutes, or until the squid is tender and the tomatoes reduced to a sauce. Taste for salt and if it is needed, add about 1–1 1/2 teaspoons.

Place rice and butter in a saucepan and cook until the rice crackles. Add 4 cups of water and the salt. Bring to a boil, stir, cover, lower heat, and cook about 12 minutes. Stir a couple of times during cooking, and when almost cooked add the squid and sauce, stir well, and cook 3 minutes more or until the rice is *al dente,* biteable, cooked but firm.

Serve in a big, deep platter. For 6.

Risotto con Frutti di Mare
RICE WITH SHELLFISH

The name of this recipe can be translated literally as "rice with fruits of the sea"—shrimp, baby squid, mussels, and small clams. Ideally it is made with Mediterranean clams, for which we substitute the slightly larger Atlantic counterpart, cherrystone clams. If you can't get mussels, you can substitute small or bay scallops.

½ pound small squid
4 tablespoons olive oil
½ cup dry white wine
1 pound mussels (or ¾ pound small scallops)
1 pound small cherrystone clams
½ pound medium shrimp

4 tablespoons parsley, coarsely chopped
3½ teaspoons salt
4½ cups water
2 cups Italian arborio or American medium-grain rice
2 tablespoons unsalted butter

Clean and cut up squid (pages 104–105), and put it in a big frying pan with 2 tablespoons of the olive oil. Cook over medium heat, stirring constantly for 1 or 2 minutes, or until the color of the squid tentacles changes to pink and lavender. Add the wine, let it evaporate, then reduce the heat to a simmer and cook for 20 minutes.

In the meantime, scrub and clean the mussels and wash the clams. Put the remaining 2 tablespoons of olive oil in a good-size pot and drop in the mussels and clams. Cover and cook on a high heat, stirring a couple of times, about 5 minutes or until all the shells are opened. Turn off the heat and cool enough to handle. Separate the mussels and clams from their shells. Let the juices drip back into the pan they were cooked in, discard the shells, and put the meat in with the squid.

Peel and devein the shrimp and add them to the squid, mussels, and clams. Put the shrimp shells in the pan in which the mussels first cooked, and add ½ cup of the water, bring to a boil, and simmer about 15 minutes. Then strain this broth through a cheesecloth-lined sieve into the frying pan with the squid and shellfish. Add the parsley with 1½ teaspoons of the salt and simmer about 5 minutes.

If you substitute fresh scallops for the mussels, be sure you use small (bay, not sea) ones. Add them to the shrimp and squid when you put in the parsley, as they should cook only a short time if they are to remain flavorful and tender.

Put the rice, butter, and the remaining 2 teaspoons of salt in a big pot and cook until the rice crackles. Add the 4 cups of water and bring to a boil. Stir, cover, and reduce the heat to simmer. Cook about 8 minutes, stirring a couple of times. Uncover and add the squid and shellfish with their sauce. Keep on cooking and stirring over low heat until the rice is tender and flavored with the fish. Serve immediately. For 6.

Risotto con Gamberetti e Cozze
RISOTTO WITH SHRIMP AND MUSSELS

3 dozen mussels (about 3 pounds, depending on size)
2 tablespoons olive oil
6 tablespoons unsalted butter
1 garlic clove
1 dried red pepper pod, seeded
1 pound shrimp

3 tablespoons Italian parsley, chopped
½ cup dry white wine
2 cups Italian arborio or American medium-grain rice
4½ cups fish broth, hot (page 105)

Scrub the mussels well and pull out their beards. Place mussels and olive oil in a frying pan or saucepan, cover well, and cook over medium heat for about 4 minutes or until the mussels have opened up. When cool enough to handle, remove the meat from the shells and reserve in a bowl. Strain the pan juices through a cheesecloth-lined strainer onto the mussels.

Melt 3 tablespoons of the butter in a sauté pan, add the garlic and pepper pods, and cook until the garlic is golden and the pepper darkened. Remove both these flavorings and add the shrimp and parsley. Stir and cook until the shrimp have turned coral pink. Add the wine and cook a couple of minutes until it is partially evaporated. Add the mussels and their juices, remove from the heat, cover, and set aside.

Put the remaining butter in a saucepan over medium heat. Add the rice and cook, stirring, until the rice crackles. Add the hot fish broth, cover, and bring to a boil. Lower the heat slightly and cook covered for 15 minutes or until the rice is tender.

When the rice has cooked, stir in the shrimp and mussels and their juices. Transfer to a hot serving dish and serve immediately. For 6.

Riso con Peoci
RICE WITH MUSSELS

Peoci is the Venetian word for mussels. The dish is lightly flavored with olive oil and a bit of onion, and cooked in fish broth to get the real, traditional flavor.

FOR THE FISH BROTH:
5 cups fish broth (page 105), or 5
   cups water
1 pound fish heads, tails, bones
1 teaspoon salt
4 peppercorns
1 small onion
1/2 carrot
1 stalk celery
1 bay leaf
1 tablespoon wine vinegar

FOR THE RISOTTO:
1/2 cup olive oil
1 medium garlic clove
2 pounds mussels
1/4 pound butter
1 small onion, minced
2 cups Italian arborio *or American*
   medium-grain rice
4 cups fish broth

If not using fish broth: Put heads, tails, and bones in a soup pot with all the flavorings and the water, bring to a boil, lower the heat, and simmer about 20 minutes. Strain through a cheesecloth-lined sieve and save the broth for cooking the rice.

In another big pot, put about 3 tablespoons of the olive oil (or enough to cover the bottom), the garlic, and well-cleaned mussels. Bring to a high heat, stir with a wooden spoon, and keep cooking until the mussels open. When the mussels are cool enough to handle, fork out their meat and put it aside in a pan bowl. Discard shells and strain olive oil and mussel juices over the mussels.

Melt the butter in a 4–5 quart pan, add the rest of the olive oil, the minced onion, and the rice. Cook over medium heat until the onion is limp and the rice crackles, glistening with butter. Add 1/2 cup of fish broth as needed to keep the rice just barely moist with liquid. After about 15 minutes, when the rice has plumped up and is nearly cooked, add the mussels and their juices. Keep on cooking and stirring over medium heat until the rice is tender. Add the last, if any, of the broth as you cook. Taste for salt, add some if needed, and serve. For 6.

Risotto con Tonno
RICE WITH TUNA

This *risotto* is quick, simple, and delightful as a summer first course, a real success at any table. Children love it.

1 small garlic clove
3 tablespoons olive oil
2 cups plum tomatoes
4 fresh basil leaves
1 6½–7½-ounce can Italian tuna,
    packed in olive oil

salt to taste
2 cups Italian arborio or American
    medium-grain rice
4 cups water
2 tablespoons unsalted butter
2 teaspoons salt

Using a good-size frying pan, sauté the garlic in the olive oil over medium heat until the garlic turns golden. Discard the clove and turn off the heat a minute. Add the tomatoes, basil, and tuna fish. (If you can't get Italian tuna packed in olive oil, look for light tuna packed in vegetable oil. White tuna packed in water simply isn't the right taste or texture for this dish.) Simmer about 15 minutes (mashing up the tuna and tomatoes with a fork occasionally) or until the juices are reduced, the color darkened, and the flavors blended. Taste for salt, and add some if needed.

Put the rice and butter in another pan. Cook until rice is coated with butter and crackling, add the water and salt and bring to a boil, stir, cover, and reduce the heat. Cook about 10 minutes, stirring a couple of times. By this time the rice is practically dry, almost cooked. Add the tuna sauce and continue stirring and cooking uncovered until the rice is tender and done. For 6.

Riso e Scampi alla Veneziana
RICE WITH SHRIMP, VENETIAN STYLE

This *risotto* uses the broth in which the shrimp are cooked to add flavor. The shrimp may be either fresh or frozen.

1 medium onion
4 fresh basil leaves
½ clove garlic
4–5 sprigs parsley
1 pound shrimp fresh or frozen, un-
    shelled
5 cups water

1 teaspoon salt
8 tablespoons unsalted butter
¾ cup olive oil
1½ cups rice
½ teaspoon salt
2 tablespoons parsley, chopped

Mince the onion, basil, garlic, and parsley sprigs and put them with the shrimp in boiling salted water. Cook for 3 minutes, or until the shrimp are coral colored. Scoop out the shrimp, peel, and set them aside. Drop the shells back into the cooking water. Bring to a boil and simmer gently for 15 minutes. Strain through a cheesecloth-lined sieve before adding to the rice.

Melt the butter in the olive oil in a large saucepan. Add the rice and cook until the rice crackles and is coated with butter. Add the shrimp and ½ cup of the shrimp broth. Cook over medium heat, adding more broth ½ cup at a time as it is absorbed. When the rice is cooked, after about 20 minutes, check for salt and add as needed. Serve with a sprinkling of chopped parsley. For 6.

Gnocchi
DUMPLINGS

A first course that defies proper description (it certainly is neither pasta, nor rice, nor soup) is *gnocchi*. If the name stops you cold, their taste will turn you on. In the singular, the word is *gnocco*—with the *gn* sounding like the *gn* in *lasagne*. In the plural, it acquires an *h* and becomes *gnocchi*—knee-oh-key. Almost every Italian region has its own version, and in some of them it is part of the local folklore. In Verona the humble *gnocco* is as much at home as Romeo and Juliet. In Rome Thursday is the day prescribed for *gnocchi*. Once eaten, *gnocchi* are supposed to leave you with a beatific smile on your face, similar to that of a simpleton, who, wouldn't you know, is called a *gnocco*.

Because they very well represent all other Italian *gnocchi* we have chosen the Florentine *gnocchi verdi*, made with ricotta, which are light, soft, vaguely cheesy and green with spinach; the Roman *gnocchi*, made with semolino; and the Veronese *gnocchi*, which are made with potatoes.

Gnocchi Verdi
GREEN DUMPLINGS

1 10-ounce package frozen spinach,
*   or 10 ounces fresh*
1 pound ricotta
1 large egg
½ teaspoon nutmeg, freshly grated
6 teaspoons salt

8 tablespoons grated Parmesan
*   cheese*
¾ cup flour
4 tablespoons unsalted butter
5 quarts water

Barely cook the spinach (if using frozen, it's done by the time the ice has melted; if using fresh, remove the stems and boil until it's limp). Drain it, pressing with a spoon against the side of the strainer to remove all water possible. Mince the spinach finely.

Put the *ricotta* in a medium-size bowl, add the spinach, and mix well. Add the unbeaten egg, the nutmeg, 1 teaspoon of the salt, and stir. Fold in 4 tablespoons of the Parmesan cheese and ½ cup of the flour. Spread some flour, about ¼ cup, on a plate. Take about 1 teaspoon of the mixture at a time and roll it with the palm of your hand around the plate (or in between the 2 floured palms of your hands) until you have a little soft ball about the size of a cherry.

If this is your first experiment with *gnocchi*, test one or two in boiling water before rolling them all. If the *gnocchi* disintegrate on cooking, add another 2 tablespoons of flour to your mixture. The amount of flour is governed by how well drained the spinach and how big the egg. Its use is to firm up the very soft cheese mixture and help the egg bind everything together.

Keep on rolling little balls in the flour until the mixture is all used. *Gnocchi* must not be stacked; line them up on a wax-papered cookie sheet.

To cook *gnocchi*, bring 5 quarts of water to a boil and salt it with the remaining salt. Drop the *gnocchi* in one by one until they cover the bottom of the pot. When done, they rise to the top. Remove with slotted spoon, drain well, and put them in a warm dish. As you remove the cooked *gnocchi* from the pot, add some more uncooked ones to it. When all are done, dot with butter and sprinkle with the rest of the Parmesan cheese.

This recipe makes between 70 and 80 *gnocchi*. Ten or so per person is a reasonable helping for a first course. If you want to double the recipe you may, but don't double the flour—use only up to ¾ of a cup. For 6 to 8.

Torta Verde di Ricotta
RICOTTA AND SPINACH PIE

This one-crust pie, filled with a mixture identical to that of *Gnocchi Verdi*, can be served hot or tepid as a first course.

FOR THE FILLING:
1 pound ricotta
10-ounce package frozen spinach, or 10 ounces fresh
1 large egg
½ teaspoon nutmeg freshly grated
⅓ cup flour
1 teaspoon salt
8 tablespoons grated Parmesan cheese

⅛ pound unsalted butter

FOR THE PIE CRUST:
12 ounces puff pastry
¼ cup unseasoned bread crumbs, approximate
1 egg yolk, beaten

Preheat the oven to 375°.

The filling has just the same ingredients as the recipe for *Gnocchi Verdi* (page 125), and is mixed exactly the same way.

Once you have made the filling, butter and sprinkle with bread crumbs the bottom and sides of a 10-inch pie pan. Roll the pastry to a thickness of ¹⁄₁₆ inch and large enough to fit the pan. Place the pastry in the pan and sprinkle it with bread crumbs.

Spread the filling in the unbaked crust. Sprinkle the top with the rest of the Parmesan cheese and dot with butter. Cut off excess dough, reroll it, and cut it into strips. Place the strips criss-cross over the filling. Paint the strips and border with the beaten egg yolk. Bake about 40 minutes (at 350°), or until the crust is light brown and the filling is puffed and toasty. Cool a few minutes before eating or you will burn your tongue. For 6.

Gnocchi di Semolino alla Romana
ROMAN *SEMOLINA GNOCCHI*

1 quart milk
1 cup semolina or cream of wheat
¾ cup unsalted butter
1 teaspoon salt

freshly ground pepper, to taste
½ teaspoon freshly grated nutmeg
3 egg yolks
1 cup grated Parmesan cheese

Bring the milk to boil over medium heat. Add the semolina in a steady stream, stirring as you add. When the semolina is well mixed in, add ¼ cup of butter, the salt, pepper, and nutmeg.

Cook about 20 minutes or until the semolina (cream of wheat) is cooked. Remove from heat, stir in the egg yolks one at a time, and finally add about 2 tablespoons of Parmesan cheese.

Butter a cookie sheet and with the aid of a spatula spread the *gnocchi* mixture to a thickness of ½ inch. Let it cool and then cut it with a cookie cutter into rounds about 1½ inches in diameter.

When it is almost time to serve, preheat the oven to 400° and butter an ovenproof casserole well. Layer it with the rounds, dot with the remaining butter, and sprinkle with the last of the Parmesan cheese. Bake in a hot (400°) oven for about 15 minutes or until the *gnocchi* are golden and the butter and cheese melted. For 6.

Gnocchi di Patate alla Veronese
POTATO DUMPLINGS FROM VERONA

2 pounds baking potatoes
¼ teaspoon salt
3–3½ cups flour (approximate), unbleached, all-purpose

6–8 tablespoons unsalted butter, melted
4–6 tablespoons grated Parmesan cheese.

Boil the potatoes with their jackets on, drain them the minute they are tender, and peel them as soon as they can be touched. Put them in a big bowl, add the salt, and beat until smooth with an electric beater or mash well with a potato masher.

Add the flour gradually, working it in with a fork. Keep adding flour until you have a workable, rather solid dough.

Generously flour the pastry board or counter and your hands, take a handful of dough, and roll it into a long cylinder no more than ¾ inch in diameter. Cut it into 1-inch slices. Press each slice with your thumb against the side of a cheese grater. Roll your thumb gently downward and away, allowing the dough to curl up a bit and be dimpled by the grater, making a shell-like shape—a *gnocco.*

Keep on rolling cylinders, cutting slices, and shaping until all the dough is used. As you finish each *gnocco,* line it up on a floured cookie sheet. *Gnocchi* should dry at least 2 hours.

When it's time to cook, bring at least 4 quarts of water to a boil in a big pot and add 1 teaspoon of salt for each quart of water. Drop in just enough *gnocchi* to cover the bottom of the pot. As they are done the *gnocchi* rise to the top. Let them cook gently as they float for a minute or two more. Remove with a slotted spoon, drain well over the boiling pot, and put into a warm serving dish. Repeat this process until all the *gnocchi* are cooked. Dress with the melted butter, sprinkle with the cheese, and serve. For 6 to 8.

Polenta

When talking of Italian food, it is impossible to avoid mentioning *polenta*. It can be translated literally as "a cornmeal dish," but that would not do it justice. Traditionally, *polenta* was, and to a certain extent still is, a major staple of the northern alpine regions, appearing as a first course, second course, side dish, bread, and dessert. This kind of wide usage seemed so inordinate to southern Italians years ago that they nicknamed the blond northern cornmeal eaters *polentoni:* made of *polenta.* The northerners replied, calling the southerners *terroni:* made of *terra*, earth, referring to their tanned complexion. All in good jest, sometimes . . .

Polenta is made with cornmeal boiled in salted water and by itself, like macaroni without a sauce, is our idea of nothing at all. With a sauce, and the northerners have many, *polenta* is as kind to the spirit and appetite as any good dish of pasta.

There is a variety of second courses, either meat or fish, that function as sauce for *polenta* to mutual advantage. We've chosen three that have stayed with us over the years as true favorites of our entire tribe:

> *Polenta e baccalà al sugo alla Romana,* with tomato and codfish
>   sauce (page 186)
> *Polenta e salsicce,* with sausages and tomato sauce (page 165)
> *Polenta con spuntature e salsicce,* with spareribs and sausages (page
>   167)

Polenta as an accompaniment for any entrée, especially grilled meat and fish, is also a great favorite: cooked *polenta* is cut in diamond shapes or whatever you wish and then briefly grilled or fried. It makes a nifty substitute for potatoes.

To Make Polenta

The real enemy of *polenta* is lumps, practically impossible to get rid of once they appear. Experienced *polenta* makers have developed the art of sprinkling cornmeal into boiling water with one hand while stirring with a long wooden spoon in the other.

For beginners, almost inevitably, this system produces not only the dreaded lumps but a considerable amount of embarrassment, since there is no known use for lumpy *polenta.* Years ago, cooking in Rome, my first go-round with *polenta* ended in enormous protests against the kind of cornmeal Italy produced . . . too prone entirely to lumps of all sizes. Today that problem has all but disappeared. Italy manufactures a splendid "instant" *polenta* that cooks in 5 to 10 minutes, mostly depending on the brand, and it has a great taste. Look in specialty shops for it usually, and oddly enough in 13-ounce boxes with complete instructions for the amount of water and salt in English as well as Italian. MR

For those who have no luck getting the instant, we recommend American cornmeal. It mixes easily in cold water and doesn't lump when that mixture is added to hot water. Hence the following untraditional method for 6 to 8 servings:

2 cups cornmeal
10 cups water
3 teaspoons salt

Bring 5 cups of water to a boil in a big pot over high heat. Mix the cornmeal in the other 5 cups of cold water, stirring rapidly. When smooth, pour the cold mixture slowly into the boiling water. Add the salt. Bring back to a boil, stirring constantly, lower the heat to almost a simmer, and let bubble slowly 50–60 minutes, stirring constantly. When cooked, *polenta* is very thick, smooth, and creamy. Pour on a platter, cool slightly, and serve (see below). For 6.

How to Serve

Polenta when cooked is a very thick affair that is poured on a *polenta* board, a slab of wood used as a serving platter (and only for this purpose), and allowed to cool a bit. With the back of a spoon, make a series of indentations or one long one down the center of the cooling surface to catch the sauce. Pour some of the sauce over the entire *polenta.* Put the remaining sauce in a serving dish. Country-style eaters then serve themselves, all eating from the common board, so to speak, spooning on more sauce as they wish. City-style diners are served *polenta* on individual plates, with a scoop of sauce on top and the remaining sauce still passed around.

Polentina, a less thick *polenta*, is served in its spoonable condition in soup plates with the sauce on top. To make it, use only 1⅓ cups of cornmeal and add 2 tablespoons of unsalted butter.

SECONDI PIATTI
SECOND COURSES

Second courses, like everything else that appears on the table, are controlled by the season as well as your own mood and shopping habits. In Italy, where daily shopping is the usual routine, the whole menu is frequently decided at the market, depending on the day's bargain or the sales pitch.

In maintaining an Italian kitchen in America, we try to keep on hand the various staples called for to flavor almost any meat or fish: tomatoes, seasoning vegetables, herbs, salt pork, and olive oil. Then we let the store's offerings dictate the week's shopping. By and large, Italians use less meat than most Americans, use as much fish as is available, and frequently make a *frittata*, which is made of eggs, do the work of either one.

In organizing the recipes for this chapter, we've simply put them in the usual order: beef, veal, lamb, pork, poultry, fish, the *frattaglie*—the assortment that includes liver, brains, and tripe, which we call the "in between" cuts—and eggs.

Manzo
BEEF

Beef is highly respected on the Italian table, and it is treated with maximum regard and parsimony. There isn't much of the animal, tongue to tail (insides included), that is not boiled, braised, broiled, fried, or stewed.

Of the cooking processes, broiling is the least common because it produces, but for sizzle and smoke, no fringe benefits. With boiling you get a delicious and abundant broth, and the meat—that is the part not consumed on the spot—is used in another preplanned manner another day.

In braising, the sauce produced in the process is as important as the meat itself, and is used partially with the meat and partially as a sauce for pasta, rice, or polenta, or even to cook other meats or vegetables.

Stewing glorifies what in other kitchens are considered poor cuts. If you have tasted *Stufatino in Umido* (Shinbone Stew) or *Coda alla Vaccinara* (Oxtail, Cowhand Style), you will have to agree.

For pan frying, beef is cut thin and then pounded even thinner so that 2 (if not 3) Italian customers are easily satisfied with the amount that would serve one American.

The only portions of beef that do not appear in a dish of their own are the trimmings on the butcher block. But even these are chopped and ground and, mixed with other ingredients, go to make the base for a *sugo* or a stuffing for vegetables. Even if in the final presentation beef is a minor ingredient, the dish is considered a meat dish, and as such we include it in this chapter.

Bollito Misto
MIXED BOILED MEATS

Northern Italy's long-simmered boiled dinner makes the broth that is traditionally used with *cappelletti*, the four meats being invariably served with *salsa verde* (green sauce of capers and parsley) or *mostarda di Cremona* (hot spiced fruit pickles).

1½ pounds beef brisket	*4 teaspoons salt*
1 3-pound chicken, or half a fowl	*10 peppercorns*
1½ pounds small beef tongue	*1 teaspoon marjoram*
4 celery stalks with leaves	*1 teaspoon thyme*
2 carrots	*2 bay leaves*
2 onions	*1 small* cotechino *sausage*
¼ medium-size turnip	*whites of 2 eggs (optional)*
4 plum tomatoes	

Put the meats with the exception of the *cotechino* into a big pot, at least 8 quarts. Add the 5 vegetables and enough cold water to cover everything. Add the salt and peppercorns. Put the pot on a high heat, bring to a boil, and scoop off any froth that forms. Add the herbs, reduce the heat, and simmer for 2 hours. If using a chicken instead of a fowl, add it after approximately 1 hour's boiling so that it won't be overcooked and fall apart.

Prick the skin of the *cotechino* on all sides and put it on to boil in a separate pot in abundant cold water. When it boils, reduce the heat and simmer 2 hours.

When it's time to serve, remove the meats and chicken from the pot, saving the broth. Remove the *cotechino* from its pot and throw away that water. Cut the chicken in the usual pieces of leg, wing, half breast, etc. Skin the tongue and slice it very thin, slightly on the diagonal. Slice the beef and *cotechino*. Put all the meats and chicken on a large, well-heated platter, baste with a bit of hot broth, and serve with *salsa verde* (page 219).

Strain the broth into another big pot. If you wish to clarify it, beat the egg whites slightly, bring the strained broth to a boil, add the beaten egg whites and let them boil, beating with a whisk for about 2 minutes, or until the little particles floating in the broth have been caught by the egg whites. Pour through a cheesecloth-lined sieve into another pan.

Use about half the broth for cooking *cappelletti* or any other *minestra* for a first course. The rest may be saved in the refrigerator a couple of days or frozen in the freezer for weeks. For 8.

Coda alla Vaccinara
OXTAIL STEW, COWHAND'S STYLE

This classic dish from Rome's Trastevere section, oxtail in a rich tomato sauce, is seasoned with garlic, onion, and dry wine, and served with chunks of celery added in the final minutes of cooking. Your wine can be red, but the *Trasteverini* always use white—usually Rome's own Frascati.

FOR THE BATTUTO:
2 slices lean salt pork
1 onion
1 stalk celery
1 clove garlic
3–4 tablespoons olive oil

3 pounds oxtails, in small pieces
1 cup dry wine, preferably white
4 cups peeled plum tomatoes
beef broth
2–3 teaspoons salt, or to taste
1 bunch celery

Make a *battuto* by chopping the salt pork with the onion, celery, and garlic, and then mincing them down to a paste. Sauté the *battuto* until golden in the olive oil in a big stew pot, and then add the oxtail pieces. (Frequently the most uniform are found in ordinary supermarkets, packed in frozen 3-pound packages; fresh ones can be obtained from Italian meat markets.)

Over medium heat, stir, turn, and cook the oxtails until they are thoroughly browned all around. Add the wine and when it has evaporated, add the plum tomatoes, mashing them a bit with a wooden spoon against the side of the pot. Add the salt. Bring to a boil, reduce the heat to a simmer, cover, and cook gently 2–3 hours, or until the meat practically falls off the bone. Stir occasionally during cooking and if the sauce gets too dense, add ¼–½ cup of broth (real or made with bouillon cubes) or water to thin it. Taste for salt, adding some more if necessary.

Remove the leaves from the bunch of celery, wash, and chop it into 2-inch chunks. Add to the oxtails, raise the heat, and cook another 10–15 minutes or so, or until the celery has lent its flavor to the sauce and is tender but still rather crisp.

Serve with generous amounts of hot Italian bread, capacious napkins, and finger bowls for those who really clean the bone by taking it in hand. For 6.

Cotolette alla Calabrese
BEEF CUTLETS, CALABRIAN STYLE

Thin slices of beef or veal dipped in egg and bread crumbs, golden fried, and served with a sauce of sweet peppers and tomato: these are the principals in this southern Italian dish. Like the Neapolitan *pizzaiola,* meat cooked this way is grand with whipped potatoes.

FOR THE SAUCE:
1 tablespoon chopped parsley
1 clove garlic
3 tablespoons olive oil
1–1½ cups peeled plum tomatoes,
*   with juice*
2 big red sweet peppers
½ teaspoon salt, or to taste

FOR THE MEAT:
1½ pounds bottom round beef (or
*   veal)*
½ cup flour
2 eggs, beaten
¾ cup sifted bread crumbs
2 tablespoons butter
2 tablespoons olive oil
½ teaspoon salt, or to taste

Mince the parsley and garlic together and sauté them in the olive oil in a medium-size frying pan over medium heat. Add the tomatoes, mashing them with a fork as they go in, and simmer about 10 minutes.

Peel the peppers either by blanching them in boiling water for 10 minutes, or stripping off the thin outer skin with a paring knife, or by roasting them over an open flame (page 14). Cut first in strips, chop coarsely, and add to the simmering tomato sauce.

Simmer another 5 minutes, taste for salt on a piece of bread, and if needed, add a dash or two of salt.

Slice the meat into thin slices no thicker than ⅛ inch. Pound them with a meat pounder or the flat of a big butcher knife to tenderize them even more.

Dip in the flour and pat well on both sides. Dip them in the beaten egg, and then in the sifted bread crumbs, gently patting on as many crumbs as will adhere. Let them sit about 5 minutes.

Heat the butter and oil in another frying pan over medium heat and fry the slices on both sides. Put them into the simmering pepper-tomato sauce. Scrape the pan well, add the butter and oil and scrapings to the sauce, and let the meat simmer another 5 minutes. For 6.

Fettine alla Pizzaiola
BEEF SLICES IN PIZZA SAUCE

Thin slices of beef round (top or bottom) are cooked in a sauce of tomatoes seasoned with a touch of oregano and parsley. Not so incidentally, mashed potatoes are a perfect complement to this dish.

Semifrozen meat can be cut very thin with the home slicer. Hence we buy a 3-pound piece, put it in the freezer until very firm but not rock hard, remove it, slice it, and store the slices, each separated by plastic wrap, in the meat drawer.

1 1/2–2 pounds top or bottom round
4 tablespoons olive oil
1 clove garlic
2 cups peeled plum tomatoes

1 1/2 teaspoons salt, or to taste
1 teaspoon oregano
1 tablespoon chopped parsley

Slice the beef into the thinnest possible slices (they should be no thicker than 1/8 inch), and then pound them to make them even thinner, bigger, and more tender.

Heat the olive oil over medium heat. Brown the meat slices quickly in the oil, turning them as soon as possible and removing them to a warm platter the minute both sides are barely done.

Slice the garlic clove in half, sauté it until golden in the olive oil, and discard it. Add the plum tomatoes, mashing them as they go in. Add the salt and oregano, and cook over medium heat for about 15 minutes, or until thickened to sauce consistency. Put the meat slices and their now accumulated juices back in the sauce. Add the parsley, stir gently, and simmer another 5 minutes. For 6.

Fettine in Padella
PAN-COOKED BEEF SLICES

In padella means "in the pan." Recipes cooked *in padella* are simple and take practically no time or thought. Beef slices cooked in this way are tasty and just different enough from the ordinary steak to warrant recognition with a recipe of their own.

12 small or 6 large slices bottom
    round (about 1 1/2 pounds)
3 tablespoons unsalted butter

salt and pepper to taste
2 lemons
2–3 tablespoons wine

You can buy bottom round already sliced or use a 3–4-pound roasting piece and slice it yourself to make enough for two meals. The first slices of the round will be large and long, and the end slices will be short. Either way, make them no thicker than ⅛ of an inch. Pound the slices to make them tender and even thinner.

Melt the butter in a big frying pan over medium heat. Put in as many slices as will fit comfortably and brown them quickly on both sides. Salt and pepper lightly. Remove the slices the minute the juices start to flow on their second sides and place them on a warm platter in a warm place. Repeat until all the slices are cooked.

Add the juice of ½ lemon to the pan's sauce, scrape the bottom and sides with a wooden spoon to collect any bits stuck there, and add a little wine and any juice from the platter to extend the sauce. Put the cooked slices back in the sauce if they've cooled, or pour the hot sauce over the cooked slices if they haven't. Serve with wedges of lemon. For 6.

Filetto alla Marco Polo
TENDERLOIN OF BEEF, MARCO POLO

Named for the famous Italian discoverer Marco Polo, this particular recipe gilds the tenderloin with seasonings from China, where the Venetian explorer stayed for years. The recipe is new and made possible with the Italian markets full of exotic things from faraway lands.

4 pounds boneless beef tenderloin
4 slices fresh ginger
2 jiggers (3 ounces) cognac
1 garlic clove, peeled and cut lengthwise into slivers

dash of soy sauce
dry red wine
olive oil

Cut off and discard all long tendons and fat around the outside of the tenderloin.

Place the meat in a dish just large enough to accommodate it. (If you don't have the right size, make one of heavy-duty aluminum foil or use a sturdy plastic bag, such as a roasting bag, and later seal it well.)

Add the ginger, cognac, garlic, and soy sauce to the bowl or bag. Pour on enough red wine to come about halfway up the side of the meat. Cover and marinate for 2 or 3 hours, turning from time to time.

Preheat oven to 500°.

Barely cover the bottom of a large sauté pan with olive oil and brown the meat in it over high heat, turning until it is evenly and nicely browned on all sides.

Transfer the beef to a roasting pan and roast in the hot (500°) oven 25 minutes. Turn off the heat and let the meat stay in the cooling oven until the meat thermometer registers 140°. Remove meat from oven and keep warm. Add pan juices to the marinade and reduce to serve as a sauce with the meat. For 6–8.

Involtini in Umido
BEEF BIRDS IN TOMATO SAUCE

The Chinese would call these wrapplings, the French *alouettes*, Americans birds. But whatever you call them, these thin slices of beef—lined with *prosciutto*, filled with chopped celery, wrapped like a package, and cooked in a sauce—taste absolutely delicious.

2–2½ pounds top or bottom round
    roast
¼ pound prosciutto
2 stalks celery
2 tablespoons chopped parsley
freshly ground pepper

3 cups peeled plum tomatoes
1 medium onion
1 carrot
2–3 tablespoons olive oil
salt
½ cup dry wine, red or white

Slice thin slices from a top round roast (or bottom round, but it will be a little chewier) and pound them well to make them even thinner and more tender. Cut the slices into 4- × 4-inch pieces, or as near to that size as possible, saving the trimmings. Cut the *prosciutto* to match the meat pieces and save those trimmings. Chop 1 stalk of celery, 1 tablespoon parsley, and the meat trimmings all together, adding a twist of the pepper mill, until the whole pile is of paste consistency. On each piece of meat put a slice of *prosciutto* and about 1 tablespoon of celery-meat paste in the middle. Roll the slice up on the diagonal, then fold over the ends, one at a time, making a little packet that you can either skewer with a wooden pick or tie with cotton thread to hold it shut during cooking.

Cut up the plum tomatoes and put them through a sieve. Mince the onion and carrot with the remaining celery and parsley, and sauté until golden in a wide frying pan in just enough olive oil to cover the bottom. When the minced vegetables are golden, add the meat packets and brown them gently all around. Add salt to taste. Add the wine and when it has almost evaporated, add the strained tomatoes. The liquid in the pan should just cover the meat. If it doesn't, add a bit of hot water. Bring the pan to a boil, cover it, reduce the heat, and simmer for about 1 hour, stirring occasionally, until the sauce has been reduced and concentrated and the meat is very tender. For 6.

Polpette di Manzo
BEEF MEATBALLS

These delectable meatballs are made of twice-ground beef, seasoned with parsley, Parmesan cheese, and nutmeg, rolled in bread crumbs, and fried in oil. They can be served with lemon wedges or Tomato-and-Onion Sauce (page 218). The same mixture makes the filling for zucchini or cabbage leaves.

2 pounds twice-ground beef
2 eggs
3 tablespoons chopped parsley
1 teaspoon freshly grated nutmeg
2½ teaspoons salt
4 tablespoons grated Parmesan
   cheese

3 slices day-old Italian bread
1 cup unseasoned bread crumbs
vegetable oil for frying
lemon wedges (or Tomato-and-
   Onion Sauce)

Put the twice-ground meat in a large bowl and add the eggs, parsley, nutmeg, salt, and cheese. Wet the bread, squeeze out the water, and shred it into the meat mixture. If the crusts are too crusty and don't shred easily, discard them. Mix everything well but not too harshly. Form the mixture into balls about the size of a large egg. Flatten them a bit so that they are not more than 1 inch thick in the middle. Roll the *polpette* in bread crumbs, patting them gently to get them well covered.

Pour the frying oil in a pan to a depth of ½ inch (half the thickness of the *polpette*). When the oil is bubbling hot, put the *polpette* in and cook them until they are nicely browned and crisp on both sides. Remove them and drain on paper towels. Serve with wedges of lemon or simmer them in Tomato-and-Onion Sauce for about 10 minutes more and then serve. For 6.

Cavoli Imbottiti
STUFFED CABBAGE LEAVES

Stuffed cabbage leaves stretch a bit of beef to make a rather special dish that is easy to double for a crowd and is very good when reheated.

1 large head cabbage
1 recipe mixture for polpette (pages
   138–39)

1 recipe Tomato-and-Onion Sauce
   (page 218)

Tear off and discard the tough outer leaves of the head of a big cabbage. With a sharp, strong knife, cut all around the core and lift out as much of it as possible. Plunge the whole cored head into boiling salted water for about 5 minutes or just long enough to let the leaves get limp but not cooked through. Drain, cool, separate the leaves, and spread on paper towels to dry off a bit.

Make the *polpette* mixture for the filling and put a rounded tablespoon of it on each leaf. Then wrap the leaf up like a neat package and tie it with cotton thread.

Make the Tomato-and-Onion Sauce. When it has simmered for about 15 minutes, add the stuffed cabbage leaves and continue simmering for another 10–15 minutes. For 6.

Stracotto di Cremona
POT ROAST IN THE STYLE OF CREMONA

Stracotto means extra-cooked, or cooked and cooked and cooked. It's a northern Italian pot roast originally from the Piedmont, but the best we ever ate was in Cremona, which is in Lombardy. Traditionally, it would be cooked in a top-of-the-stove earthenware pot taller than it is wide with a very tight cover. After the first 3–4 hours simmering, the heat would be turned off and the *stracotto* left to cool. The next day the pot would be uncovered, the sauce stirred, and half a glass of red wine added, Barbera usually but at any rate a full-bodied dry red wine. The *stracotto* would then be covered and brought back to a simmer for another 3–4 hours. By that time, as an old Cremonese friend used to say, just a whiff of *stracotto* was the equivalent of a meal. Above and beyond the time consumed in its making, the essential elements are simply a nice piece of chuck, top or bottom round, seasoning vegetables, spices, and dry red wine—all of which blend to an incredible richness.GFR

3-pound pot roast (boneless chuck
    top or bottom round)
2–4 slices lean salt pork
6 whole cloves
1 medium onion
1 medium carrot
1 stalk celery
1 quart dry red wine (or 2 cups wine
    and 2 cups water)

1 stick of cinnamon
3 tablespoons olive oil, or enough to
    cover pot bottom
flour
1 teaspoon salt
½ teaspoon ground pepper
2 tablespoons tomato paste (diluted
    in 1 cup water)

If your meat is very streaked with fat, use only 2 good slices of salt pork. If it is fairly lean, use 4 slices. Cut the salt pork slices crosswise into little strips. Make a whole series of slits in the roast on all sides and stuff them with the strips of pork. Stick in the cloves at random. Then tie the piece of meat with butcher string as you would a sausage or a neat parcel.

Put the roast in a bowl just wide enough to fit it snugly and deep enough to cover the roast with the marinade. Mince the onion, carrot, and celery as finely as possible and sprinkle over the meat. Add the wine and the cinnamon and marinate at least 8 hours.

Remove the meat from the marinade and drain it well. Put the olive oil in a stew pot that has a good cover. Flour the meat, patting it well to get it evenly covered. Add the meat to the oil and brown slowly over medium heat. Once browned, salt and pepper the meat. Scoop the minced vegetables out of the marinade and add them to the pot. When these are golden, add the marinade. Add the tomato paste diluted in warm water and, if necessary, more warm water enough to cover. Bring the pot to a boil, reduce the heat to a very low simmer, and cover. Put a piece of heavy brown paper between the pot and its cover to seal it well. Cook very, very slowly for at least 4 hours. Uncover the pot, stir the sauce gently, and continue cooking uncovered until the sauce has reduced and thickened. The sauce should be smooth, like a fine gravy. The meat should be tender enough to cut with a spoon.

Use half the sauce with pasta *(rigatoni* or *fet-* *tuccine)* as a first course, and the rest with the meat for a second course. Serve with whipped potatoes or slices of hot Italian bread in order to take full advantage of the sauce. For 8 to 10.

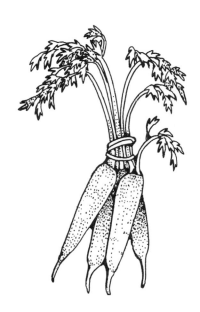

Vitello
VEAL

Everyone knows that veal cuts are just about the most expensive pieces of protein to reach the table. There are times, however, when expense is justifiably set aside, and happily, most of the ways in which Italians use veal are fairly parsimonious anyway.

Italian veal, like Italian lamb, has a short professional life. Once the animal reaches 4–5 months of age its meat becomes known as *vitellone* (big veal), and as such is not as highly appreciated, nor is it as costly. Experienced Italian cooks and shoppers recognize, or some think they do, the age of the veal by the color of the meat: pale pink for the youngest and rosy pink for the oldest. It isn't at all unusual to get involved in long erudite discussions with the butcher and a handful of total strangers while only waiting to be served. The color, size, age of the meat, and the recipe planned all undergo scrutiny.

The crucial dimension of a veal cutlet or chop is one matter that is rarely challenged: it should be as close to ⅛ inch thick as possible and then should be pounded down even thinner. About 2 pounds cut like this serves 6 people. All the little pieces left after cutlets and chops or an extraordinary roast have been cut are sold for veal stew, a more delicate dish than its beef cousin. Breast of veal, probably the least expensive part of the animal, can be boned, stuffed, rolled, and cosseted in a sauce so that it becomes a dish worthy of a feast.

Cima alla Genovese
STUFFED VEAL BREAST, IN THE STYLE OF GENOA

One of Italy's most delicious, rather fancy entrées, which is ideal for large parties. At one point in our career, we directed a crew of about 15 amateur chefs and turned out 15 of these as well as the necessary vegetables and *Zuppe Inglesi* for a fund-raiser. One hundred and fifty guests cheered. In your own kitchen you'll find the assembly rather simple, and of course the real prize is that, made a day before, there is an enhanced flavor as well as a relaxed cook on the day of the feast. MR

1 veal breast (approximately 9 pounds), boned

1½ pounds lean pork butt, minced

1 pound boneless veal stew meat, minced

1 pound cooked ham or tongue, minced

1 garlic clove, minced

2 large raw eggs

1 cup grated Parmesan cheese

1 pint whipping cream

½ cup sweet gherkins cut in ½-inch pieces

4 ounces frozen peas

1 cup unsalted pistachio nuts, shelled

2 packets unflavored gelatin (2 tablespoons)

1 quart chicken broth (approximate)

4 hard-cooked eggs

8 ½-inch-square strips mortadella

FOR THE PAN:

4 large carrots

4 onions

4 outer stalks celery, with leaves

Optional: aspic for decoration (pages 242–43), hearts of lettuce, tomato roses, parsley

Pound the veal breast well to make it as even as possible in thickness and to stretch it. Trim the edges to make a fairly respectable rectangle and then trim out any excess cartilage or fat here and there. Score patches where the meat is still thicker than that surrounding.

Mix the minced meats with the garlic, raw eggs, cheese, whipping cream, gherkins, frozen peas, and pistachio nuts. Dissolve the gelatin in ½ cup of the chicken broth and mix it in.

Spread the mix on the veal breast, leaving a bare border of about 1 inch on all sides. Line the 4 eggs down the center of the breast and the strips of *mortadella* end-to-end, making two lengths on either side of the eggs. Bring the two long sides of the rectangle of veal together, skewer them, and then sew them together. Finally skewer or sew together the two ends. Wrap the whole roll in cheesecloth and then tie it like a salami but not too tightly.

Place the roll in a shallow roasting pan. Surround it with the carrots, onions, celery. Add the rest of the chicken broth. Place the pan over two burners of your stove, bring the broth to a boil, cover the entire pan with aluminum foil, and lower the heat. Cook 2 hours. Remove the veal to a platter, weight it down, and let it cool.

When cool, place the roll in refrigerator until the following day. A half hour before the serving time, remove the cheesecloth. Slice the roll into ½-inch slices on a platter. Decorate with aspic cubes or shapes, tomato roses, a leaf or two of parsley here and there, and/or hearts of lettuce. Serves about 15 people.

Costolette alla Milanese
VEAL CHOPS, MILANESE STYLE

Milan is famous for its traditional way of preparing veal chops: they are pounded thin, dipped in beaten egg, then in fine bread crumbs, and fried to a golden brown. They're always served with a bit of lemon juice. If you can't find the chops, you may use slices of veal round, cut thin, and achieve veal cutlets *alla Milanese.*

12 very thin veal rib chops
2 large eggs, beaten
1–2 cups fine unseasoned bread crumbs

¾ stick unsalted butter
3 tablespoons olive oil
1 teaspoon salt, or to taste
1½ lemons

Only the smallest veal chops should be used to prepare this dish, as the bone should be approximately ½ inch thick and the resulting chop the same. With a sharp knife, or just by pulling, loosen the meat around the handle of the chop and bend it back over the fleshiest part. Pound that part with the flat of a big butcher knife or a meat pounder to make it thinner and to get the little bent-back pieces to stick to the bigger one. Dip the chops, one by one, in the beaten egg so that they are completely covered. Then dip in fine bread crumbs, patting them gently to get as many crumbs as possible to adhere. Let them sit about 5 minutes.

Melt the butter with the oil in a big frying pan over medium heat and sauté the chops, turning them the minute they are golden brown on one side. Salt lightly. When both sides are nicely colored, remove to a hot serving plate and serve with lemon wedges. For 6.

Piccata di Vitello
VEAL IN LEMON-AND-WINE SAUCE

Veal slices, pounded thin, floured, cooked in butter, and then generously covered with a white wine and lemon sauce: this is a basic recipe used for white meat of poultry as well for veal. It gives a taste of both delicacy and sharpness that is hard to beat.

2 pounds veal round, sliced 1/8 inch thick
1/2 cup flour
6 tablespoons unsalted butter

1 teaspoon salt, or to taste
1/2 cup dry white wine
1 lemon
sprigs of parsley

This amount of veal usually cuts up into 8–12 thin slices, some larger than others. Pound them with a meat pounder to make them uniform and even more tender. Flour them by pressing them in the flour and patting them gently to get as much as possible to adhere.

Melt the butter in a big frying pan over medium heat and add the veal slices. Turn them the minute their edges whiten and salt them lightly. When both sides are done, pour in the wine and let bubble until its vapors cease to tingle the nose. Add the juice of 1/2 lemon and stir gently with a wooden spoon. Taste for both salt and lemon. Sometimes 1/2 lemon is too little for that nice tang that lemon juice should give to this sauce. If more lemon is needed, squeeze it on, stir, and cook a moment more. Serve with the sprigs of parsley, which many find adds still a third distinct flavor to the sauce and meat. For 6.

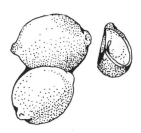

Cotolette alla Bolognese
VEAL CUTLETS, BOLOGNESE STYLE

You could call this a doubly blessed dish. It's made with thin slices of veal dipped in flour, egg, and finally bread crumbs, and is golden fried in butter. To crown this delicacy, the Bolognese add a thin slice of *prosciutto* and one of *mozzarella,* toast the cutlets in the oven, and before serving top them with a bit of tomato sauce.

2 pounds veal round, sliced ⅛ inch thick
½–¾ cup flour
2 large eggs, beaten
1 cup fine bread crumbs

1 teaspoon salt
¼ pound unsalted butter
⅓ pound prosciutto, *sliced thin*
½ pound whole-milk mozzarella
12 tablespoons tomato sauce (page 43)

Preheat the oven to 300°.

Pound the veal slices with a meat pounder or the flat side of a big butcher knife to make them thinner and as even as possible. Pat them into the flour, dusting both sides. Dip in beaten eggs and press the slices into the bread crumbs, again patting on both sides to make as many crumbs stick as possible.

Melt the butter and sauté the slices in it over medium heat, turning them over when the first side is golden brown. When both sides are done, remove, salt lightly and drain on paper towels. Put a slice of *prosciutto* on each piece of veal and then a thin slice of *mozzarella.* Place in an oven (300°) just long enough to melt the *mozzarella.* Before serving, top each slice with a couple of tablespoons of tomato sauce. For 6.

Involtini di Vitello e Prosciutto
VEAL AND *PROSCIUTTO* BIRDS

12 thin slices veal round (1½–2 pounds)
12 slices prosciutto (about 6 ounces)
12 tablespoons mozzarella cheese, grated

1½ teaspoons dried sage, crumbled, or 1 fresh sage leaf, minced
3 tablespoons unsalted butter
¼ cup olive oil

Pound the veal with a flat side of a meat pounder or the flat side of a heavy knife to make it even and thin.

Place a slice of *prosciutto* to cover each slice of veal. Sprinkle with *mozzarella;* add a sprinkling of sage.

146

Roll up each piece of veal, being careful to keep the filling in place. Skewer shut with a wooden pick.

Heat the butter and oil in a small skillet, add the veal rolls, and cook for about 5 minutes, turning the rolls as they brown.

Serve immediately. For 6.

Ossobuco
VEAL SHANKS

Literally, *ossobuco* means "bone with a hole," and in this case it is the small veal shinbone (shank), complete with its marrow, cooked in a bouquet of herbs and zest of lemon. The Milanese are the real patrons of this delicate dish, and they pair it with their *risotto*, one of the rare occasions when the first and second courses are served at the same time. It is a meal most people never forget.

FOR THE BATTUTO.
1 teaspoon rosemary
3–4 fresh sage leaves
1 small clove garlic
2 tablespoons chopped parsley
4 slices lemon zest

6–8 pieces veal shinbone
flour
4 tablespoons unsalted butter
3 tablespoons olive oil
1 cup dry white wine
1 teaspoon salt
freshly ground pepper
½–1 cup chicken broth

Have the veal shank sawed into pieces 1½–2 inches long. These pieces vary in width, so 2 small ones or 1 large makes a portion. If by any chance the skin around the meat of the bone is broken, tie butcher's string around the slice before flouring and browning in order to hold the meat snugly in place.

Flour the pieces thoroughly and brown them well in butter and oil over medium heat. Use a frying pan that will accommodate the *ossobuchi* snugly without crowding. If the pan is too big, the sauce will be too spread out and shallow to cook the veal properly.

Make a *battuto* of the rosemary, sage, garlic, parsley, and lemon and add to the browned veal bones. Spread the herbs around and cook for a moment or two. Add the wine and stir. Add the salt and a few grinds of pepper. When the wine has partially evaporated, add enough broth to bring the sauce to the top of the veal slices without covering them. Lower the heat and simmer about 40 minutes, or until really tender. Serve hot with the sauce. For 6.

Rollato di Vitello
ROLLED BREAST OF VEAL

A boned breast of veal, smothered in chopped flavorings of carrot, celery, sage, parsley, and layered with cheese, *mortadella*, and *prosciutto*, is rolled and cooked as gently as possible on top of the stove. This is a dish for special occasions, and can be served either warm or cold.

FOR THE BATTUTO:
½ stalk celery, with leaves
1 carrot
1 jumbo or 2 medium eggs, hard-boiled
1 fresh sage leaf
4 sprigs parsley
¼ shallot (or ⅛ onion)

1 small breast of veal, boned
¼ pound grated whole-milk mozzarella
3 slices mortadella
6 slices prosciutto
4 tablespoons olive oil
1 teaspoon rosemary
1 cup dry white wine
1 cup chicken broth

Have the butcher bone the veal breast, and be sure he gives you the bones. Spread the veal out, smooth side down, and pound it to an even thickness. Make a *battuto* of the celery, carrot, egg, sage, parsley, and shallot. Salt the rough-cut (boned) side of the veal and spread it with the *battuto,* leaving an inch bare on the long sides as well as the wider end. Cover the *battuto* with the grated *mozzarella,* then with the slices of *mortadella,* and finally with the *prosciutto.*

Starting with the smaller end of the veal breast, roll it up slowly into a big sausage. Be careful not to squeeze too hard; push the filling in place with your fingers as you roll so that it will not come out at the wide end. Temporarily skewer shut the lengthwise opening. Then tuck in and skewer each rolled end. Finally, tie up the whole roll like a sausage, using butcher's string, and remove the skewers.

Heat the olive oil over medium high heat in a big, heavy pot (a Dutch oven would be perfect) and put in the veal roll and bones. Sprinkle with the rosemary. Brown thoroughly, turning slowly, to seal in all the juices. Once it is browned, add the wine and let it evaporate. Then cover the pot, lower the heat, and cook for 1½ hours. Check it from time to time and turn the roll over so that it will cook evenly. Baste it with the juices in the pot; if they seem to be cooking away (you should have about ¾ inch of them in the pot), add some chicken broth.

When the meat is cooked, cool it on a platter at least 15 minutes before slicing. While it is cooling, add a bit more chicken broth to the juices in the pot, heat, scrape well to get any bits of meat from the sides and bottom, then strain into a sauceboat and serve hot with the sliced veal roll. If you prefer a thicker sauce, cook a few minutes over medium heat, or until thickened, before serving. For 6.

Spiedini alla Siciliana
VEAL ON SKEWERS, SICILIAN STYLE

Traveling in Sicily one wonderful summer, a group of friends asked us for a "buffet" dinner with promises of a local specialty to be cooked on site. We were told to dress casually and thus, in working clothes, we arrived, Franco's cameras and cases beginning to weigh heavily on both our shoulders. The friends were grand, albeit dressed in white linens, the table spread with as many Sicilian delicacies as it would hold, and our host, on a terrace just off the dining room, had the fire going. We all stood around watching and commenting while Frederico carefully painted his skewers with oil, turned them properly, and urged everyone to have a glass of wine. The dinner was indeed superb and presented with as much chic as any feast anywhere. Of all the dishes, watermelon sherbet tinged with chocolate included, these little packets of veal remained the most securely in our palate-memory. MR

3 pounds veal round, preferably
    semifrozen for easy slicing
½ pound Sicilian or dry salted
    ricotta, or feta cheese
½ pound thinly sliced prosciutto
½ cup coarse unseasoned bread
    crumbs

½–¾ cup olive oil, approximately
3–4 small onions, peeled
3 dozen bay leaves
1½ teaspoons salt (approximate)
2 teaspoons dried oregano

Slice the veal as thinly as possible—to make at least 24 slices. Pound with the flat side of a meat pounder to make the slices even thinner. Trim off and discard all fat. Cut each slice of veal in half.

Chop the cheese and mince the prosciutto. Mix cheese and prosciutto with the bread crumbs. Dampen with a bit of the olive oil, just enough to hold the mixture together.

Put a teaspoon of cheese-ham mixture in the center of each slice of meat. Fold the corners of the veal in and over the filling to enclose it.

Cut the onions in quarters lengthwise. Cut off the root end at the base of each quarter.

Slide a wedge of quartered onion onto a skewer. Follow with a bay leaf and a filled packet of veal, and continue with onion, bay leaf, and meat until each skewer holds 4 veal packets. Finish each skewer with a bay leaf and onion piece. Slide a second skewer up through the various pieces to hold them firmly.

Mix the rest of the olive oil together with the salt and oregano. Brush the filled skewers with the flavored oil and place them over hot coals on an outdoor grill or in a preheated broiler. Grill, turning as the meat browns, and brush several times with oil as the veal cools. For 6.

Saltimbocca
VEAL CUTLETS WITH *PROSCIUTTO*

The translation for this delicacy is "jump in the mouth." Tender veal slices are seasoned with fresh sage, salted by the thin pieces of *prosciutto* they're layered with, and then are cooked in butter. It's really a quick dish, tastes like a banquet, and is synonymous with Rome.

2 pounds veal round, in palm-size slices, ⅛ inch thick
¼ pound prosciutto, *thinly sliced*
fresh sage leaves, 1 per slice of veal

6 tablespoons unsalted butter
salt
freshly ground pepper

Pound the veal slices gently to make them even. Cut the *prosciutto* slices so that there is a piece to cover each piece of veal. Put a leaf of fresh sage on each veal slice and cover with *prosciutto.* Pin the ham to the veal with a wooden pick or roll the slices up with the ham inside and fix with a wooden pick.

Put half the butter in a good-size frying pan, melt it over medium heat, and put in the *saltimbocca* with just a touch of salt and pepper (the prosciutto will take care of the major salting). The minute the edges of the veal start to whiten, turn the pieces over. Total cooking time is approximately 2 minutes to a side.

When they are cooked, remove the slices or rolls to a hot platter. Over medium heat, melt the rest of the butter, stir, and scrape the edges and bottom of the pan to get all the bits off and into the butter. Pour it over the *saltimbocca* and serve. For 6.

Scaloppine al Marsala
VEAL CUTLETS WITH MARSALA WINE SAUCE

By now the very name of this dish (either veal scallops, veal *scaloppine,* or a version thereof) has taken its place in the international vocabulary, but the original dish remains the same, far simpler and tastier than the many variations on the theme.

If you have to sauté the meat in two batches, put all the cutlets back in the pan before you add the Marsala. Once you have added the wine, turn them over to get them well coated with the sauce on both sides. Then remove them, add the broth, and proceed as above.

2 pounds veal round, sliced 1/8 inch
    thick
flour
1/4 pound butter

salt
freshly ground pepper
1/2 cup Marsala wine
4–5 tablespoons chicken broth

Pound the veal slices gently with a meat pounder or the flat side of a heavy butcher knife. Pat with flour so that as much as possible adheres to both sides of the cutlets.

Melt the butter in the widest sauté pan you have and put in the slices in one layer. Salt and pepper lightly. Sauté quickly both sides over medium high heat. As soon as both sides are done, pour in the Marsala and cook another 2 minutes.

Remove the slices to a hot platter.

Add just enough broth to the liquid in the pan to make a pourable sauce. (If you don't have real chicken broth available, use a bouillon cube in hot water.) Scrape the bottom and sides of the pan to collect any bits stuck there, stir, and cook for another 1–2 minutes. Pour over the veal slices and serve. For 6.

Spezzatino di Vitello con Piselli
VEAL STEW WITH PEAS

This is a stew of bite-size chunks of veal, flavored with white wine and tomatoes, and combined at the end of its cooking with tiny peas.

For the extra fancy dinners, place *spezzatino* in puff pastry shells, 2 to a person, or serve it with slices of grilled *polenta*.

2 pounds boneless veal stew meat
1/2 cup flour
3–4 tablespoons olive oil
1 clove garlic
2 teaspoons salt

freshly ground pepper
1 tablespoon minced parsley
1 cup dry white wine
2 cups peeled plum tomatoes
10-ounce package frozen tiny peas,
    defrosted

Cut the veal into bite-size pieces and flour them lightly by shaking in a bag with about 1/4 cup of flour.

Put enough olive oil in the bottom of a stew pot just barely to cover, add the garlic, sauté until golden, and then discard the clove. Add the floured veal pieces and brown them thoroughly and slowly. Add the salt, pepper, parsley, and wine. When the wine has evaporated, add the plum tomatoes, mashing them up a bit as they go in. If

needed, add enough water so that the meat is barely covered. Cover the pot and simmer on low heat for about an hour.

Stir once in a while, and if the sauce has reduced too much, add a bit of hot water or chicken broth to thin it. Taste for seasonings and tenderness. When the meat is really tender, add the defrosted peas and cook for another 10 minutes. Serve hot with hot Italian bread. For 6.

Vitello Tonnato
VEAL WITH TUNA SAUCE

Vitello tonnato is a favorite Italian cold dish for a summer's day. Famous in the Piedmont and Lombardy, loved by the French, who call it *veau tonné,* and the English, who call it tunnied veal, it is easy to make. Most people prepare this dish, with its wine-and-tuna sauce, the day before serving so that all its flavors blend perfectly.

FOR THE BATTUTO:
1 tablespoon capers
1–2 fresh sage leaves
1 small onion
2–3 anchovy fillets

2-pound boned roast of veal
2 cups dry white wine
1 tablespoon wine vinegar
salt to taste
1 6½-ounce can Italian tuna
freshly ground pepper
½ cup olive oil
juice of 1 lemon

Make a *battuto* of the capers, sage, onion, and anchovy fillets and put it in a pan just big enough to hold the meat snugly. Tie the meat with butcher's string and put it on top of the *battuto.* Add the wine, the vinegar, and as much water as necessary just barely to cover the meat. Bring to a boil, reduce the heat, and cook at a slow boil for about 1½ hours, or until the liquid is reduced to about ⅔ of the original amount. Taste for salt and adjust if necessary. Add a few grinds of pepper.

Drain the tuna, saving the oil if it's olive oil. Put the drained tuna in with the meat, mashing it up with a spoon, and cook another 15 minutes. Remove the meat and put it on a cool platter.

If you don't have a blender or a food processor: let the tuna sauce cool slightly and then put it through a sieve into a bowl. Add the olive oil (that reserved from the tuna if it was olive oil, plus enough to make ½ cup) and the lemon juice, and blend well.

If you do have a blender or a food processor: put the tuna sauce in it and blend at high speed. When it is smooth and homogeneous, add the olive oil and lemon juice and blend at low speed. The sauce should be smooth, relatively thick, and creamy. It should not be runny.

When it is cool, cut the veal into very thin slices. Pour a bit of sauce in the bottom of a deep platter. Arrange the veal slices on the sauce so that they barely overlap. Pour the rest of the sauce over them. Decorate with a few more capers or tiny sprigs of parsley, as you wish. (Some cooks like to add a garnish of sliced hardboiled eggs just before serving to accent the edges of the platter.) Cover with another inverted platter or aluminum foil and refrigerate for at least 24 hours. This dish keeps well in the refrigerator for a long time—up to a week—and actually improves with time. For 6.

Agnello o Abbacchio
LAMB

Italian lambs seem to reach the slaughtering age sooner than their American or Australian cousins. They weigh in at 18–20 pounds at the point of sale. Knowing the frugality of shepherds in general and Italians in particular, this waste of potential poundage may appear illogical, but perhaps it can be explained by the answer we got from an old hand in the Abruzzi, "We have limited pastures, so we have to limit the flock."

"Fine," we said, "but why not slaughter the big ones and let the little ones grow?"

He considered a second whether he would answer such a stupid question, and then he told us, "Because the little ones taste better."

All this is to say that in Italy only young baby lamb *(abbacchio)* deserves the title of lamb. Once past that stage it becomes mutton.

Nonetheless, there are several dishes that can be prepared with excellent results using older lamb *(agnello)* like that available on the American market. Also in many Italo-American markets, especially around Easter, one can find true baby lamb for *abbacchio al forno* (roast lamb). What little fat there is on an 18-pound lamb is very delicate and digestible, and the cuts cook in practically no time. As the lamb grows beyond the 20-pound stage, its fat loses these qualities, and it is advisable to trim off as much as possible, cook in a very slow oven (if roasting), or cut and trim and cook on top of the stove, making good use of wine and/or wine vinegar to soften and season the meat. The best cuts, American style, are the leg, the rack or ribs, then the fore, and finally the breast and neck.

Abbacchio al Forno
ROAST LAMB

Baby lamb, a traditional Easter dish, uses almost half a lamb, which should weigh no more than 6–8 pounds (only the fore is saved for other dishes). Flavored with a whisper of garlic and a breath of rosemary, it is roasted with thin wedges of potatoes.

FOR THE BATTUTO:
½ clove garlic
3 teaspoons dried rosemary, or 2 sprigs fresh
2 teaspoons chopped parsley
1 teaspoon salt
pepper (3–4 twists of the mill)
1 teaspoon olive oil

half baby lamb, 6–8 pounds
½ cup olive oil
1 teaspoon rosemary
2 teaspoons salt
pepper, to taste
6–8 potatoes, cut into quarters or eighths to make thin wedges

Preheat the oven to 400°.

Chop up all the dry ingredients of the *battuto,* mince them further, pile them up, and add 1 teaspoon olive oil to make a paste. With a sharp knife make 6–8 slits in the lamb and fill them with the *battuto.*

Put the ½ cup olive oil in an open roasting pan, add the lamb, and turn it over and over in the oil to coat all sides. Sprinkle with the remaining 1 teaspoon rosemary, 2 teaspoons salt, and pepper to taste. Surround the lamb with the thin wedges of potato, giving them a turn to coat with oil, and place the pan in the 400° oven for 10 minutes. Reduce the heat to 375° and roast for approximately 45 minutes more, or until the meatiest part of the lamb reaches 150–160° on the meat thermometer. Remove the lamb from the pan, test the potatoes, and if they are not done, return the heat to 400° and finish roasting the potatoes. During the 55 minutes' roasting time, baste the lamb 3 or 4 times, and turn the potatoes with a spatula in order to get them evenly browned and roasted. For 6.

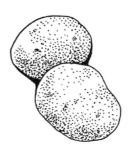

Abbacchio alla Cacciatora
HUNTER'S LAMB

Here lamb chunks are prepared the way the hunters of yesterday cooked venison, spiced with rosemary and garlic, simmered in wine and wine vinegar.

Buy the smallest lamb possible for the best of flavor and texture. Originally this dish was made with acidulous wine, wine starting to go to vinegar, which was common in Italian households, especially in the wine-producing areas.

3 pounds lamb fore
2 cloves garlic
3–4 tablespoons olive oil
3 teaspoons rosemary

2 teaspoons salt
pepper to taste
½ cup wine vinegar
½ cup dry white wine

Have the butcher chop the lamb into chunks, as for stew. Cut off any extra fat, but leave the bones in, as they add flavor.

Peel the garlic cloves, split them, and sauté them in a large frying pan over medium heat in just enough olive oil to cover the bottom of the pan. When the garlic is golden, remove it and add the chunks of lamb, rosemary, salt, and pepper. Raise the heat and brown the meat thoroughly on all sides. Add the vinegar and quickly cover the pan for a few seconds, or until you hear that the vinegar has stopped steaming. Then uncover and stir with a wooden spoon to loosen any bits of browned meat stuck to the sides and bottom of the pan. Add the wine and stir some more. When the wine has almost evaporated, lower the heat and cook until tender, about 15 minutes.

If your pan is not large enough to accommodate the meat in one layer, either do the browning in two pans, each containing garlic-flavored olive oil, or brown one portion at a time. When all the pieces are evenly and thoroughly browned, combine them in one pan before adding the vinegar and wine. With a bit of vinegar, rinse out the pan in which you browned the lamb, scraping to detach all the bits that may have stuck to the side of the pan, and add to the lamb pieces to enrich the wine sauce. Cook about 15 minutes more, or until tender. Serve with the sauce. For 6.

Costolette d'Abbacchio Panate
BREADED LAMB CHOPS

Loin lamb chops, no more than ½ inch thick, are dipped in beaten egg and bread crumbs, fried crisp, and served with lemon. Chops cooked this way are in that category of delicate foods best eaten with the hands in order to get every last tasty morsel.

12 thin (½-inch) loin lamb chops
3 eggs
1½–2 teaspoons salt, or to taste

1 cup unseasoned fine bread crumbs
4–6 tablespoons olive oil
1½ lemons

It's not always easy to find thin-cut lamb chops, so ask the butcher to cut them that way. Trim off any excess fat and cut a bit of the meat away from what could be called the handle of the chop. Turn it back on the meaty end and pound with a meat pounder to thin it a bit more and to make the folded meat stick to the main part of the chop. Beat the eggs well and add the salt. Dip the chops, one by one, into the eggs, then press them into the bread crumbs, first one side and then the other. Pat them well so that as many crumbs stick as possible. Let stand a few minutes.

Heat the oil in a wide frying pan, put in the chops, and fry on both sides until they are a golden brown. Drain on paper towels and serve hot with lemon wedges. For 6.

Spiedini d'Agnello
LAMB ON SKEWERS

1½ pounds lean lamb, boneless
4 tablespoons olive oil
*3 sprigs fresh rosemary, or 2 tea-
     spoons dried*
1 teaspoon salt
freshly ground pepper to taste

dash of Tabasco sauce
juice of 1 lemon
5 small artichokes
3 leeks
2 red sweet peppers
4 ounces mushrooms

Cut the lamb in bite-size pieces. Place in a bowl and sprinkle with the oil, rosemary, salt, pepper, Tabasco, and 1 tablespoon of lemon juice. Turn over and over to coat all the pieces with the seasonings. Cover and refrigerate for at least an hour.

Prepare the artichokes (pages 226–27) and cut in half. Soak in water to which you have added the remaining lemon juice.

Cut off and discard roots and green tops of the leeks. Blanch the whites of the leeks in salted boiling water for 3 minutes. Drain immediately.

Roast the peppers (page 14), slip off their skins, core, and cut in bite-size pieces.

Clean the mushrooms as necessary and cut off the bases of their stems; cut in half if very large.

When the leeks are cool, slice in ½-inch rounds.

The above is enough to fill about 1 dozen 10-inch skewers. Count your meat pieces so that you can allow about the same number for each skewer, with a piece of lamb at each end.

Skewer a piece of lamb, add a slice of leek, then follow with pepper, artichoke, lamb, mushroom, and so forth, finishing the skewer with another piece of lamb. The vegetable line-up is up to you, but do not brush off any pieces of rosemary clinging to the meat.

Skewers may be cooked on an oiled hot griddle, in an oiled broiler, in a large frying pan, or, even better, over the coals of an outdoor grill.

Brush the kebabs with any remaining marinade during cooking. Add a sprinkle of salt and pepper after the meat has browned. Remove from heat when the meat is cooked and browned on all sides, but still pink inside. For 4 to 6.

Coscia d'Agnello al Gin
LEG OF LAMB WITH GIN

1 leg spring lamb (about 4 pounds)
2 slices lean bacon, salt pork, or pancetta
1 tablespoon fresh rosemary leaves, or 2 teaspoons dried rosemary
1 small garlic clove, peeled
½ teaspoon salt (approximate)
freshly ground pepper to taste

2 tablespoons juniper berries
6 anchovy fillets
1 tablespoon Dijon mustard
5 tablespoons olive oil
1 tablespoon fine unseasoned bread crumbs (approximate)
½ cup dry white wine
½ cup gin

Preheat the oven to 425°.

Trim the lamb of all excess fat, leaving just a thin layer on the top side of the roast.

Mince together bacon, salt pork, or *pancetta*, rosemary, and garlic. Add salt and a generous amount of pepper to the mince. Mix well.

Make slits in and around the leg and insert portions of the mince in each.

Crush the juniper berries with the anchovy fillets. Add the mustard, a scant tablespoon of the olive oil, and just enough bread crumbs to make a paste.

Spread the paste over the top and sides of the lamb.

Put 3 tablespoons of olive oil in the bottom of a roasting pan. Place the lamb in the pan and roast for 15 minutes in the hot (425°) oven.

Pour the wine and one more tablespoon of olive oil over the lamb. Baste and bake another 15 minutes.

Pour gin over the leg and baste once. Then reduce heat to 390° and continue roasting 1 hour. Baste occasionally.

Reduce heat to 375° and continue roasting for 30–40 minutes more or until meat thermometer registers 160°.

Place the lamb on a warm serving platter.

Sieve the pan juices into a saucepan, taste for seasoning, and adjust as necessary. Heat and serve with the lamb. For 6.

157

Costolette d'Abbacchio a Scottadito
GRILLED LAMB CHOPS

A scottadito (to scorch the fingers) is a Roman way of describing cooking swiftly over the high heat of a hot, open grill. The melted fat raises the flame to sear the outside of the chop quickly, leaving the inside tender and moist.

12 thin shoulder lamb chops
4 tablespoons olive oil
salt, pepper

2 teaspoons rosemary
1 1/2 lemons

Get your charcoal grill started.

Flatten the chops with a meat pounder or the flat side of a heavy butcher knife. Put the olive oil on a platter and dip the chops in it, oiling both sides. Let the chops marinate in the oil for about 5 minutes.

When the coals are red hot, remove the chops from the oil, salt and pepper them, and put them on the grill. Sprinkle them with the rosemary and turn them the minute they are crackling brown on one side. Brown the other side and serve with lemons cut in wedges. For 6.

Agnello alla Marchigiana
LAMB STEW IN THE STYLE OF THE MARCHES

The *Marchigiani,* the people of the Marches region of central Italy, know and understand good food and wine as well as any. This, their recipe, is one of the most appetizing ways of serving lamb stew.

2–3 pounds lamb fore, cut in chunks
1/2 cup flour
1 clove garlic
sprig of fresh rosemary, or 1 tea-
*   spoon dry*
1/4 cup olive oil

2 1/2 teaspoons salt
freshly ground pepper
1 cup dry white wine
1 cup plum tomatoes
1 teaspoon tomato paste, diluted in
*   1/4 cup warm water*

Put the lamb chunks and flour in a paper or plastic bag and shake well. Chop the garlic and rosemary to tiny bits and sauté them until golden in the oil in a fair-sized pan over high heat. Add the lamb and brown it thoroughly, turning it over and over on all sides. Add the salt, a few grinds of pepper, and the wine. When the wine has evaporated, add the tomatoes and the tomato paste diluted in warm water. When the whole mixture is back to a boil, lower the heat and simmer for about 1 hour, or until the meat is tender. Stir occasionally while the stew is simmering. For 6.

Agnello al Barolo
LAMB WITH BAROLO

*2 pounds boneless lamb, shoulder or
        leg*
flour for dredging
1 onion, peeled
4 tablespoons olive oil
*1 tablespoon fresh rosemary leaves,
        or 2 teaspoons dried rosemary*
1 small garlic clove, peeled

leaves of 3 sprigs Italian parsley
2 cloves, crushed
2 teaspoons salt (approximate)
freshly ground pepper to taste
*2 cups Barolo or other robust red
        wine*
*1 beef bouillon cube dissolved in ½
        cup hot water, or ½ cup beef
        broth*

Cut the lamb into 1½–2-inch cubes, dredge in flour, and pat gently to remove excess flour.

Slice the onion paper thin and sauté in the olive oil until limp. Add the cubed lamb and brown it thoroughly.

Mince together the rosemary, garlic, parsley, and cloves. Add to the lamb. Add salt and pepper.

Add the wine and the bouillon cube and its water to the stew.

Cover the pan, bring to a boil, lower the heat, and simmer 25 minutes, stirring occasionally. Then uncover and cook another 15 minutes or until the meat is tender, the sauce reduced a bit.

Serve with the meat sauce and mashed potatoes. For 4 to 6.

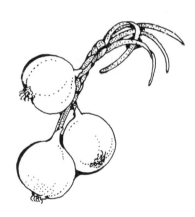

Maiale
PORK

Unlike cattle and sheep, which are raised only in some parts of Italy, pigs fare well—in fact, prosper—all over the country. Depending on climate and feed, they differ in size and taste from region to region. Most of the animal, after its demise, reaches the market cured and in an infinity of preparations. Almost every region, if not town, has its own cured pork specialty. For example, Parma is known for its *prosciutto,* cured, unsmoked ham. Bologna is the home of *mortadella,* the original bologna sausage. The Abruzzi is famous for all sorts of sausages, Modena for its *zamponi* (stuffed pigs' feet) and *cotechino* (cooking salami). Milano and Genoa vie for honors in the preparation of their salami.

The pork cuts perhaps most frequently called for are also cured: *pancetta* and *guanciale* (unsmoked bacon). They appear in pasta sauces and stuffings, as the base for gravies and soups, and in some top-of-the-stove meat dishes.

Thus very little of the pig gets to market fresh. The most common fresh cuts are the chops and the loin roast. Italian chops are generally cut thinner than their American counterparts, but most butchers don't mind adjusting their cut to your recipe, and some supermarkets even make a policy of offering both thick and thin chops. In recent years American markets have begun featuring boned tenderloin of pork, which lends itself superbly to Italian recipes.

Dishes that are also common on the Italian table include fresh sausage, the liver, the rind, the feet, and the knuckles. Pigs' feet and knuckles are particularly popular in the North, especially as winter dishes.

Costolette di Maiale Panate
BREADED PORK CHOPS

This is the same sort of recipe as Veal Chops, Milanese Style: thin pork chops, dipped in beaten eggs and bread crumbs, are fried crisp and golden and served with lemon.

12 thin pork chops (½ inch thick)
1–1½ cups unseasoned bread crumbs
3 eggs
1 teaspoon salt, or to taste
1½ lemons
½–1 cup oil

Have your butcher cut the pork chops so they are no more than ½ inch thick. Cut off any excess fat around the edges and pound them with a meat pounder or the flat side of a big butcher knife to make them even thinner. Put the bread crumbs on a big plate. Beat the eggs in a shallow bowl, adding salt. Dip the chops, one by one, in the beaten eggs, then press them into the bread crumbs. Pat them well to make as many crumbs as possible stick to the chops. Let stand a few minutes.

Heat the oil in a wide frying pan, put in the chops, and fry them on both sides to a golden brown. Drain on paper towels and serve hot with lemon slices. For 6.

Cotolette di Maiale all'Erbe
HERBED, BREADED PORK CUTLETS

1½ tablespoons fresh rosemary leaves, or 2 teaspoons dried rosemary
1 bay leaf
8 juniper berries
10 sprigs Italian parsley
1 cup unseasoned bread crumbs
2 large eggs
1 teaspoon Dijon mustard
2 pounds lean pork cut in thin slices (may be from leg, boned loin, or thin chops without bone)
vegetable oil for frying
salt to taste
freshly ground pepper to taste
1 lemon, cut in wedges

Place the herbs, including the parsley leaves and some tender stems, in the bowl of a food processor or on a chopping board and mince. The juniper berries may be a bit recalcitrant, in which case crush them with the flat of a knife on the chopping board before adding to the other flavorings. Add the bread crumbs and mix well. Place the mixture in a soup bowl.

Beat the eggs in another bowl. Add mustard to the eggs and mix.

Trim the pork slices of any extra fat. Dip them in the beaten egg, then in the herbed bread crumbs. Let rest a few minutes and repeat dipping and breading.

Fry the cutlets in the smallest amount of vegetable oil necessary, about ¼ inch deep. When golden brown on both sides remove to drain on paper toweling. Sprinkle with a little salt and pepper to please. Serve with lemon wedges. For 6.

161

Lombo di Maiale all'Arancia
BONELESS PORK LOIN WITH ORANGE SAUCE

2½ pounds pork loin, boneless
6 tablespoons olive oil
1½ cups dry white wine
2 oranges
2 tablespoons wine vinegar
1 tablespoon fresh rosemary leaves,
*   or 2 teaspoons dried rosemary*

1 tablespoon juniper berries (if avail-
*   able)*
2 bay leaves
½ teaspoon salt
1 teaspoon freshly ground pepper

Tie the loin with butcher's string, like a sausage.

Make a marinade with 2 tablespoons of the oil, the wine, the juice of 1½ oranges, the vinegar, and the rosemary.

Put the pork loin in a container that fits it snugly. Add the marinade and let stand for at least an hour, turning the loin occasionally.

Grind and mix together the juniper berries, bay leaves, salt and pepper.

Lift the loin from the marinade, let it drain a bit, and then roll it in the juniper berry mince.

In a flameproof casserole with a close-fitting cover, large enough to hold the loin neatly, put the remaining 4 tablespoons of olive oil. Brown the loin thoroughly in the oil.

Peel a spiral of the zest of one of the squeezed oranges and add to the casserole. Add also the mari-nade and any of the juniper mince that did not cling to the pork.

Bring to a boil, cover, lower the heat, and let simmer for about 1¼ hours, turning the loin occasionally. If the liquids in the casserole should evaporate too fast, add some hot water. The loin is done when it is tender and no pink juice appears when you prick it with a fork.

Once done, lift the loin from the casserole and let it rest 10 minutes before removing the string and cutting into slices. Pour pan juices over the sliced pork and decorate with thin slices of the remaining half orange. In the event that the pan juices are too concentrated, add a little hot water, bring to a boil, then use. If the juices are too thin, boil them down a bit before serving over the pork. For 6.

Lombo di Maiale Martini
LOIN OF PORK MARTINI

Having watched any number of Italian chefs put a dash of wine, brandy, or liqueur in a roasting pan, we decided to experiment and liked the vermouth-gin combination of cocktail fame very much. The two blend nicely with the herbs, while the gin seems to cut any extraneous fat.

*2½ pounds boned pork loin, blade
    end*
*½ pound thick-cut very lean bacon
    or* prosciutto *end*
*1 cup very loosely packed parsley
    leaves with some tender stem*
1 heaping tablespoon juniper berries
*4–6 tablespoons grated Parmesan
    cheese*

ground pepper to taste
olive oil to cover pan bottom
handful of celery leaves
½ small onion
1 small carrot
1 lemon
¼ cup dry white vermouth
½ cup dry gin

Preheat the oven to 325°.

Make the slits (where the bones were) even deeper into the roast without cutting all the way through.

Place the bacon, parsley, and juniper berries in the bowl of a food processor with the steel cutting blade and process on and off until nicely minced but not puréed. Sprinkle in the cheese and process on/off to blend only.

Stuff the two pockets of the loin with the mince, packing it in rather well. Sew the openings and then tie the roast like a salami. Roll the roast in freshly ground black or white pepper.

Place a bit of olive oil in the baking pan, put in the celery, onion, carrot, and any parsley stems you may have left over. Add the meat, sprinkle with lemon juice, and cut the rind into 4 pieces and put them in the pan. Roast at 325° for 1½ hours or until the meat thermometer registers 160°. After the meat is in the oven ½ hour, splash it with the vermouth. After another half hour, splash it with half the gin, scrape the pan bottom, and baste the roast with the liquids. Turn the meat over for even browning.

Toward the end of roasting, add the final bit of gin and baste well. Mash the lemon rinds well and get all the juice out of them.

Let the meat stand 10–15 minutes before slicing. Serve with strained pan juices. For 6 to 8.

Maiale Arrosto alla Senape
ROAST PORK WITH MUSTARD

1 5-pound loin of pork
1 tablespoon fresh rosemary leaves,
    or 2 teaspoons dried rosemary
10 juniper berries, crushed

1 clove garlic, peeled
4 teaspoons salt
10 peppercorns
4 tablespoons mustard

Preheat the oven to 325°.

Trim off and discard excess fat of the loin, leaving only a moderate layer on the top.

Mince rosemary, juniper berries, garlic, salt, and pepper. Place ⅓ of the mince here and there in the pork's natural cavities or between the bones.

Mix remaining ⅔ of the mince with the mustard and spread it over the top of the loin.

Roast in moderate oven (325°) about 3 hours or until the meat thermometer registers 160° and the mustard-mince topping is crisp and browned. Let stand 10 to 15 minutes before carving.

This roast reheats well; it is also very good cold. For 6 to 8.

Porchetta alla Perugina
ROAST PORK IN THE STYLE OF PERUGIA

This is an old-fashioned way to prepare a nice pork loin. The final taste is very similar to that of the real *porchetta,* a full-grown pig cooked on a spit over an open fire and then sold in slices at street corner stands. We recommend, as do the *Perugini,* this recipe as practical for the family kitchen.

FOR THE BATTUTO:
2–3 fresh sage leaves
1 sprig rosemary
2 fresh basil leaves
1 clove garlic
1 bay leaf

1 teaspoon salt
freshly ground pepper

4–5 pound pork loin, boned
1 teaspoon salt
¼–½ cup olive oil

Prepare the *battuto* by mincing all the ingredients together until they are practically a paste. Spread this mixture on the thinner side of the loin (where the bones once were), and then tie the meat up as if it were a sausage, so that the herbs are held tightly inside. Put it in a heavy pot, just big enough to hold the roast (a stainless steel small fish poacher is ideal), add enough water almost to cover the meat, add 1 teaspoon salt, and put over a low heat. Cover and bring slowly to a boil, and then uncover and boil slowly until all the liquid has evaporated. Pour on enough olive oil to coat the loin thoroughly, and continue cooking, turning the meat over and over until a good golden crust has formed. Slice and serve. For 6.

Salsicce in Umido
SAUSAGES IN TOMATO SAUCE

This is a classic way to cook sausages to serve as a second course. When coupled with *polenta,* this recipe gives you a mountaineer's one-dish meal, good for any after-ski crowd.

3–4 tablespoons olive oil
3 cups peeled plum tomatoes
1½ teaspoons salt

12 sweet Italian sausages
freshly ground pepper

Put the olive oil in a big pan over medium heat and add the tomatoes, mashing them as they go in. Add the salt, raise the heat, and once the tomatoes are bubbling, lower the heat to a simmer.

In the meantime prick the sausages around and about with a fork and put them in a frying pan with ½ inch of water. Bring to a boil, reduce the heat, and simmer until all the water has evaporated, the sausages have given up some of their fat (you may want to prick them again), and are lightly browned on all sides. Add them to the simmering tomato sauce.

Cook 25–30 minutes, or until the sauce has really thickened and the sausages have lent their flavor to the tomatoes. Taste for salt, adding some more if necessary and add the pepper. Serve as a second course or with *polenta* as a one-dish meal. For 6.

Salsicce con Fagioli
SAUSAGES WITH BEANS

This is a variation on a theme: Sausages in Tomato Sauce are combined with a generous amount of boiled beans. For the sausage-tomato sauce, see the preceding recipe.

1 recipe Sausages in Tomato Sauce
4 cups shell or kidney beans

½ cup warm water

If using fresh or dried beans: boil them in salted water until cooked. Then drain them and add to the cooked Sausages in Tomato Sauce.

If using canned beans: be sure they have been put up without sugar. Drain them and add to the cooked Sausages in Tomato Sauce.

Add ½ cup warm water and simmer another 10–15 minutes. Serve with hot Italian bread. For 6.

Salsicce con Lenticchie
SAUSAGES WITH LENTILS

Although lightly flavored with vegetables (carrot, onion, celery, tomato, and garlic) lentils remain the main characters in this recipe. The sausages are an everyday addition, but if you wish to make a traditional New Year's Day dish, add a *cotechino* (northern Italian sausage) or a *zampone* (sausage-stuffed pig's foot) in place of the sausages themselves. According to folklore, lentils eaten on New Year's make you rich all year. Both *cotechino* and *zampone* are available in Italian specialty shops at Christmastime.

2 cups dried lentils
8 cups cold water
1 clove garlic
1 carrot
3–4 plum tomatoes
1 onion

1 stalk celery, with leaves
3–4 teaspoons salt, or to taste
freshly ground pepper
12 sweet Italian sausages, or 1 cotechino, *or 1* zampone

Sort through the lentils, a handful or so at a time on a plate, and remove any bits of chaff or stone. Wash them quickly by putting them in a colander under cold water. Put the lentils, water, and all the vegetables into a big pot. Bring to a boil, scoop off any froth that may have formed, add the salt and a few grinds of pepper, and reduce the heat. Simmer for about 45 minutes–1 hour, or until the lentils are soft and the liquids have reduced to practically nothing. Check the level of the liquid toward the end of the cooking time, because a heat that is too high can reduce the liquid too quickly, in which case a little water must be added.

If using sausages: prick them liberally all around, cook them in ½ inch of water in a wide skillet. When the water has evaporated and the sausages' fat has begun to run, brown the sausages all over for another 10 minutes. Drain, add to the cooked lentils, and simmer about 10 minutes before serving.

If using *cotechino* or *zampone:* prick them as you would the sausages and put them in cold water to cover amply. Bring to a boil, reduce the heat to a simmer, and cook for 1 hour. Remove either the *cotechino* or *zampone* from the cooking water, cool a bit, and then slice into ¼-inch slices. Place the slices down the center of a big platter and surround them with boiling hot, cooked lentils.

As you serve the lentils, be sure to search for the garlic and remove it. Also remove the now limp celery stalk, the carrot, and any piece of onion that hasn't disintegrated as the tomatoes have. For 6.

Spuntature (e Salsicce) al Sugo
SPARERIBS (AND SAUSAGES) IN SAUCE

This is a worthwhile, versatile recipe, especially valuable for the rich sauce it produces. It can be made also with the added attraction of sausages. Either way it is great with *polenta* as a one-dish meal. The sauce alone is exceptional with *rigatoni,* while the spareribs with the addition of beans make a glorious second course. This recipe serves 6 to 8 generously and is easily stretched for a crowd.

3 tablespoons olive oil
1 red pepper pod, seeded
1 pound pork spareribs, cut into 3-inch lengths (not country style)

½ teaspoon salt
freshly ground pepper
1 cup dry red wine
4 cups plum tomatoes
6 sweet Italian sausages (optional)

Cover the bottom of a big pot with olive oil and put the red pepper pod in to cook over medium heat. When the pod is dark brown, discard it. Add the spareribs, salt, and a few grinds of pepper. Cook over high heat until thoroughly browned, and then add the wine and stir carefully. Add the tomatoes, mashing them a bit as they go in.

If you use sausages: put ½ inch water in a medium-size frying pan, add the sausages, and prick them with a fork to let their fat flow. Cook over medium heat until the water has evaporated, the sausages have released their fat (you may want to prick them again midway in the cooking), and they are nicely browned. Add to the tomato-sparerib pot. Bring that pot to a boil, then lower the heat to simmer and cook for at least 1 hour, stirring from time to time. This simmering can go on longer, for even 2 hours, in which case you may have to add a bit of water to maintain a good consistency in the sauce. It should be dark, thick, reduced to about half the original amount. Taste for salt and add some if necessary. Serve hot. For 6.

Spuntature (e Salsicce) con Fagioli
SPARERIBS (AND SAUSAGES) WITH BEANS

The ingredients for this dish are exactly the same as in the preceding recipe, plus ½ cup of water and 4 cups of kidney or shell beans.

Proceed exactly as for *Spuntature al Sugo,* with or without the sausages, but 15 minutes before serving add 4 cups of drained kidney or shell beans, with ½ cup of water, and simmer. The beans may be canned, or they may be prepared by boiling dry or fresh ones in salted water until cooked. In any case, be sure that the canned ones have been put up without sugar and are drained and rinsed. Serve with hot bread. For 6.

Zampetto
PIGS' FEET

A favorite dish in northern Italy: the pigs' feet are boiled in flavored, salted water until tender, and are served with *salsa verde,* page 219.

2 little pigs' feet or 1 big one per person	*1 onion*
2 tablespoons wine vinegar	*1 carrot*
salt	*1 stalk celery*
	4–5 peppercorns

Put the pigs' feet in a pot, cover well with water, add the vinegar, salt (1 teaspoon per quart), vegetables, and peppercorns. Bring to a boil, reduce the heat, and simmer for about 1½ hours, or until tender, so tender the meat practically falls away from the bone. Serve with *salsa verde* and kidney bean salad, or any vegetable *all'agro* you desire.

Pollame
POULTRY

There are probably only two basic differences between American poultry and its Italian counterpart: the Italian product is still frequently sold in its entirety (head, feet, sometimes even feathers), and it is less fat than the American bird.

The feet are put in broth to strengthen it with natural gelatin, and the crest is used in sauce for rice or pasta. Because it's been years since either heads or feet were sold in the average American market, we've not included them in our recipes.

At the same time, the current way of selling poultry in parts lends itself admirably to buying a bit at a time for such things as pasta stuffing.

As for the fat in both turkeys and chickens, cut it off anywhere you find it, and either throw it out or use it in some other way.

The American turkey is somewhat bigger and plumper than the Italian, so much so that it is a big item on Italy's import list, but self-basting birds are not advised for Italian recipes, as they are too fat and overpower their stuffings. The self-basting fat makes the breast fall apart when sliced for cooking in a pan.

Besides these few pointers, all we can say is that poultry is versatile, easy to prepare, and a genuine favorite in Italian cooking, North to South.

Pollo Arrosto con Patate
ROAST CHICKEN WITH POTATOES

This is the simplest way to cook a chicken without giving it much attention. All it needs is just the careful insertion of rosemary, basting with oil, and a hot oven to turn it crisp and golden brown on the outside, tender and moist on the inside.

6–8 medium potatoes
1 4-pound roasting chicken
1 lemon
2–2 1/2 teaspoons salt

3 sprigs fresh rosemary (or 3–4 tea-
*   spoons dried)*
olive oil

Preheat the oven to 375°.

Peel the potatoes, cut them into wedges, and soak them in cold water.

Take out the giblets and neck of the chicken; save them for future use. Wash the bird, rinsing out the cavity thoroughly. Cut the lemon in half and scrub it around inside the cavity, squeezing it as you work so that a lot of juice coats the bird. Lightly salt the cavity and put in a few rosemary leaves. Make small slits in the body of the bird, under the wings, where the leg meets the body, in the fleshy parts of the breast. Stuff these with the rest of the rosemary leaves. Place the bird breast down on a poultry rack in a big shallow roasting pan. Add drained potatoes all around. Sprinkle with olive oil and add a bit of salt. Roast (at 375°) for 1/2 hour. Take the bird out, turn it breast up, baste with oil and pan juices 2 or 3 times, sprinkle with a touch of salt, flip potatoes and baste them, and return bird to the oven for another 1/2 hour or so of roasting. (Chicken usually is done if one allows about 18 minutes per pound.) For 4.

Pollo Ripieno alla Romagnola
STUFFED CHICKEN IN THE STYLE OF ROMAGNA

In Romagna, as in the other northern regions of Italy, little touches of flavoring are blended together with butter and wine to change the whole idea of stuffing. Incidentally, roast potato wedges, as prepared with *pollo arrosto* (above), are the usual as well as the perfect accompaniment to this.

1 Italian sweet sausage
1 4-pound roasting chicken (includ-
*   ing giblets)*
1 small onion

1 small stalk celery
2 tablespoons butter
3–4 ounces mushrooms, chopped
*   coarsely*

½–1 cup shredded Italian bread
(crusts not included)
¼ cup dry white wine

2 teaspoons salt
1 teaspoon rosemary
olive oil

Preheat the oven to 375°.

Skin the sausage. Clean the giblets. Boil the gizzard 5–10 minutes and skin it. Send the sausage, gizzard, heart, and liver of the chicken through a meat grinder. Mince the onion and celery into tiny bits, and sauté them gently in the butter over medium heat until golden. Add the ground meats and chopped mushrooms, and continue cooking until the meats have lost their rosiness. Put the shredded bread in a bowl, dampen with the wine, and add the meats with their flavorings and juices. Add 1 teaspoon of the salt and mix lightly.

Rinse the cavity of the chicken and drain well. Spoon in the stuffing and skewer or sew shut. Make slits in the joints and fill them with the rosemary. Sprinkle with a little olive oil.

Proceed as for ordinary roast chicken: cook it (at 375°) breast down for the first half an hour; then turn it, salt it, and baste during the last half an hour or so. For 4.

Pollo alla Diavola
CHICKEN, DEVIL'S STYLE

Anything cooked *alla diavola* in Italy usually means it's been grilled over abundant hot coals, of which the devil himself should have enough, and the seasonings are also hot, but not so hot as to ruin the taste buds. In this chicken's case, the flavor is heightened with hot red pepper, black pepper, and lemon.

½ cup olive oil
3 red pepper pods, seeded (or 3–4
dashes Tabasco sauce)
2 small broilers

2 lemons
salt to taste
freshly ground black pepper

Heat the olive oil in a small pan over medium heat, add the pepper pods, and sauté them until they are deep, dark brown. Turn off the heat, cool the olive oil, and throw away the browned peppers. (The alternative is just to add Tabasco to the olive oil to make it hot.)

Cut the chicken in half, crack the legs and wing joints loose, and spread out, skin side up, on a board or clean counter. Pound the chicken halves well with a meat pounder and really flatten them out.

Add the juice of 1 of the lemons to the seasoned olive oil along with 3 or 4 twists of the pepper mill. Put the chicken halves in a big bowl, pour the seasoned olive oil over them, and turn the pieces over and over to coat them well. Let stand 1 or 2 hours, turning the pieces from time to time.

When your grill is heaped with hot, hot coals, put the marinated chicken halves on to cook, skin side down. Add salt, a bit more pepper, and grill thoroughly, turning frequently, basting from time to time with any leftover marinade. The chicken is done when it is tender and has acquired a dark brown crust all over and the juices run clear.

Serve hot with lemon wedges. For 6 to 8.

Pollo alla Cacciatora I
HUNTER'S CHICKEN I

Chicken prepared in the way, according to tradition, hunters cooked their venison, using wine and wine vinegar to make a sauce flavored with rosemary and a hint of garlic. For today's nonhunters, this dish is fast and easy to make on top of the stove. A large frying chicken will serve 6, because the sauce (and the inevitable bread dipped in it) is an integral part of the dish.

1 large frying chicken
3 tablespoons olive oil
1 clove garlic
2 teaspoons rosemary

1 1/2 teaspoons salt, or to taste
1/4 cup wine vinegar
1/2 cup dry white wine

Fryers usually come cut into 4 pieces, but for this dish you should cut these in half again, so that you have 8 pieces. If you have the patience, try for 10 to 12 pieces, because the smaller the piece, the quicker the cooking and browning, and the tastier it is. Cut off any bits of fat you see.

Heat the oil with the garlic in a deep frying pan (a chicken frying pan with its high edges is ideal, but a deep, cast-iron pot is almost as good). When the garlic is golden, discard it. Put in the chicken, rosemary, and salt and brown thoroughly, turning the pieces on all sides. When the chicken is a deep golden brown, add the wine vinegar and quickly cover the pan until the sizzling stops. Then add the wine and cook on high heat until it has evaporated (when its vapors no longer tingle the nose). Reduce the heat and simmer about 20 minutes, or until the chicken is tender. Put the pieces on a warm platter in a warm oven.

Add about 1 tablespoon of water to the juices in the pan, turn up the heat, and with a wooden spoon scrape clean the sides and bottom of the pan to detach any little bits that may have cooked on. This will turn the sauce a golden amber. Pour the sauce over the chicken and serve with Italian bread. For 6.

Pollo alla Cacciatora II
HUNTER'S CHICKEN II

A fancier version of the traditional *cacciatora* uses a *battuto* of parsley, celery, and garlic, plus bay leaves as the herb seasoning.

FOR THE BATTUTO:
1 tablespoon chopped parsley
1 1/2 stalks celery, with leaves

1 clove garlic

172

3-pound frying chicken
3 tablespoons olive oil
2 bay leaves
1 cup dry white wine

4 tablespoons chicken broth
1 1/2 teaspoons salt
freshly ground pepper

Cut the chicken into at least 10 small pieces. Make a *battuto* of the parsley, celery, and garlic. Brown the chicken for 10 minutes in the olive oil over high heat in a good-size frying pan. Add the *battuto* and continue to cook over medium high heat, turning everything over and over so that all the chicken pieces are well browned and the little bits of vegetable don't burn or stick to the bottom of the pan. Don't worry if some do, for they will be taken care of by the next step.

Add the bay leaves and wine and cook over high heat until the wine has almost completely evaporated. Add the broth. With a wooden spoon scrape all the little bits off the sides and bottom of the pan. Add the salt and a few grinds of pepper. Simmer for 20 minutes, or until the chicken is tender and the sauce has cooked away a bit and darkened. Serve with Italian bread. For 6.

Gallina in Umido
CHICKEN STEEPED IN SAUCE

FOR THE BATTUTO:
1 medium onion
1 stalk celery
1 carrot
1 tablespoon chopped parsley

1 frying chicken (3–4 pounds)
2–3 tablespoons olive oil
1/2 cup dry white wine
1 1/2 teaspoons salt
freshly ground pepper
3 cups plum tomatoes, cut up

Cut the chicken up into 10 pieces and remove all the fat you can.

Make a *battuto* of the onion, celery, carrot, and parsley, mincing them to a paste. Cover the bottom of a medium-size stew pot with olive oil and add the *battuto.* Cook everything until golden over medium heat, and then add the chicken pieces and slowly brown them in the flavored oil. Add the wine and scrape the sides and bottom of the pot to collect any bits that may have stuck. Add the salt and pepper. When the wine has almost evaporated, add the tomatoes and bring to a boil. If the liquids don't quite cover the chicken pieces, add enough warm water to do so, and cover the pot. Simmer very slowly for 1 hour, stirring occasionally, or until the chicken is very tender and the sauce has thickened and has reduced to about half its original quantity. For 6.

Cosce di Pollo al Vino
CHICKEN LEGS IN WINE SAUCE

6 chicken legs with thighs (about 2¼ pounds)
flour for dredging
2 tablespoons olive oil
2 tablespoons unsalted butter
1 medium onion, peeled
1 large carrot, scrubbed
1½ celery stalks with leaves, washed
1 teaspoon salt, or to taste
freshly ground pepper to taste
½ teaspoon paprika
1½ cups dry wine (red or white)
2 tablespoons chopped parsley

Separate thighs from drumsticks and dredge all the chicken pieces in flour.

In a sauté pan sauté chicken in the oil and butter until browned.

Mince the onion, carrot, and celery together and add to the chicken. Continue cooking uncovered until the mince is limp. Add salt, pepper, paprika, and wine.

When the wine has evaporated, cover the pan.

Simmer about 25 minutes or until the chicken is cooked. Stir 2 or 3 times as the chicken simmers. Place the chicken on a serving platter, strain the sauce over the chicken, sprinkle with parsley, and serve. For 6.

Petti di Pollo Farciti
STUFFED CHICKEN BREASTS

4 chicken breasts, boned and skinned, cut in half (8 pieces)
4 slices Fontina or Muenster cheese
2 tablespoons Italian parsley, chopped
2 tablespoons capers, rinsed
4 thin slices of prosciutto
flour for dredging
5 tablespoons unsalted butter
¼ cup olive oil (approximate)
salt to taste
freshly ground pepper to taste
6 tablespoons very dry sherry

Cut off and discard any fat clinging to the chicken.

Place the chicken pieces between sheets of wax paper or plastic wrap and pound them with the flat side of a meat pounder. Lift the paper, overlap any pieces that may have split in pounding, replace the paper, and pound the overlapping pieces gently to make them stick together.

Cut or fold the cheese to cover half of each piece of chicken breast.

Add a piece of prosciutto to cover.

Mince the parsley and capers together and spread on the prosciutto.

Fold each chicken piece to enclose the stuffing, pressing the edges together to seal.

174

Dredge the stuffed chicken in flour, pat well, and let rest a few minutes.

Sauté the chicken in butter and olive oil 3 minutes on each side or until golden brown. Sprinkle with a little salt and pepper and remove to a warm plate in a warm place.

Add the sherry to the pan. Stir and cook over medium heat about 1 minute or until a sauce has formed. Pour over the chicken breasts and serve. For 6.

Pollo Fritto
BATTER-FRIED CHICKEN

FOR THE BATTER:
1 recipe yeast batter, diluted with 1/4 cup water (page 220)
1/4 teaspoon white pepper

FOR THE CHICKEN:
2 2-pound frying chickens
5 tablespoons lemon juice
1 teaspoon salt
1/4 teaspoon white pepper
1 tablespoon Tabasco sauce

1 rounded tablespoon Italian parsley, chopped
2 garlic cloves, peeled and thinly sliced lengthwise
leaves of 2 sprigs fresh rosemary, minced, or 2 teaspoons dried rosemary
1/2 cup dry white wine
flour for dredging
vegetable oil for frying
2 lemons, cut in wedges

Mix the batter. Add the pepper and let rest in a warm place (such as an oven with a pilot light) for at least an hour.

Cut the chickens into small pieces; remove and set aside (for broth or other uses) the wing tips, end of drumsticks, backs, necks, and giblets.

Make a marinade of all the remaining ingredients except the flour, lemons, and oil.

Place chicken pieces and marinade in a snugly fitting dish or sturdy plastic bag and turn it around and about to get the marinade to coat all the meat. Let rest for 2 hours, turning two or three times.

Remove chicken from marinade, drain on absorbent toweling, pat dry, and dredge in the flour.

To fry: put ample vegetable oil (3–4 inches) in each of two pans. Bring one of the pans to low frying heat (360°) and the other to higher frying heat (375°).

Stir batter and dip the chicken pieces in it.

Place as many pieces of chicken as will fit comfortably in the first pan and turn them back and forth to let the batter swell and begin to turn golden. Remove and place in the second and hotter pan to finish cooking to a deep brown, very crisp stage.

Drain well on absorbent toweling. Serve hot (or cold: they are ideal for a picnic) with wedges of fresh lemon. For 6–8.

Anitra allo Spiedo
GRILLED DUCKLING ON A SPIT

Anitra alla griglia—in the absence of a spit, cut the duck in half and pound it as flat as you can. Use same procedures as for the *spiedo* and then grill.

1 garlic clove, peeled and quartered
2 sprigs fresh rosemary, or 2 tea-spoons dried rosemary
12 juniper berries, crushed
2 tablespoons soy sauce
1 tablespoon Worcestershire sauce
1 teaspoon Tabasco sauce
3 tablespoons grappa
1 lemon
1 2–3-pound duckling

Make a marinade using the first seven ingredients plus the juice of the lemon. Save the empty lemon halves.

Remove the giblets and neck from the duck and set aside for another dish. Cut off and discard (if the butcher hasn't already done so) the oil sacks above the duck's tail. Cut off any extra fat at the cavity opening.

Rinse the duck thoroughly and rub the cavity with one half of the lemon whose juice you used in the marinade. Place the other half in the cavity.

Put the duck in a plastic bag or covered dish large enough to hold it comfortably. Add the marinade and cover, or seal the bag and place it on a platter, about 2 hours before it is time to grill. Turn the duck from time to time to ensure a good soaking.

Get a grill going with ample hot coals.

Tie the wings and legs of the duck tightly to the body and place the duck on a spit. Put the marinade in a bowl or jar for use during cooking.

Keep a spray bottle of water handy so that as the duck's fat falls on the coals and ignites, the flames can be brought under control. This happens at the beginning of the grilling and the spraying prevents the duck from being too blackened by smoke.

Allow the duck to rotate slowly over the hot coals for approximately 40 minutes, basting often with the marinade.

At the end of cooking, the duck's juices will run clear when the meaty portions are skewered or pierced with a fork; the skin will be dark and crisp.

Cut the duck into 4 pieces with poultry shears; brush once more with any remaining marinade and serve. For 4.

Galletto Ripieno con Mandorle e Prugne
ROCK CORNISH HEN WITH ALMOND-PRUNE STUFFING

1 Rock Cornish hen
1 Italian sweet sausage, skinned
5 dried prunes, pitted
1/4 cup blanched, slivered almonds
1 thick slice day-old Italian bread,
    crustless
1/2 cup milk

1/2–3/4 teaspoon salt
2 slices lean bacon
freshly ground pepper
2–3 tablespoons olive oil
1/2 cup dry white wine, or 1/4 cup dry
    vermouth

Remove and discard the hen's neck; clean and reserve the giblets. Cut the sausage into small pieces. Cut the prunes into quarters. Chop the almonds coarsely. Break up the bread and put it to soak in the milk.

Add the sausage, giblets, and prunes to the almonds and chop or process until all the ingredients are well chopped and about the same size.

Squeeze the milk from the bread and add it to the stuffing. Mix well.

Salt the hen's cavity, then stuff both cavity and neck pouch with the almond-prune mixture. Skewer both openings closed.

Place the bacon on the bird's breast and tie the wings and legs close to the body. Sprinkle liberally with pepper.

In a skillet brown the hen in the oil.

Preheat oven to 400°. Place the hen in a baking dish just large enough to hold it. Bake for 15 minutes. Add the wine and baste the hen.

Lower the heat to 375° and continue baking 30 to 40 minutes, or until the meat is tender.

Once the hen is cooked, place it on a hot platter. Degrease the pan, if necessary, and serve the pan's juices with the hen. Cut in half with a pair of poultry scissors. For 2. Multiply for more.

Galletto alla Povera Zingara
POOR GYPSY'S CHICKEN

This is a formula originally worked out for pigeon and squab. American Cornish hens are the perfect birds to receive a poor gypsy's touch of herbs, mushrooms, and mustard.

3 Cornish hens (about 1 pound each)

FOR THE MARINADE:
3 tablespoons olive oil
3 tablespoons lemon juice
1½ teaspoons pepper, freshly ground
1½ teaspoons dried rosemary, crumbled
¾ teaspoon salt
1 dash Tabasco, or to taste

FOR THE SPREAD:
12 ounces fresh mushrooms, cleaned
3 tablespoons unsalted butter
salt to taste
freshly ground pepper to taste
3 tablespoons Dijon mustard
¼ teaspoon Tabasco
3 tablespoons tomato ketchup
¼ cup lemon juice
1 teaspoon freshly ground pepper

Cut off and discard wing tips from the hen. Remove the giblets and reserve. Cut the hen in two along the breast bone. Open the hen, dry the cavity with paper towels, and pound the bird flat with a meat pounder.

Prepare the marinade by mixing well the olive oil, lemon juice, pepper, rosemary, salt, and Tabasco. Place the hen on a plate and baste it with the marinade, turning it over and over.

Preheat the broiler for 10 minutes.

Chop the mushrooms coarsely. Clean and chop the hens' giblets. Melt the butter in a sauté pan and put in the giblets, mushrooms, and salt and pepper to taste. Cook for 4 minutes or until the mushrooms have released their moisture. Let cool.

Chop or grind the giblets and mushrooms to a paste. Add any pan juices, the mustard, Tabasco, ketchup, lemon juice, and ½ teaspoon additional pepper. Taste for salt and adjust if necessary.

Place the hen halves, cavity up, in the broiler pan; broil 5–6 minutes or until well browned, brushing with marinade once or twice as they cook.

Turn and brown the hen's skin side, basting as you did before. When the skin is browned, turn again, spread the cavity with the mushroom mixture, and broil 3 to 4 minutes until the spread is cooked and beginning to crisp. Turn the skin side up, brush with remaining spread, and broil another 3–4 minutes. For 6.

Galletto con Salsa di Fragole
CORNISH HEN WITH STRAWBERRY SAUCE

For the hen and marinade, use the same ingredients, amounts, and procedures up to marinating as in the preceding recipe. While the hen marinates, make the sauce:

1 cup strawberry jam
⅓ cup soy sauce
¾ cup wine vinegar

1 teaspoon Tabasco
1 tablespoon unsalted butter
2 slices lemon

Place all of the ingredients with the exception of the soy sauce in a saucepan. Add only ½ of the soy sauce to begin with. Stirring constantly, lower the heat and let boil slowly until mixture is thickened and saucey and coats a spoon.

Taste for salt and add more soy sauce if you wish. (Do not overboil or you will have sauce that turns to cement on cooling.)

Place the hen halves, cavity up, in the broiler pan. Brush with the marinade and broil 5–6 minutes on each side or until well browned, brushing with marinade once or twice. Serve half a hen to each diner and pass the sauce. For 6.

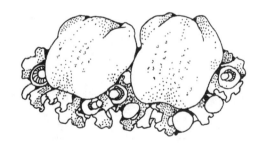

Tacchino Ripieno alla Lombarda
ROAST STUFFED TURKEY IN THE STYLE OF LOMBARDY

Beef, sausage, chestnuts, and giblets combine with mushrooms, sage, and rosemary to make a completely different kind of stuffing. This is a real production, and gives the American turkey a whole new appeal.

1 turkey (10–15 pounds)
1 carrot
1 stalk celery
2 small onion
2 teaspoons salt
½ pound chestnuts
3 sweet Italian sausages
½ pound twice-ground beef
2 eggs
4 tablespoons grated Parmesan cheese

½ teaspoon nutmeg
½ pound mushrooms
1 lemon
1–2 teaspoons rosemary
2 fresh sage leaves
2 slices lean salt pork
olive oil
1 cup dry white wine
1 tablespoon flour

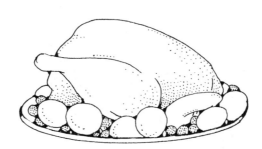

Remove the giblets and neck from the turkey, and put them in a saucepan with the carrot, celery, onion, 1 teaspoon of salt, and enough water to cover. Bring to a boil, cover, reduce the heat, and let it bubble along on a simmer until the giblets are tender, about ½ hour or so.

With a sharp paring knife make an incision through the outer shell of each chestnut. Put them in a saucepan with enough water to cover, bring to a boil, reduce the heat, and cook gently for ½ hour or until tender. Drain, cool slightly, and peel off the outer shell and inner skin as quickly as possible. Mash up the chestnuts, but don't make a purée—little nuggets of nut are necessary for the proper texture.

Skin the sausages and send them with the beef through a meat grinder. Put in a bowl and add the eggs, cheese, nutmeg, and chopped mushrooms. When the giblets are done, strain their broth and save it. Chop up the liver and heart, skin and chop the gizzard, and add the chopped mixture to the bowl. Add the chestnuts and stir and mix well. Add salt to taste, perhaps ½–1 teaspoon.

Preheat the oven to 325°.

Rinse the turkey well and wipe the cavity with wedges of the lemon, squeezing as you wipe to cover all the surface with juice. Stuff the turkey cavity and neck pouch and skewer shut. Make little slits in the skin under the wings where the legs join the body and a few in the fleshiest part of the white meat. Stuff each slit with a bit of rosemary and sage. Put the bird in a big roasting pan.

Put the salt pork crosswise on the breast. Cut a double piece of cheesecloth big enough to drape over the entire bird and lay it on. Dribble olive oil over the cloth to moisten it slightly. This keeps the bird from drying out excessively in the first hours of cooking.

Put the stuffed turkey in the oven (325°). When the breast begins to brown (after about 40 minutes), pour 1 cup of white wine over it and baste thoroughly 3 or 4 times. Continue to baste frequently and if more liquid is needed, use the giblet broth. Half an hour before the estimated cooking time is over, remove the cheesecloth and salt pork and baste again. When the turkey is done (the leg moves easily and is about to break away from the body), put it on a platter. Add the remaining giblet broth to the juices in the pan, scraping the bottom and sides to collect any bits stuck there. You may thicken this sauce by cooking it, stirring constantly, about 4 minutes at medium heat.

Serve turkey in slices with spoonfuls of the rich stuffing and sauce. For 10.

Tacchino di Natale con Ripieno di Riso
SEMIBONED CHRISTMAS TURKEY WITH RICE STUFFING

FOR THE STUFFING:
giblets of 1 turkey
giblets of 3 chickens
5 tablespoons unsalted butter
1 bay leaf
½ teaspoon dried oregano
3½ teaspoons salt
freshly ground pepper
3 cups water
1⅓ cups extra long-grain rice
5 large mushrooms, cleaned and sliced
2 sweet peppers (1 green and 1 red, if possible) cored and diced, or *3 stalks celery, washed and diced*
1 tablespoon grated Parmesan cheese

FOR THE TURKEY:
1 10-pound turkey, not self-basting
1 teaspoon salt
½ teaspoon freshly ground pepper
¾ teaspoon freshly grated nutmeg
5 tablespoons unsalted butter
2 tablespoons olive oil or vegetable oil
1 bay leaf
1 celery stalk, washed and chopped
1 onion, peeled and quartered
2 cloves
4 or 5 peppercorns
1½ cups dry white wine
1½–2 cups chicken broth (page 88)
juice of 1 lemon

Trim all the giblets, chop them coarsely, and sauté in butter with the bay leaf and oregano for 5 minutes. Sprinkle with ½ teaspoon salt and freshly ground pepper to please.

Bring the water to a boil and add remaining 3 teaspoons salt and rice. Bring back to a boil, stir, cover, and cook 10 minutes. Drain.

Add rice to the giblets. Add the mushrooms and peppers (or celery) and the Parmesan cheese.

Stir and cook over medium heat for about 1 minute or until well mixed. Taste for seasoning and adjust if necessary.

The rice will still be a bit undercooked and this amount of stuffing will seem a bit too little for the bird. However, the rice swells and cooks during the roasting and fills the cavity nicely.

Place the turkey, breast down, on a chopping board. Slit the skin along the back from neck to tail. Pull the skin open a bit and with the point of a sharp knife separate the meat from the ribs and breast bone, following the contour of the bone. When you reach the wing joint, snap it with your fingers, then cut through the joint, detaching the wing from the carcass but not breaking the skin.

Follow the same procedure for the legs of the bird, cutting through the joint connecting the thigh to the carcass and that connecting thigh to drumstick, but leaving the thigh meat and drumstick attached to the skin. Remove the thigh bone itself. Pull the carcass away, leaving skin, breast meat, wings, thighs, and drumsticks spread out on the cutting board. Sprinkle with salt, pepper, and nutmeg.

Thread a needle with strong cotton thread and at the tail begin to sew the skin back together along the original slit. Leave an unsewn opening big enough to spoon in the rice stuffing.

Stuff the bird and complete the sewing of the opening. The stuffed turkey will look somewhat limp but will plump up with cooking.

Melt the butter and oil in a flat-bottomed roasting pan. Add the bay leaf, celery, onion, cloves, and peppercorns and sauté until limp.

Preheat the oven to 325°.

Place the turkey in the roasting pan and brown on all sides over medium heat. Add the wine and continue cooking 5 minutes. Let the turkey cool off a bit, then lift it up and put a rack under it with the turkey breast up.

Cover the turkey with 2 layers of cheesecloth. Pour about ½ cup of broth over the breast and place the roasting pan in the moderate oven (325°).

Roast for 3½–4 hours, basting from time to time with the remaining broth and the pan juices.

After 3 hours remove the cheesecloth.

When the turkey is cooked, remove it to a serving platter and let it rest about 20 minutes before carving.

Strain and degrease the pan juices and put them in a saucepan over medium heat. Add the lemon juice and stir and cook for 4 minutes. Adjust salt and pepper to your taste. Serve with the roast turkey. For 16.

Piccata di Petto di Tacchino
TURKEY BREAST IN A PIQUANT SAUCE

Thin slices of white meat of turkey cooked in a lemon-and-wine sauce are another favorite. The same process can be used for chicken breasts or slices of veal with the same mouth-watering effect.

1 small breast of turkey
flour
¼ pound unsalted butter
1 tablespoon olive oil

½ cup dry white wine
juice of 1 lemon
½–1 teaspoon salt

Remove the skin from the breast and cut into 12 thin slices no more than ⅛ inch thick. Pound them gently with the side of a big butcher knife or a meat pounder. Dredge them in flour, patting it on to make sure it sticks. Melt the butter in a big frying pan over medium heat, adding 1 tablespoon olive oil to help prevent the butter from browning. Sauté the slices in the butter and oil, turning them when the edges get white (this takes about 3 minutes). Cook the second sides another 3 minutes. Since hardly anyone but a restaurant has a huge frying pan, you'll probably have to cook two batches. Remove the first to a warm platter. When the last slices in the second batch are cooked, don't remove them from the pan. Just add the wine and stir and cook for a moment. Then add the lemon juice and stir again. Taste the sauce on a bit of bread and if desired, add salt. Put all the cooked slices back in the pan and see that each one is coated with the sauce. Simmer about 2 minutes. Serve hot with the sauce. For 6.

183

Petto di Tacchino Fritto Dorato
GOLDEN-FRIED TURKEY BREAST

This is a classic way to cook the white meat of poultry. The golden and crisp outside leaves the meat moist and tender inside, and everything has its flavor heightened with lemon juice. If your market doesn't carry turkey cutlets, a 7–8 pound breast of turkey, frozen, yields more than enough slices for 6, and the carcass can be used in making a broth, while the little bits of meat remaining on it can be used for various pasta stuffings. The turkey breast slices marvelously when almost defrosted.

12 slices turkey breast
flour
2–3 large eggs, beaten well
½ pound unsalted butter

1 tablespoon olive oil
1 teaspoon salt
1½ lemons

Remove the skin from the turkey breast and slice the meat into thin (about ⅛-inch) slices, and pound them to make them even thinner. Make small incisions around the edges to cut any membrane, otherwise the slices tend to curl while cooking.

Dust the slices with flour and dip them in the beaten eggs.

Melt the butter in a big frying pan, add the olive oil, and cook the turkey slices quickly over medium heat. Turn them over as soon as they are golden on one side. Sprinkle lightly with salt as soon as they are cooked and remove to a warm platter in a warm oven. Serve with lemon wedges. For 6.

Pesce
FISH

The first thing to know about Italian fish is that they are Mediterranean and as such don't swim the Atlantic. Even when of the same family, they are different from the ocean fish, sometimes in size and variety, sometimes in color and texture, but not much in flavor if the same Italian cooking techniques are followed. It is a matter of marinating, grilling, frying, seasoning, poaching in a sauce in the Italian way.

The second thing to know is that Italian recipes, regardless of fish family lineage, do wonders with almost any creature of the sea. They make especially good use of squid and mussels as well as the ubiquitous cod, one of the few fish found easily on both sides of the Atlantic. By and large, little fish are fried, medium are grilled or poached, and big fish are sliced and done in a sauce.

The third thing to know is that if you stick to these general rules of shopping, handling, and cooking, the palate will be more than pleased:

(1) Buy fresh fish whenever possible.

(2) Keep the heads and tails, which add to flavor (especially in soups) and to shape (when being grilled).

(3) If using frozen fish, defrost on the least cold shelf of the refrigerator and reduce the cooking time.

(4) Look for fish frozen whole (not fillets) with their heads and tails.

(5) If using frozen shrimp, when possible get those with their shells still on.

(6) In choosing squid, look for the smallest ones you can find, for they are more tender.

(7) If grilling fish, you may use a stove broiler, which is adequate, but for ideal results use a charcoal grill.

(8) If using dried salt cod, the whole beast (split open, dried with skin and bones) or that which is dried, skinned, boned, and boxed is recommended. All dried salt cod must be soaked in cold water, which is changed from time to time, up to 24 hours or until it is soft and fleshy. The whole cod that is sold in Italian shops takes a 24-hour soaking, but it is frequently found already soaked and can be purchased by the piece. The boxed cod, more easily found in the average American supermarket, should be soaked at least 12 hours (or according to directions on the box).

In choosing recipes, we have tried to be impartial as to region of origin.

We have also tried to select the most representative recipes whose ingredients could be found or duplicated easily on this side of the ocean, using either oceanic cousins of fish found in the Mediterranean Basin or good counterparts.

Baccalà al Sugo alla Romana
SALT COD IN A ROMAN SAUCE

Dried cod, soaked to fleshiness, is cooked in a tomato-and-onion sauce and accented with raisins. Leave out the raisins, and serve with *polenta* for a Northern variation. The Romans serve it with bread alone.

2 pounds dried cod
3 medium Bermuda onions
3 tablespoons olive oil
3 cups plum tomatoes

¾ teaspoon pepper
2 tablespoons white raisins
salt to taste

Soak the cod, changing the water a couple of times, skin and bone it if necessary, and cut it into 4-inch chunks.

Slice the onions into thin slivers. Sauté them in olive oil until translucent, golden, and limp. Let the pan cool a moment, and then add the tomatoes and pepper and simmer for 15–20 minutes, or until the mixture has amalgamated a bit. Add the fish chunks and the raisins and cook over low heat for about 15 minutes, or until the fish flakes. Taste for salt and add if needed. Serve with *polenta* or generous pieces of Italian bread. For 6.

Filetti di Baccalà Fritti
BATTER-FRIED SALT COD FILLETS

Salt cod fillets, dipped in batter and deep-fried, are an old, old Roman favorite. The batter is made with yeast and flour; the frying ideally is done in 2 big cauldrons, but a good deep pan in your own kitchen will do almost as well.

2 pounds dried cod
1 recipe Pastella *II (page 219)*

vegetable oil for deep-frying
1½ lemons, cut into wedges

Soak the cod, changing the water a couple of times, skin and bone it if necessary, and cut into pieces about 5 inches long, 1½ inches wide.

Prepare the *pastella* and let it stand in a warm place at least an hour, or until it has doubled in bulk and is rather full of bubbles.

Put frying oil in a deep pan to the depth of at least 2½ inches and bring it to high (375°) heat.

Dip the cod in the batter, coating all sides well, and put the pieces in the hot oil. When they are deep golden on one side, turn them over and continue frying until they are golden all around. Take them out with a slotted spoon and put them in a second pan of hot oil. Fry until very crisp, remove, and drain on paper towels. Serve hot with the lemon wedges. For 6.

Capesante e Gamberi
SHRIMPS AND SCALLOPS

1 pound scallops
1 pound large shrimp
1 garlic clove, peeled and quartered
4–5 tablespoons olive oil
¾ teaspoon salt
freshly ground pepper, white if possible

1 tablespoon capers, rinsed and drained
5–6 sprigs Italian parsley, chopped
10 drops Tabasco sauce
2 tablespoons brandy
juice of 1 lemon

Wash the scallops thoroughly. If they are very large, cut them in half. Peel, clean, and rinse the shrimp. Pat both fish dry with paper towels.

Cook the garlic in olive oil over medium heat until golden, then discard. Let the oil cool a moment or two.

Add scallops and shrimp, raise the heat, and sauté for 4 minutes, turning occasionally. Sprinkle with salt and pepper and sauté 2 minutes more.

Mince the capers and parsley leaves together to make at least 3 full, rounded tablespoons, and add to the pan along with the Tabasco. Cook 1 minute.

Add the brandy and lemon juice. Cook and stir 2 minutes. Taste for salt and adjust to please. Serve hot. For 4 generously.

Branzino alla Brace
GRILLED STRIPED BASS OR ROCKFISH

This is a good way to marinate other fish similar to the striped bass such as small halibut, red snapper, even the humble rose fish. If larger than 2 pounds, double the marinade.

1 2-pound striped bass or rockfish

FOR THE MARINADE:
2 lemons
½ cup dry sherry
½ cup olive oil
1 sprig fresh rosemary, or 2 teaspoons dried rosemary

½ teaspoon salt
3 to 4 drops Tabasco sauce, or ½ red pepper pod, seeded
pinch of sugar

Have the fish cleaned (or do it yourself), but leave the head and tail on.

Squeeze 1 lemon and mix the juice with the sherry and all the other ingredients in a bowl. If using the red pepper pod, break it up into pieces before adding to the marinade.

Put the fish in a suitable deep dish and pour the marinade in. Let the fish marinate for at least 1 hour, turning it over a few times. While the fish marinates, start your grill.

When the coals are ready, oil the grill and set it about 4 inches above the coals. Take the fish out of the marinade and put it on the grill. Cook each side until the skin blisters and crackles, brushing frequently with the marinade.

When the fish is done, remove it to a platter, skin and bone it, and serve with the remaining lemon cut in wedges and a dribble of good olive oil. For 4.

Fritto Misto di Pesce
MIXED FRIED FISH

There's hardly a fishing town in all Italy that isn't able to come up with this combination of golden-fried fresh shrimp, small squid, and fish no more than 2–3 inches long. Any one of these fried by itself is grand, but the combination gives a delicious contrast of taste and texture. The choice of small fish depends on your fish market, but we found that small fresh smelts are a good substitute for the tiny fish frequently found in Italian markets.

1½ pounds fresh small squid (or frozen)
1 pound fresh medium shrimp
1 pound fresh (very small) smelts, or other tiny fish when available

1 cup flour
vegetable oil for deep frying
salt to taste
2 lemons, cut into wedges

Defrost the fish if necessary.

Clean the squid (pages 104–105), cutting the bodies into rings and tentacles in half. Shell and devein the shrimp. Clean the smelts. Dredge all the pieces by shaking them in a sturdy bag with the flour.

Bring the frying oil to a high heat (375°). Drop the fish in a few at a time, so that the pan is full but not overcrowded. Keep turning the pieces as they become golden, and remove them with a slotted spoon when they are really crisp and thoroughly golden. Drain on paper towels on a cookie sheet and sprinkle with salt. Serve on a hot platter with the lemon wedges. For 6.

189

Gamberi alla Capri
SAUTÉED SHRIMP WITH CHERRY TOMATOES AND OLIVES

olive oil to cover the bottom of your
   sauté pan
2 cloves garlic
2 pounds medium shrimp, peeled
   and deveined
3 teaspoons capers
2 dozen olives, pitted and halved
4–6 tablespoons unsalted butter

salt to taste
several twists of the pepper mill
3 tablespoons Italian parsley,
   chopped
2½ dozen cherry tomatoes, halved
1 cup dry white wine (approximate)
1 teaspoon lemon juice

Flavor the olive oil by sautéing the garlic in it until dark brown. Discard the garlic and add the shrimp. Stir-fry over high heat for 90 seconds. Add capers, olives, butter, salt, and pepper and cook 1 minute.

Add parsley, tomatoes, wine, and lemon juice and cook about 1 minute. Serve with some of the sauce and generous pieces of Italian bread. For 6.

Gamberi alla Casalinga
SHRIMP, FAMILY STYLE

Originally this dish used shrimp just as they come from the sea, skin, tail, head and all to be eaten with the fingers. But for those who prefer forks, buy fresh shrimp with their jackets on, peel them, and dry them on paper towels before you begin with the seasoned olive oil.

2 pounds medium shrimp
1 clove garlic
1 red pepper pod, seeded (optional)
4 tablespoons olive oil

2 tablespoons chopped parsley
1 tablespoon capers
juice of 1 lemon
1 teaspoon salt, or to taste

Clean the shrimp by shucking off the shells, breaking off the tails, and deveining if necessary.

Sauté the garlic clove (and a red pepper pod if you like a hot touch in your dish) in olive oil over medium heat until golden and then discard it (with the red pepper after it has turned a deep brown).

Cook the shrimp in the olive oil, stirring constantly until they've turned a nice coral pink. Add the parsley and capers with the lemon juice. Stir, add salt. Taste the sauce for flavor on a morsel of bread and add a bit more salt if necessary. Cook another 3 minutes and serve.

Remember that if you keep the shrimp over high heat too long they'll lose both flavor and texture. The secret of this dish is speedy cooking, which leaves the shrimp cooked through but still firm. For 6.

Merluzzo alla Siciliana
FISH FILLETS IN ANCHOVY SAUCE

*2 pounds fresh fillets of hake, cod,
   haddock, or whiting*
2 large eggs
½ cup (approximate) flour
*1 cup unseasoned bread crumbs (ap-
   proximate)*

12 salted anchovy fillets
6 tablespoons olive oil
vegetable oil for frying
3 tablespoons chopped fresh parsley
1½ lemons

If the fish fillets are unmanageably long (more than 7 or 8 inches), cut them in half.

Beat the eggs until they are light in color and foamy.

Put the flour on one plate and the bread crumbs on another. Dredge the fillets in flour, pat them well to shake off any extra flour that doesn't adhere, dip them in the beaten eggs, and finally press them into the bread crumbs, first one side and then the other, and pat well. Set aside.

Mince the anchovy fillets to a paste. Warm the olive oil in a small saucepan over low heat and stir in the anchovy paste. Cook, stirring constantly, until the anchovies have disintegrated. (Do not overheat as the anchovy bits will just fry.) Once the mixture looks like a sauce, which usually oc-

curs after about 5 minutes, set it aside in a warm place.

Heat the vegetable oil to 375°, or medium heat, in a big frying pan and sauté the fish fillets on both sides to a golden brown. (If the oil isn't hot enough, the fillets just absorb it and become soggy; if too hot, the oil tends to darken the bread crumbs and egg coating too much before the inner fish is cooked.)

When the fish fillets are nicely browned on both sides, remove them and put them on absorbent paper to drain.

Once all the fish is cooked, place it on a warm serving platter. Add the parsley to the anchovy sauce, stir, and pour it over the fillets. Serve with lemon wedges. For 4–6.

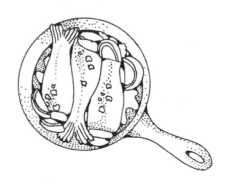

Pellegrine alla Fiorentina
SCALLOPS FLORENTINE STYLE

FOR THE VEGETABLES:
1 ½ pounds fresh spinach
1 teaspoon salt
2 tablespoons unsalted butter
¼ teaspoon freshly grated nutmeg
3 ½ cups freshly cooked mashed potatoes
¾ teaspoon salt
⅛ teaspoon white pepper
2 tablespoons unsalted butter
1 tablespoon grated Parmesan cheese
1 cup milk (approximate)

FOR THE SCALLOPS
2 pounds sea scallops, cleaned and dried
2 tablespoons unsalted butter
1 tablespoon olive oil
2 tablespoons snipped fresh or freeze-dried chives
½ garlic clove, peeled and minced
1 tablespoon minced Italian parsley
½ cup dry white wine
½ teaspoon salt, or to taste
⅛ teaspoon white pepper
2 tablespoons flour
⅔ cup whole milk
½ cup medium (all-purpose) cream
6 tablespoons grated Parmesan cheese

Wash fresh spinach well, discard the heaviest of the stems, and cook the remainder in the water that clings to the leaves. Add the salt and cook and stir until just tender. Drain well. Squeeze dry.

Place cooked spinach in a saucepan with the butter. Sprinkle with nutmeg and heat and stir until the butter has melted and coated the spinach.

Season fresh mashed potatoes with the salt, pepper, butter, and cheese. Add as much milk as needed to make smooth whipped potatoes.

For the scallops: melt the butter in the olive oil in a sauté pan large enough to hold all the scallops in one layer. Add the chives and minced garlic and parsley. Add the scallops. Pour the white wine over the scallops; add salt and pepper. Bring to a boil, cover, lower the heat, and cook 5 minutes.

Preheat oven to 450°.

Divide the spinach equally into 6 ovenproof gratin dishes. Using a pastry bag with a wide nozzle, pipe the mashed potatoes around the spinach. (You can arrange it with a spoon or fork, but the pastry bag is better.)

Take the scallops from their pan, reserving the juices, and place them on the spinach.

Add flour to the scallops pan, mix with a whisk, add the milk and cream, and bring to a boil slowly, whisking all the time. Taste for salt and pepper and correct to please. Cook at least 4 minutes.

Pour the sauce over the scallops in each dish. Sprinkle with Parmesan cheese.

Bake in a hot (450°) oven for 5 minutes or until slightly golden here and there. Let stand at least 10 minutes before eating or you'll burn your tongue and miss the combination of flavors and textures. For 6.

Persico alla Milanese
OCEAN PERCH, MILANESE STYLE

An everyday, old-fashioned way to prepare any fish fillet, illustrated here with perch. Slices of the fish are dredged in flour, dipped first in beaten egg then in fine bread crumbs, and fried golden in butter. This is another easy recipe for many of the fish fillets found on the American market.

2 pounds ocean perch fillets
1/2–3/4 cup flour
2 eggs
1 cup unseasoned bread crumbs

1/2 cup unsalted butter
1 teaspoon salt
2 lemons, cut into wedges

Press the fillets into the flour, patting it on them gently so that they absorb as much as possible. Knock off any excess flour. Beat the eggs and then dip the fillets in them, and then into the bread crumbs, patting the bread crumbs as you did the flour. Melt the butter in a heavy frying pan over medium heat and sauté the fillets quickly until golden, first on one side and then on the other. Drain on paper towels, sprinkle with the salt, and serve with lemon wedges. For 6.

Pesce Spada Dorato
GOLDEN-FRIED SWORDFISH

Swordfish (or halibut) steaks, cut no thicker than 1/2 inch, dipped in flour and egg, and then fried golden in olive oil, retain the delicacy and moistness of the fish.

2 1/2–3 pounds swordfish (or hali-
    but)
3/4 cup flour
1 teaspoon salt

2–3 eggs
4 tablespoons olive oil
2 lemons, cut into wedges

If you can't have the swordfish or halibut cut to the 1/2-inch thickness on purchase, cut it yourself, carefully slicing through the steaks. Mix the flour and salt on a big plate and dredge the steaks well, gently patting the flour on them so they absorb as much as possible.

Beat the eggs well and dip the fish in them.

Heat the olive oil in a heavy frying pan over medium heat and fry the fish steaks to a golden brown on each side. Drain on paper towels. Serve with lemon wedges. For 6.

Pesce all'Anconetana
FRIED FISH IN TOMATO SAUCE FROM ANCONA

FOR THE FISH:
*2–2½ pounds pollack, fresh cod,
    salt cod fillets (page 185)*
flour
vegetable oil for frying

FOR THE SAUCE:
3 garlic cloves
4 tablespoons olive oil
3 cups peeled plum tomatoes
3 tablespoons chopped fresh parsley
½ teaspoon salt
freshly ground pepper to taste

Cut the fish in pieces approximately 2" × 3", dredge them in flour, wait 5 to 10 minutes, and then dredge them again, patting the flour on well.

Put at least 1 inch of vegetable oil in a frying pan and bring it to 375° or medium heat. Fry the fish pieces a few at a time until both sides are golden brown. Then let them drain on absorbent paper. Keep them in a warm place while making the sauce.

In a saucepan, sauté the garlic in the olive oil until golden and then discard the cloves. Let the flavored oil cool a bit.

Put the tomatoes through a food mill or coarse sieve, add them to the cooling olive oil, and bring the pan back to a boil, stirring as it heats. Add the parsley, salt, and pepper (a few twists of the mill), lower the heat, and simmer the sauce for about 15–20 minutes, or until it has reduced somewhat and darkened in color. Put the fried fish pieces on a serving platter, cover them with sauce, and serve immediately. For 4–6.

Scorfano al Forno
BAKED GROUPER

In the Mediterranean, the *scorfano rosso* is used as one of the solid fish in soups and stews. Its Atlantic cousin, the grouper, is used a great deal for frozen fish fillets, bearing no name whatsoever. But if you are lucky enough to live where grouper is sold, either in fillets from the larger fish or whole if small, here is a recipe which is also equally good with sea bass or red snapper.

*1 6-pound grouper, or 2 fillets of the
    same weight*
*1 sprig fresh rosemary, or 1 teaspoon
    dried*

3 small bay leaves
2 garlic cloves, peeled
1½ teaspoons salt, or to taste
freshly ground pepper

½ cup olive oil
1 teaspoon dried oregano
5 sprigs Italian parsley

1 tablespoon wine vinegar
¾ cup plain tomato juice
3 ounces black Sicilian olives

Have the fish cleaned but leave the head and tail on for a more flavorsome dish.

Preheat the oven to 400°.

Mince the rosemary, bay leaves, and garlic together and sprinkle the mince throughout the cavity (or over the fillets). Add 1 teaspoon of the salt and a generous sprinkling of pepper.

Put the oil in a dish just large enough to hold the fish well. Add the oregano to the oil. Place the parsley sprigs down the center of the dish. Put the fish on top of the parsley and sprinkle with ½ teaspoon salt and a little more pepper.

Add the vinegar and tomato juice to the dish and baste the fish 3 or 4 times.

Surround the fish with the olives.

Bake in a hot 400° oven approximately ¾–1 hour; cover the dish with aluminum foil for the first ½ hour, then remove the foil and baste thoroughly and continue baking another 15–30 minutes. Taste the now diminished sauce for salt and add more if desired.

Serve the fish with olives surrounding it and its sauce poured over it. For 6.

Seppie all'Umido alla Genovese
SQUID, GENOESE STYLE

Squid, Genoese style is very like the Roman versions except that the sauce is more abundant, filled with tomatoes, and flavored with a bit more garlic. The dish can accommodate squid that are a little larger because you do have more sauce to go around for longer simmering.

3-pound package frozen squid
4 tablespoons olive oil
2 cloves garlic
2 tablespoons fresh chopped parsley
2 teaspoons salt

½ teaspoon ground pepper
1 cup dry red wine
3 cups plum tomatoes
1 package frozen peas (10 ounces)

Clean the squid in the usual fashion (see pages 104–105) and cut it into squares or rings, the tentacles in half.

Heat the olive oil in a big frying pan, add the garlic, and cook until golden. Discard the garlic and add the squid, parsley, salt, and pepper. When the squid start to turn pink (after about 2 or 3 minutes over medium heat), pour in the wine, and cook until the alcohol has evaporated and the vapors no

longer tingle the nose. Add the tomatoes, mashing them with a wooden spoon against the side of the pan. Bring to a boil, lower the heat, and simmer about 15–20 minutes or until the sauce has reduced and concentrated a bit and the squid is tender. Add the peas and continue simmering another 10 or 15 minutes, or until the peas are cooked. Taste for salt, adding some if necessary. Serve hot with Italian bread. For 6.

Seppie coi Piselli alla Romana
SQUID WITH PEAS, ROMAN STYLE

Small squid, fresh or frozen, cooked in flavored olive oil, white wine, and parsley, are joined by peas toward the end of their simmering. A delicate dish loved by Romans, this has many variations up and down the coast of Italy.

3 pounds fresh or frozen squid
4 tablespoons olive oil
1 clove garlic
1 red pepper pod, seeded
1 cup dry white wine

2 tablespoons chopped parsley
1 teaspoon salt, or to taste
1 package frozen peas (or 1 pound fresh)

If using frozen squid: defrost them either at room temperature or under running cold water. Clean and cut as on pages 104–105.

Put the olive oil in a big, wide frying pan over medium heat. Add the garlic and the pepper pod. When the garlic is golden and the pepper a deep brown, remove them both and put in the squid. Cook for about 3 minutes, or until the squid has changed its color to pink and purple. Add the wine and continue cooking until it has evaporated. Lower the heat and add the parsley and salt. Simmer about 20 minutes, or until the squid is tender. Add the peas (frozen take about 10 minutes, the fresh about 15, to cook). When everything is tender to the bite, check the sauce for salt, adding more if necessary. Serve piping hot with hot Italian bread. For 6.

Seppie Ripiene
STUFFED SQUID

With a little bit of patience and dexterous fingers nearly anyone can stuff a squid's body, which is then poached in sauce (basically wine and tomatoes) and served as a second course. If you use medium-size squid, about 6 or 7 inches long, plan 2 to a person.

12 medium squid
1 small clove garlic
1 cup parsley leaves
1/4 teaspoon oregano
2 teaspoons salt

1 teaspoon freshly ground pepper
4 tablespoons olive oil
3–4 slices Italian bread
1/2 cup dry white wine
6 plum tomatoes (optional)

Clean the squid as on pages 104–105, letting the bodies dry on paper towels. Put the tentacles, garlic, parsley, oregano, salt, and pepper together on a chopping board and chop them well. Shred the Italian bread, discarding the crusts, into a bowl. You should have about 1 cup of shredded bread. Add the chopped tentacles and herbs and mix well. Moisten with a bit of the olive oil to make a coarse paste.

Fill the squid with the paste until they are ½–¾ full. Don't stuff them too tightly or they'll burst in the pan. Skewer shut with plain round wooden picks. Save any leftover stuffing.

Cover the bottom of a big frying pan with the rest of the olive oil and put in the stuffed squid in one layer. Brown gently over medium heat. Move the squid about a bit with a spatula or wooden spoon while they are browning to keep them from sticking. Then, if there is any, add the remaining stuffing and sauté it for a moment or so. Add the wine, stir well, and keep on medium heat until the wine has nearly evaporated.

At this stage, if you wish tomato-flavored sauce, put the plum tomatoes through a sieve or food mill, and add the resulting thick juice to the pan. Add enough warm water just barely to come up to the top of the squid. If you don't want to include the tomatoes, add water only. Stir around with a wooden spoon to loosen any bits that may have stuck to the sides and bottom of the pan. Lower the heat and simmer uncovered for 20–30 minutes, or until the squid is tender and the sauce has condensed. Turn the squid over a couple of times while simmering them in order to ensure even cooking.

Remove the squid to a platter, pour the sauce over them, and serve. For 6.

Sogliole Fritte Dorate
GOLDEN-FRIED SOLE

The tiniest sole, no bigger than the palm of your hand, are ideal for this dish, and are most authentically Mediterranean, but fresh fillets of larger sole are just as good and more frequently available.

6 large or 12 small sole fillets
flour
2 eggs

¾ teaspoon salt
olive oil
1½ lemons

Gently press the fillets into the flour, covering both sides well. Beat the eggs lightly and add salt. Dip the fish into the beaten eggs, then fry in about ½ inch hot olive oil. When the fillets are golden on one side, turn them and do the second side. Remove the minute both sides are a good golden color. Serve with lemon wedges. For 6.

Spiedini di Rana Pescatrice
SKEWERS OF MONKFISH, MUSHROOMS AND TOMATOES

2 pounds monkfish
2 green sweet peppers, cut into 1½-inch squares
½ pound large brown mushrooms, washed, stems removed
1½ dozen cherry tomatoes, washed, hulls removed
½ cup olive oil
½ cup dry white wine

2 tablespoons snipped fresh or freeze-dried chives
1 tablespoon chopped Italian parsley
1 teaspoon fresh rosemary, or ½ teaspoon dried
½ teaspoon dried oregano
freshly ground pepper

Trim the fish of the central bone and the skin. Cut the fish into 1½-inch squares.

Place a piece of pepper at one end of a skewer. Add a mushroom, tomato, piece of fish, tomato, mushroom, fish, tomato, mushroom, fish, mushroom, tomato, and finally a second piece of green pepper. Send another skewer up along side the first to hold all the pieces well.

Repeat on other skewers; the aim is to get 3 pieces of fish on each skewer and begin and end with the pepper which is sturdy enough to protect the other pieces.

Place the skewers in a platter.

Put oil, wine, herbs, and pepper in a jar, shake well, and pour over the skewers. Let marinate, basting from time to time, for at least ½ hour.

Grill skewers on an open grill or in a preheated broiler, turning as one side is cooked, about a total of 6 minutes. Baste with any remaining marinade and serve when the fish is cooked, the tomatoes and mushrooms just barely cooked, and the peppers still green and crisp. Makes about 8 9-inch skewers. For 4.

Trance di Pesce alla Griglia
GRILLED FISH STEAKS

Almost any of the more fleshy types of fish lend themselves well to cooking over an open grill. This simple treatment includes rosemary and parsley as the herbs, together with a bit of olive oil and lemon juice to keep the fish moist while it cooks.

FOR THE BATTUTO:
1 small clove garlic
5 sprigs fresh rosemary (or 2 teaspoons dried)
2 tablespoons chopped parsley
1 teaspoon salt
freshly ground pepper

3 pounds thick slices or fillets of fish (turbot, halibut, perch, haddock, or fresh cod)
⅓ cup olive oil
2 lemons

Get your grill going.

Make a *battuto* of the garlic, rosemary, parsley, salt, and pepper.

Mix the olive oil and the juice of 1 of the lemons together in a small bowl, and brush both sides of the fish slices with the mixture. Spread the fish slices out on a platter and sprinkle them evenly with half the *battuto*. Place the slices, herbed-sides down, on a hot open grill. Sprinkle the up-sides with some of the *battuto*. When the first sides are well browned, turn the slices carefully (using two spatulas helps to do this easily). Sprinkle again with the remaining *battuto*, brush with the oil-lemon mixture, and cook until the second side is thoroughly browned. Serve with the remaining lemon cut into wedges. For 6.

Trotelle alla Salvia
BAKED TROUT WITH SAGE

6 small rainbow trout (½ to ¾ pounds each)
salt to taste
12 fresh sage leaves

6 tablespoons butter
freshly ground pepper
1½ lemons

Preheat the oven to 450°.

Clean the fish but leave the heads and tails on.

Salt the cavities of the fish lightly. Chop 6 of the sage leaves well and sprinkle them inside the fish. Cut 1 tablespoon of the butter into 6 bits and put a bit in each fish.

Butter a baking dish just large enough to hold the fish. Distribute the remaining 6 sage leaves along the bottom. Put in the fish. Sprinkle with salt and a few twists of the pepper mill. Melt the remaining butter and dribble it over the fish.

Bake (at 450°) for 6–8 minutes, basting once during baking. Serve with lemon wedges. For 6.

Frattaglie
THE "IN-BETWEEN" CUTS

Frattaglie aren't just "in-between" cuts, they're the interior organs—kidneys, liver, sweetbreads, brains, and tripe—of all those noble beasts who've been to market. Depending on where you shop, you can find perhaps all or only a few of them. Sometimes they're very much the fashion: the elegant New York brunch features sweetbreads, the British dinner its mixed grill, a French lunch a delicate dish of brains. In Italy the presence of a dish of veal kidneys isn't merely a matter of fashion. It has traditionally made a regular, weekly appearance, although our Italian butcher has admitted that a time-honored group of menus is being ignored in this decade by the modern housewife. Yet there is hardly a reputable restaurant from the top to the toe of Italy that doesn't include one or more *frattaglie* on every menu.

In the United States we easily find calf's liver as well as beef and baby beef liver in our local markets. Tripe also is usually available. To buy pig's liver, we frequently have to go to Italian butchers, as we do also for brains and sweetbreads. Again it just depends on market supply and demand.

We don't know why the modern housewife has begun to ignore *frattaglie,* but we do know that most of the ways of cooking them are easy, and that their taste makes any search for them well worth the effort. To tell the truth, when we come across them, as well as pork rind, while shopping for something else, we're likely to abandon any previously planned menu in their favor. Try them. You'll see.

Fagioli e Cotiche
BEANS WITH PORK RIND

This is Italy's contribution to the pork-and-bean recipes of the world, another very hearty, very inexpensive, very nutritious dish for a crowd. The idea of ham or pork rind doesn't appeal to a lot of people at first, but they don't have to eat the rind, and invariably they go wild for the beans and the sauce; eventually they end up eating the rind after all. Of course the rind is not a cut, but we frequently find it where we find the livers and other organ meats.

½ pound pork rind

FOR THE BATTUTO:
2 slices lean salt pork
1 clove garlic
1 small onion
1 tablespoon chopped parsley

3 tablespoons olive oil
2 cups peeled plum tomatoes,
  coarsely chopped
salt to taste
freshly ground pepper
2 cans white beans (cannellini), *or 2*
  cups dried

Cut the pork rind into 1- × 2-inch pieces. Put them in a pot with at least 2 quarts of water and boil, covered, for at least 1 hour, or until tender.

Make a *battuto* with the salt pork, garlic, onion, and parsley, and sauté it until golden in the olive oil in a large stew pot. Add the plum tomatoes, salt and pepper to taste, and the now tender pork rind. Cook for 30 minutes, to reduce the sauce and blend its flavors. Drain and rinse the canned beans and add them to the pot. Heat through, taste for salt, and adjust seasonings if necessary. Serve hot.

If you wish, you can use dried beans. Boil them in 1½ quarts water for 2 minutes. Remove them from the heat and let stand 1 hour. Return them to the heat and simmer until tender. For 6.

Fegatelli di Maiale
PORK LIVERS

Little bundles of pork liver, cut just bigger than bite-size and wrapped in a rete *(caul). The rete* is the intestinal membrane, a white lacey looking thing you can purchase uncut in Italian meat markets. If you find the liver already cut and wrapped in the *rete,* make sure the butcher wasn't too generous with it, because it is fat, and all you need is just barely enough to wrap and cook the liver in.

1–1½ pounds pork liver
½ pound of rete *(caul)*
bay leaves

2 tablespoons olive oil
salt and pepper
3 tablespoons wine vinegar

To prepare the bundles yourself, cut the pork liver into chunks about the size of a small egg. Cut the membrane just big enough to wrap up the chunks. Stick a bay leaf under the last flap of each bundle and skewer the packet with a wooden pick.

Pour the olive oil into a big frying pan and add the liver chunks as the pan is heating. The membrane will start to melt the minute the pan gets hot.

Salt and pepper generously. Sauté quickly, 1–2 minutes on a side, until the liver is nicely browned and the juices start to flow. The minute they do, add the wine vinegar, cover, and cook another 2 minutes, or until the vinegar stops sizzling. Serve with just a touch of the pan's sauce and big chunks of hot Italian bread. For 6.

Fegato alla Toscana
LIVER, TUSCAN STYLE

Baby beef liver, which is a little meatier than calf's liver, dusted in flour and cooked in herb-flavored olive oil, is a quick dish whose flavor is heightened by lemon juice.

2 pounds baby beef liver
flour
½ cup olive oil
1 clove garlic

2–3 fresh sage leaves
salt to taste
freshly ground pepper
1½ lemons

Cut the liver into slices no thicker than ¼ inch. (Slices this thick are sometimes found precut and frozen, in which case defrost in the refrigerator before using.) Dredge the slices in flour, patting it on well to make as much as possible firmly adhere. Shake off any loose, excess flour.

Heat the olive oil with the garlic and sage in a big frying pan over medium high heat. (If you can't get fresh sage, use bay leaves. Dried sage doesn't have the same effect on the liver as does the fresh.) Add the floured liver and sauté quickly, turning it as soon as the bottom side has browned. Cook the second side only until the juices run. The liver should be almost crisp on the outside, tender and moist inside. Add salt, pepper, and the juice of ½ lemon to the pan, and heat for a moment. Put the slices on a warm platter and pour on some of the flavored olive oil. Cut 1 lemon into thin wedges, arrange them around the platter, and serve. For 6.

Fegato alla Veneziana
LIVER, VENETIAN STYLE

Calf's liver, sliced no thicker than ¼ inch, cooked quickly in olive oil with thinly sliced onions, is unbelievably kind to the palate in taste and texture.

2 Spanish onions
3 tablespoons unsalted butter
¼ cup olive oil

½ teaspoon salt
2 pounds calf's liver
2 tablespoons chopped parsley

Cut the onions in half, and then sliver each half into the thinnest possible slivers to make about 1½ cups. If using regular all-purpose kitchen onions, slice them as you would the Spanish onions, but soak them about 10 minutes in ice water and drain them carefully before using.

Heat the oil and butter over medium heat in a big frying pan. Add the slivered onions and sauté them until translucent. Add the salt as they cook.

If the liver is cut into the usual ½-inch-thick slices, put them down on a cutting board and cut horizontally through them to get slices no more than ¼ inch thick.

Add the thinly sliced liver to the onions and sauté quickly, only 30 seconds per side. If cooked longer, the liver loses both flavor and texture, becomes dried out and dull. It should be just barely pink and moist when you cut into it. Add the parsley, stir, and cook another ½ minute.

Serve with the onions and flavored olive oil on top of the liver. For 6.

Fegato con Vino Bianco
BABY BEEF LIVER IN WHITE WINE

4 tablespoons unsalted butter
2 bay leaves
2 pounds baby beef liver, sliced no
*   thicker than ¼ inch*

½ cup dry white wine
1–2 tablespoons chopped parsley

Melt the butter in a wide frying pan over high heat. Add the bay leaves and the liver. Sauté 1 minute on each side and then pour in the wine. Continue cooking another moment or so, until the wine has just about evaporated.

Put the slices of liver on a serving platter, sprinkle with parsley, and pour over them any remaining butter-wine sauce. For 6.

Fritto Misto alla Romana
FRIED BRAINS (OR SWEETBREADS) MIXED WITH VEGETABLES, ROMAN STYLE

Fritto misto has many variations, depending on what's available in the regional market. A most frequent combination includes zucchini, artichokes, cauliflower, and either brains (calf's or lamb's) or veal sweetbreads. It can also include potatoes, *ricotta*, liver, and apple slices.

Four main ingredients make a decent choice. Everything is cut into approximately the same bite-size bits, dipped in an egg batter, deep-fried quickly, and served hot with lemon wedges.

It's the kind of production in which two cooks in the kitchen make more than good sense. Both can clean and cut while the *pastella* sits. Then one can dip while the other fries. The bigger the pan, the faster the frying and the better the eating, because this dish should not sit around but be served immediately.

1 double batch pastella	*3 artichokes*
½ pound brains (calf's or lamb's)	*1 head cauliflower*
1 tablespoon vinegar	*vegetable oil for deep-frying*
or *½ pound sweetbreads*	*4 lemons*
1 teaspoon salt	*salt*
3 zucchini	

Mix up a double batch of *Pastella* I (page 219) and let it sit for 2 hours.

If using brains: soak them in ice water for about half an hour. Then drain them, remove the skin and membrane, and put them in fresh water to cover. Add the vinegar and simmer for about 15 minutes. Drain and cut in bite-size pieces, and they're ready for the *pastella.*

If using sweetbreads: soak them in salted ice-cold water for at least 1 hour. Drain them, put them in a quart of fresh water with the teaspoon of salt, and simmer until tender (about 15 minutes). Drain, and then put them into fresh cold water. Drain again, cut away any fat or membrane. Cut them in bite-size pieces, and they're ready for batter and frying.

Trim off and discard zucchini tops and bottoms. Cut the trimmed zucchini into long, finger-size spears. Trim and prepare the artichokes (pages 226–27), cutting them finally into wedges no wider than ¼ inch at the base. Soak the artichoke wedges in a quart of water mixed with the juice of 1 lemon until frying time. Break the flowerets off the cauliflower stem, wash them, and they're ready.

Put oil to a depth of at least 2½ inches into a big pan and heat to 375° (or until hot enough so that a dollop of batter frizzles and fries immediately on contact). Dip a few morsels of prepared ingredients into the batter, then put them on to fry. (Use your fingers for this; it's messier but easier and quicker.) The pieces will sink to the bottom immediately and slowly rise as they turn golden and cook. They do cook rather quickly, and must be turned over (a slotted spoon is good for this) as soon as they're golden on one side. Remove them when golden crisp all around, replacing them with more battered pieces. Drain thoroughly, first over the hot oil, so that as much oil as possible falls back into the pan, and then on paper towels. Keep the oil at a very high heat during frying, and the process will go quickly. Serve immediately with wedges of lemon. For 6.

Rognoncini Trifolati
VEAL KIDNEYS AND MUSHROOMS

1 ¾ pounds veal kidneys
½ pound large mushrooms
2–3 anchovy fillets
3 tablespoons olive oil
1 garlic clove

3 tablespoons unsalted butter
juice of ½ lemon
1 tablespoon chopped parsley
salt and pepper to taste

Remove any fat from the kidneys and cut them into thin slices. Clean and cut the mushrooms into thin slices (cut them in half first and then cut each half into as many thin wedges as possible). Mash the anchovies to a paste.

Heat the oil in a medium-size frying pan. Add the garlic, sauté until golden, and then discard it. Add the kidney and mushroom slices and sauté over high heat 2 or 3 minutes, adding the butter and anchovy paste and stirring everything all the while. As soon as the kidneys and mushrooms start to give up their juices, add the lemon juice and chopped parsley. Stir and continue cooking another moment or two until the sauce has thickened a bit. Taste for salt, adding some if needed. Add pepper to taste and serve immediately. For 6.

Frittate
OMELETS

The easiest way of translating *frittata* is as "omelet." But the very word *omelet* conjures up a host of white-clad chefs who, at the end of a long professional life, having mastered special tools and techniques, finally turn out the Perfect Omelet: puffy, golden, slightly crisp on the outside, filled or unfilled, almost a soufflé. The *frittata* is not necessarily difficult, not exactly filled, because all the additions to the eggs are mixed and blended with them, and most of the time it's not puffy. In fact some of the time it must be spooned rather than cut.

Moreover, the Italian *frittata* is much humbler, more a peasant dish. For centuries it was the working man's lunch. A loaf of bread, slit open, was filled with a *frittata* and taken along on the job. On today's Italian table, it appears as a second course in a lunch, as part of a light supper, or is carried on picnics. Restaurants have been serving them up cold as *antipasti,* but the true followers of the *frittata* cult insist on serving them hot, at table.

In many regions the word is used as an exclamation: "What a *frittata!*" people say, to comment on any sort of action that ends up as a scrambled mess.

The *frittata* pan is a normal frying pan, copper, iron, or aluminum (in order of historical appearance on the market). It is usually cured by age and by the simple fact that it is never washed. Once used, and preferably while still hot, it is rubbed clean with salt and a paper towel. An aged, well-seasoned pan is considered an heirloom. The heavy iron or aluminum omelet pan available on the American market is of course marvelous for making *frittate,* but you can be successful without one.

If you're a novice or buy a new pan, choose a wide, heavy aluminum pan, fill it with fresh cooking oil, bring it to a very high heat, let it cool overnight, empty it, and wipe it dry. From then on, use it only as a *frittata* pan, with butter or olive oil as the recipe dictates. Wipe it clean each time you use it; don't soak or soap it.

If the right size pan is not available, the *frittata* can be cooked in two batches. The ingredients, other than the eggs, are usually prepared first in a pan and then divided in half, as are the eggs. This ensures the proper texture for each batch as well as the correct thickness of no more than about ¾ of an inch.

Northern Italians traditionally use butter, while the Southerners use olive oil. The Northerners tend to use more eggs and less of the other ingredients, the so-called filling. The Southerners use fewer eggs, considering them to be mainly a binder for the filling. On the average, 1 ½ eggs per person is the right amount if the eggs are medium size. Most of our recipes call for 7 large eggs for 6 people (about the equivalent of 9 medium eggs). Experiment for yourself, and adjust the number to your taste.

When you've decided how many eggs to use, you should warm them to room temperature while you prepare and cook the filling. Once beaten, the eggs can be salted before you add them to the vegetables, or you can salt them during cooking. Some *frittate* (for example, the zucchini one) taste better if salted after cooking.

When you are ready to combine the vegetables and the eggs, raise the heat so that you'll be able to cook quickly. There should be no need to add more oil or butter, but if the vegetables look a little dry, use your own judgment and add a bit of butter or oil if it seems necessary. Then pour in the eggs, stirring right away. As the edges of the *frittata* start to solidify, lift them gently with a spatula to get the uncooked eggs down to the bottom of the pan. Once the bottom of the *frittata* is solid and golden, it should slide back and forth when the pan is shaken.

Then it's time to turn the whole thing over and cook the second side. Some champions can just flip it, and of course the smaller the *frittata,* the more easily it is flipped. The most revered way to turn it, whether it's large or small, is to slide it out, cooked side down, onto a big plate. Cover the plate with the pan and turn plate and pan together, letting the uncooked side of the *frittata* plop back into the pan. Return it to high heat and cook until this second side slides back and forth. Then once more slide it out onto that big plate, cut like a pie, and serve.

Frittata di Carciofi
ARTICHOKE OMELET

A *frittata* makes a few artichokes go a long way. This one is eaten cold as an *antipasto* or on picnics. Hot, it is a most delicate second course.

3 artichokes
juice of 1 lemon
3 tablespoons olive oil
    (approximately)

7 large eggs
salt to taste

Prepare the artichokes for cooking as on pages 226–27. Slice from the top to stem into ⅛-inch slices. Soak in water with the lemon juice. Drain and dry before using.

Heat the olive oil in a big frying pan, add the sliced artichokes, and cook them until tender over medium heat, stirring from time to tame.

Beat the eggs and salt to taste. Raise the heat and put in the eggs, shifting the artichokes back and forth with a fork to make sure the eggs seep down to the bottom of the pan. As soon as the bottom crust is formed, turn the *frittata*. When golden brown on both sides, it's ready to serve and eat. For 6.

Frittata con Erba Cipollina
CHIVE OMELET

4 tablespoons unsalted butter
7 large eggs
handful of chives, finely chopped

1 teaspoon salt, or to taste
freshly ground pepper

Melt the butter in a omelet pan over low heat. Beat the eggs well.

Raise the heat, put in the beaten eggs, sprinkle with chives, salt, and freshly ground pepper. When the bottom is golden brown, turn the omelet and continue cooking until the second side is done. Serve hot. For 6.

Frittata con Fagiolini
OMELET WITH GREEN BEANS

1 cup water
1½ teaspoons salt
1 9-ounce package frozen cut green
    beans

4 tablespoons olive oil
7 large eggs

Bring the water to a boil and add 1 teaspoon of the salt and the frozen beans. When the water comes back to a boil and the beans are thoroughly thawed but not completely cooked, drain and pat dry with paper towels.

Heat the olive oil in an omelet or frying pan, add the drained beans, and sauté about 4 minutes, or until tender, turning the beans with a spoon as they cook.

Beat the eggs well, add the last of the salt, and pour the eggs over the cooked beans. Shake the pan to get the eggs well distributed, and when the bottom is solid and golden brown, turn the omelet and cook the other side. Serve hot. For 6.

Frittata al Formaggio
CHEESE OMELET

6 large eggs
3 tablespoons unsalted butter
½ pound fresh mozzarella cheese,
    shredded, or whole milk mozza-
    rella, cubed

½ teaspoon salt, or to taste
1½ tablespoons minced Italian
    parsley or minced fresh basil
freshly ground pepper

Beat the eggs lightly.

Melt the butter in the omelet pan, add the eggs, then sprinkle with the mozzarella.

Add the salt.

As the eggs start to set around the edges, go around with a spatula to make sure they don't stick. Lift the edges here and there and tilt the pan to let some of the uncooked egg slip down underneath.

Sprinkle with the parsley or basil.

When the underside is cooked and golden, turn and cook the second side.

Slide the frittata onto a warm serving plate, sprinkle with a bit of pepper, and serve. For 4.

Frittata ai Funghi
MUSHROOM OMELET

½–1 pound mushrooms
3 tablespoons unsalted butter
salt to taste

5 sprigs parsley, chopped (optional)
7 large eggs

Clean the mushrooms. Just cut off a thin slice at the bottom of the stem, throw it away, and slice the rest of the mushroom. The small ones slice nicely from top to bottom, each piece including a tiny bit of stem. The big ones should have their stems sliced separately into tiny rounds and the tops into thin slices.

Melt enough butter to cover the bottom of the pan and put the sliced mushrooms in to cook. At first they will absorb the butter, and then they will give out their own delicious liquid just as they are about done and are ready to have the eggs added. At this point the mushrooms are cooked but still slightly crisp. Sprinkle with a bit of salt. Add parsley, if desired, to the mushrooms.

Beat the eggs thoroughly and pour them onto the cooked mushrooms. Stir gently with the tip of a spatula to get the egg to slip down and around and in between the mushroom slices. As soon as the bottom has browned and the top begun to solidify, turn the *frittata* to complete cooking. Sprinkle with a bit of salt and serve. For 6.

Frittata al Prosciutto e Tre Formaggi
OMELETS WITH HAM AND THREE CHEESES

¼ cup fresh ricotta
2 tablespoons Parmesan cheese
2 ounces fresh mozzarella cheese, grated
2 ounces cooked ham, diced

1 tablespoon cream
5 large eggs, well beaten
2 tablespoons unsalted butter
salt to taste

Mix the three cheeses with the ham and add the cream to make a soft filling.

Pour ¼ of the beaten egg into a hot, buttered omelet pan. When the underside is well browned and the top is beginning to set, place ¼ of the filling down the center of the omelet, fold the sides up over the filling, and continue cooking a moment or two longer. Cook the remaining egg with filling to make 3 more omelets. Sprinkle with salt to your taste. Serve hot. For 4.

Frittata Rognosa
TOMATO-AND-ONION OMELET

The *rognosa* isn't really an omelet in the usual sense of the word, since it isn't supposed to be crisp and shapely. The perfect *rognosa* is just moist and spoonable, not unlike scrambled eggs. For years and years it has been the working man's lunch, as a filling inside a loaf of bread called a *pagnottella*. Today it's the cook's selection for a quick snack or second course when there is no meat.

1 large Bermuda onion
2–3 tablespoons olive oil
1½ cups plum tomatoes

salt to taste
7 large eggs

Sliver the onion by cutting it in half, eliminating the core at the bottom and slicing each half into the thinnest possible slices the shape of new moons. If you don't have a big Bermuda, use 2 medium all-purpose onions, slivered and soaked in cold water for about 10 minutes, and then drained and dried. Put the onion in a big frying or omelet pan with the olive oil (just enough to cover the bottom), and sauté until golden and translucent over medium heat. Add the tomatoes and mash them up with a wooden spoon. Bring to a boil, reduce the heat, and simmer about 15 minutes, or until the liquids are reduced and the color deepened. Salt lightly.

Beat the eggs to a froth and add them. Raise the heat to medium and stir the eggs into the tomato sauce until the whole thing starts to solidify. Stir once or twice more as the eggs and sauce unite to make a moist, almost solid *frittata.*

If your pan won't accommodate this many eggs and the tomatoes, proceed by installments. Cook the tomatoes and onion to the point where they're ready for the eggs. Remove half the tomato mixture and add half the eggs, making a *frittata* for 3. Serve on a hot platter. Put the last half of tomato and onion back in the pan, add the rest of the eggs, make a second *frittata,* and serve. For 6.

Frittata con Spinaci
SPINACH OMELET

Another *frittata* commonly used by working men for lunch on the job, this omelet of spinach with a hint of Parmesan cheese can be made with the frozen or fresh vegetable.

½ pound fresh spinach, or ½ package frozen (5 ounces)
7 large eggs

2 tablespoons grated Parmesan cheese
salt to taste
3 tablespoons butter

Cook the spinach in boiling salted water. Drain it, squeezing it against the side of a sieve to get out as much water as possible. Chop it, if it isn't already chopped.

Beat the eggs well. Add the Parmesan cheese and a pinch of salt, and then beat in the chopped spinach.

Heat the butter in a big, heavy frying pan, and when it is melted and bubbly (not browned), pour in the eggs with their spinach and cheese. Cook over medium high heat, lifting the sides of the *frittata* from time to time and tilting the pan to let the uncooked egg run down to the bottom. When the bottom is a golden brown and the top is fairly solid, turn the *frittata,* using either a spatula or the plate system, and cook the second side to a golden brown. Sprinkle with salt and serve. For 6.

Frittata con Zucchine
ZUCCHINI OMELET

Once a summer dish, this *frittata* made with the smallest of zucchini is a year-round possibility in America. Many people consider a zucchini omelet the only way to get the real flavor of zucchini.

2 medium or 4 small zucchini
3–4 tablespoons olive oil

salt to taste
7 large eggs

Cut the zucchini into very, very thin rounds. Heat the oil in a heavy frying pan and put in the zucchini. Cook over medium high heat until they are just wilted and slightly golden. Sprinkle with salt.

Beat the eggs well and pour them over the zucchini, stirring gently to get the eggs down to the bottom of the pan and all around the edges and in between the slices. As soon as the bottom is golden brown and solid, slide a spatula under one side, tilt the pan, and let more uncooked egg go to the bottom. When the whole pan is fairly solid, turn the *frittata* and finish cooking. Sprinkle with salt. Serve hot or cold. For 6.

Frittatine al Sugo
LITTLE OMELETS WITH TOMATO SAUCE

Omelets, thin as French *crêpes*, are stacked like layers in a cake, with basil-flavored tomato sauce in between each *frittatina.* The little extra effort that goes into making this transforms an everyday dish into a Sunday treat.

FOR THE SAUCE:
4 tablespoons unsalted butter
1 1/2 cups plum tomatoes
4–5 fresh basil leaves
1 teaspoon salt

FOR THE FRITTATINE:
8 large eggs
2 tablespoons flour
1/2 teaspoon salt, or to taste
2 tablespoons water
2–3 tablespoons butter
3–4 tablespoons grated Parmesan cheese

The sauce: melt the 4 tablespoons butter in a large saucepan, then add the tomatoes and their juice, mashing the tomatoes as they go into the pan. Tear the basil leaves into little pieces and add them. Add the salt and let the mixture come to a boil, lower the heat, and simmer for about 15 minutes, or until reduced to sauce consistency.

The *frittatine:* beat the eggs well, adding the flour, salt, and water. Melt 2 tablespoons of the butter in a heavy omelet or frying pan. When the butter is melted and bubbly, spoon enough beaten eggs into the pan to make a thin round about 5 inches in diameter. As soon as its bottom is solidified and golden, turn it over. As soon as its second side is cooked, take it out and put it on a warm serving platter on which you have placed 1 tablespoon of sauce. Cover the finished *frittatina* with a bit more sauce.

Continue cooking the *frittatine,* layering them as they are done with a bit of sauce. Add the last tablespoon of butter to the pan when it is needed. When all the beaten egg is used up (you should have made about 10 thin *frittatine*), pour the remaining sauce over the layers. Cut as you would a cake and serve hot.

An alternative way of serving *frittatine* is to roll each one up as it is cooked and put it into the simmering tomato sauce. For 6.

Frittata all'Amatriciana
OMELET WITH *BUCATINI* AND HOT TOMATO SAUCE

This is an easy way to be creative. Make an omelet with the pasta of your choice in it; just be sure the two main ingredients are compatible.

FOR THE OMELET:
1 tablespoon butter
2 large eggs

FOR THE FILLING:
1 portion of bucatini *dressed with hot tomato sauce (page 43)*

Heat up your omelet pan. Add the butter. Beat the eggs well with a whisk. Chop coarsely the dressed *bucatini* and mix with the eggs.

Pour the mixture into the hot pan and cook over medium heat until firm on the bottom. Slide off onto a large plate. Turn the omelet pan upside down over the plate. Turn plate and pan right side up, letting the omelet fall, uncooked side down, into the pan. Cook the second side until it is firm on the outside, moist on the inside. For 1.

Salse e Pastelle
SAUCES AND BATTERS

Here are three marinades, four familiar sauces to use in cooking and serving meats and fish, plus two favorite batters for fish, meat, and vegetables.

Marinade for Poultry #1

juice of 1 lemon
2 tablespoons olive oil
1 tablespoon soy sauce
1 teaspoon mustard
1 teaspoon hot pepper sauce
    (Tabasco)

1 sprig fresh rosemary, or 1 teaspoon
    dried
freshly ground pepper

Place all of the ingredients in a small bowl and whisk or beat well. Pour over chicken pieces and let marinate for at least ½ hour, turning the pieces 3 times. Enough for 1 broiler.

Marinade for Poultry #2

⅓ cup lemon juice
2 teaspoons soy sauce
4 dashes Tabasco
⅓ cup dry white vermouth
1 teaspoon sugar

salt
freshly ground pepper
1 tablespoon olive oil
1 small garlic clove
2 sprigs rosemary

Marinate ½ to 1 hour.

Marinade for Poultry #3

juice of one orange
2 tablespoons olive oil
½ tablespoon vinegar
1 tablespoon Worcestershire sauce
1 tablespoon Tabasco

salt
abundant freshly ground pepper
2 tablespoons mixed rosemary,
    oregano, thyme

Marinate ½ to 1 hour.

Maionese
MAYONNAISE

The Italian mayonnaise is the reduction to basics of all the mayonnaises in the world. It contains no spices, just a pinch of finely ground white pepper. The only variation allowed is the substitution of first-quality white wine vinegar for the lemon juice. By law it should be made by hand: the color and texture are incomparable. Lawbreakers may use a blender or a food processor at the expense (minimal) of color and texture, and an egg white, countered by the saving of time and nervous energy.

1 egg (room temperature)
¼ teaspoon salt
¾ cup olive oil

juice of ½ lemon
finely ground white pepper

The lawful way to make mayonnaise (by hand): put the egg yolk and the salt in a bowl. Stir well with a wooden spoon. Add a few drops of oil and stir constantly. As the oil is amalgamated, add a few more drops. This should be done without missing a beat, otherwise the mayonnaise *impazzisce*, literally goes crazy: it curdles. Keep stirring and adding oil by drops until half of the oil has been used. By now the mixture has the look and feel of mayonnaise, but it isn't. Add a few drops of lemon juice and keep stirring. The mixture gets thinner and lighter with the addition of lemon, so you add a few drops of oil to bring back the thickness. If the mixture hasn't gone crazy by this time, you're home safe.

If it has, you need another bowl and another egg yolk. Stir the egg yolk and add a teaspoon of the crazy mixture. Keep stirring, and when the newly created mixture is well amalgamated, add a bit more of the crazy mixture, and so on until you have a sane mixture.

Keep stirring and watch your pace until all the oil and lemon are gone. Add a pinch of white pep-

2 eggs
½ teaspoon salt

per (don't add black if you have no white), stir well, and you have *maionese*, unforgettable on any poached fish (except for cod) or in *insalata russa*.

The unlawful way to make mayonnaise (with a blender): break the whole egg into the blender. Add the juice of ½ lemon, the salt, the white pepper, and 2–3 tablespoons of the olive oil. Blend until the mixture is homogeneous and thick. Then pour the oil in a steady trickle into the vortex at the center of the blender. Stop pouring oil only, and if, a small bubble of oil forms in the center. Blend until it disappears, and then add the remaining oil in a steady trickle. Blend a moment more. The final consistency of mayonnaise should be creamy and thick, not runny. When spooned, it should not peak but should slowly search out its own level of rest.

This recipe makes about 1 cup of mayonnaise, enough for 4 *maionese* lovers or 6 discreet admirers, and it doubles easily for more.

There is a third way of making mayonnaise, also unlawful for the purists, and that is with a food processor, using the steel blade:

½ teaspoon pepper, preferably white

¼ teaspoon mustard, or to taste
2 cups olive oil

¼ cup lemon juice

Put the eggs, salt, pepper, and mustard in the food processor bowl and process for at least 1 minute. Add ½ cup of the oil and process until the mixture starts to thicken. Slowly begin to add the remaining oil, processing all the time, and continue to process until the mixture has thickened. Slowly add the lemon juice, processing as you add.

If the mayonnaise is too thick, add more lemon juice, and if it is too thin, add more oil. Consistency may vary according to the temperature of the eggs and the brand of oil. You may change the thickness, of course, to fit the use you wish to make of the mayonnaise. By and large, many people like thin mayonnaise for poached fish and thicker mayonnaise for composed salads. Makes 3 cups approximately. If keeping in the refrigerator for a few hours or a day, place plastic wrap right down on the surface to prevent a "skin" from forming.

Salsa di Noci per Pesce
WALNUT SAUCE FOR FISH

This was developed for our restaurant, and we found the use of an aluminum "sizzle pan" (available at cookware stores) quite beneficial to a fish fillet. A "sizzle pan" holds the fish and sauce and butter together nicely, and, well seasoned, never sticks.

3 cloves garlic, minced
4 egg yolks
1¾ cups olive oil
¼ cup dry white wine

2 tablespoons lemon juice
1 cup chopped walnuts
¼ cup chopped Italian parsley

Put the garlic in the work bowl of the food processor with the steel blade. Add the egg yolks and process on/off until fully mixed. With the motor running, slowly pour the olive oil into the egg mixture. Keep the motor on and add the white wine and lemon juice. Stop the motor and stir in the walnuts and the parsley.

When it is time to broil the fish, brush the broiler "sizzle pan" with butter. Broil both sides a total of 2 minutes. When cooked, remove the "sizzle pan" from the broiler, spoon each fish fillet with about 2 tablespoons of sauce, and put the pan back for 30 seconds. Serve at once.

This recipe makes about 2 cups of sauce, and it is delicious on most broiled fish.

217

Salsa di Pomodoro e Cipolla
TOMATO AND ONION SAUCE

This sauce is used with *Polpette*, boiled beef, and with fish fillets.

*3 medium cooking onions (or 1 huge
    Bermuda)*
3 tablespoons olive oil
*3 cups whole plum tomatoes, peeled
    (fresh or canned)*

2 teaspoons salt, or to taste
freshly ground pepper

Cut the onion(s) in half, scoop out the little center core, and slice the halves in the thinnest possible slivers. If using regular all-purpose kitchen onions, you may want to soak them 5 or 10 minutes in cold water to make them milder tasting. Drain well on paper towels.

Put the olive oil in a large frying pan over medium heat. Add the onions and cook them until they are limp and transparent. Turn off the heat for a few minutes to allow the oil to cool, then add the tomatoes. If using fresh tomatoes, cut them in bite-size chunks before you add them. If using canned plum tomatoes, mash them a bit as they go in. Add the salt and a few grinds of the pepper mill to the sauce, and turn up the heat until the whole pan boils. Then lower the heat and simmer, stirring occasionally, for 20–25 minutes, or until the tomatoes have practically disintegrated and the liquids have reduced almost by half and the color has darkened. For 6.

Salsa Verde
GREEN SAUCE

This sauce of parsley, garlic, and capers, held together with oil and vinegar, is a must for *bollito misto.* When made with lemon, it fancies up any fish in the market. It shouldn't be made in a blender, however, because that homogenizes it and spoils the texture.

2 cups parsley leaves
2 tablespoons capers
1 clove garlic
½ cup olive oil

½ cup wine vinegar (or the juice of
1½ lemons)
salt (or 2 chopped anchovy fillets)

Chop the parsley, capers, and garlic into fine bits. If using the anchovies instead of salt, add them to the pile and mince everything some more. Put it all in a mortar and grind to a paste. Add the olive oil, 1 tablespoon at a time, and keep on grinding until a very thick sauce consistency is reached. Then add the vinegar (or lemon, as the case may be) a little at a time in order to dilute the sauce until it is really spoonable. Taste for salt on a bit of bread and adjust the seasonings if necessary.

This sauce can be made ahead of time and keeps well in the refrigerator with an extra drop or two of olive oil on top. It must, however, be brought to room temperature and stirred vigorously before serving. For 6.

Pastella per Friggere I
BATTER FOR FRYING I

Here is the basic batter used to fry vegetables like zucchini, artichokes, broccoli, and zucchini flowers, or apples, brains, shrimp, and squid. It's light, tasty, and crisp. This makes enough to fry zucchini for 6 people, for example.

2 eggs
1½ tablespoon olive oil
⅔ cup warm water

½ teaspoon salt
¾ cup flour

Break the eggs into a bowl; add the oil, water, and salt. Beat until nicely mixed and homogeneous. Slowly sprinkle in flour, beating constantly, until the mixture has the consistency of a good pancake batter. Let it sit for a couple of hours before using.

When you use this batter to coat cut-up vegetables or anything else, drop in only a few pieces at a time, turn them slowly with a fork to coat all sides, and then take them out and immediately put them into hot frying oil.

Pastella (con Lievito) II
BATTER (WITH YEAST) II

This even lighter, crisper batter is traditionally used to fry cod, but it is also delicious with vegetables.

1 square fresh yeast (or 1 packet dry)
1 1/4 cups warm water

1/2 teaspoon salt
1 1/2 cups flour

Dissolve the yeast in the warm water, breaking it up a bit with a spoon and stirring to make sure it all melts. Add the salt and slowly sprinkle in the flour, beating with a whisk or a fork until all the flour is absorbed and the batter is smooth. Let rise in a warm place for at least 1 hour, or until it has doubled in bulk and become light and full of bubbles. Stir and use immediately.

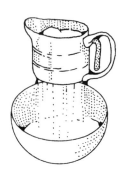

IV

CONTORNI
VEGETABLES AND SALADS

Contorni are not just side dishes in the American sense. They are an integral part of second courses, sometimes even bearing the brunt of the course. They are the vegetables and salads whose choice, until recently, depended entirely on the season.

Where garden produce is concerned, the pride and joy of most Italian cooks are the *primizie,* the first of the crop. They are smaller and, because they come from local truck gardens, they are the freshest. Even when crops have traveled a long way to the market, Italians still have a predilection for the smaller vegetables. It's a matter of taste.

Examples of the-smaller-the-better philosophy are the 4-inch zucchini, the 6-inch eggplant, tiny peas, and green beans about the size of matchsticks. All of these make exquisite eating. The search for such produce is rewarding and brings to shopping a sort of breathless quality. We hope you'll find yourself exclaiming over new greens at the vegetable stand as we always do.

Our recipes stick with the vegetables usually found in the average American market or those that might show up in the home garden, hence the inclusion of stuffed zucchini flowers. When we recommend fresh plum tomatoes for a sauce, or fresh beans for a salad, we do so because the flavor is not only better but in some cases so different from the canned variety that only if fresh is used will the results be satisfactory. We have found fresh plum tomatoes at harvest time in Italian markets, while shell beans have shown up in the supermarket. For the really devoted cook-gardener, homegrown plum tomatoes aren't any more difficult to raise than salad tomatoes.

When we recommend frozen vegetables we are simply recognizing the advantages of their enormous convenience: they're clean, cook rapidly, and, if watched and timed properly, are almost as satisfactory in taste and texture in certain dishes as the fresh. They are certainly better than nothing at all out of season.

When it comes to cooking vegetables, the same rigid rule applies as for pasta: they are cooked to the *al dente* stage. Like pasta, many are served with a sauce. The same vegetables also appear dressed with olive oil or deep-fried in basic batter. Some are stuffed, but for those vegetable dishes that have a meat filling, you must turn back to Part III.

Asparagi all'Agro
ASPARAGUS WITH OIL AND LEMON

The quickest and simplest of dressings for nearly all the green vegetables is olive oil and the juice of a lemon or good wine vinegar.

The same treatment works well with broccoli, cauliflower, spinach, zucchini, green beans, and fresh or canned shell (cranberry) beans. Choose either fresh lemon juice or the best of red wine vinegar. We like to toss the vegetable in oil first and well and then add the juice or vinegar. Salt and pepper to your taste.

3 pounds asparagus
2 teaspoons salt (for the water)

3 tablespoons olive oil
juice of 1 lemon

Break off the root end of the asparagus stalk by stalk. It breaks exactly where the edible part begins, and cutting it arbitrarily either leaves a bit of root on or robs you of a bit of tender stalk. Wash carefully and put in boiling salted water just to cover. (A big frying pan is ideal for this.) Bring the water back to a boil, cover, and reduce the heat a bit. Boil slowly about 5 minutes, or until a fork can easily pierce the broken end of the stalk. Lift the asparagus out with tongs, draining off as much water as possible.

After you've settled them on a serving platter, drain them once more by tilting the platter and spooning out the last of the water. Pour the olive oil over the asparagus and baste 2 or 3 times. Add the lemon juice and baste again, scooping up the dressing with a big spoon until all the stalks are dressed. (If you haven't a lemon on hand, use ½ tablespoon of wine vinegar.) Serve warm or cold, as you wish. For 6.

Asparagi al Prosciutto
ASPARAGUS WITH *PROSCIUTTO*

Here is asparagus in one of its most elegant guises: fresh stalks are cooked *al dente,* wrapped in thin slices of *prosciutto,* and sprinkled with Parmesan cheese.

2½ pounds asparagus
1½ teaspoons salt (for the water)
¼ pound prosciutto

¼ pound butter
4 tablespoons grated Parmesan cheese

Preheat the oven to 400°.

Break off the root ends of asparagus stalk by stalk and discard them. Wash thoroughly and put in boiling salted water to cover. Bring to a boil, cover, and cook about 5 minutes, or until a fork goes through the base of the stalk easily. Lift out with tongs and drain on paper towels.

When they are cool enough to handle, divide the stalks into 6 even bundles. Wrap each bundle in a couple of very, very thin slices of *prosciutto,* securing them with a wooden pick. Butter a cookie sheet and line the bundles up on it, sprinkle with the Parmesan cheese, and put in a hot oven (400°) for about 3 minutes, or until the cheese has melted. Melt the butter in a saucepan, and when the bundles come out of the oven, put them on a platter, pour the melted butter over them, and serve. For 6.

Carciofi Fritti Dorati
GOLDEN-FRIED ARTICHOKES

Thin slices of artichokes, dipped in flour, then in beaten egg, and deep-fried to a golden crispness: these can be served alone as a *contorno,* or can be part of a *fritto misto* (pages 204–205). This definitely is one of the dishes that really merits two cooks: one to dip and one to fry.

6 medium artichokes
2 lemons
1 cup flour

4 medium eggs
1 teaspoon salt
vegetable oil for frying

Prepare the artichokes as on pages 226–27. Then slice the quarters so that the base of each piece is no thicker than ¼ inch.

As one by one the artichokes are cut and de-choked, put them in water with the juice of 1 lemon (to keep them from discoloring). When all are prepared, drain them and pat dry with paper towels. Put the flour in one bowl. Beat the eggs in another and add ½ teaspoon of the salt.

Pour frying oil into a big pan to a depth of at

least 2 inches and heat to 375° (or to the point where a drop of beaten egg sizzles and fries instantly). Dredge a few wedges of artichoke at a time in the flour, dip them into the beaten eggs, and fry. Don't overcrowd the pan. As the artichokes turn golden, turn them to crisp the other side. Take them out when they're a nice toasty color, using a slotted spoon to let as much oil as possible drip back into the pan. Place them on paper towels on a hot platter. Keep on flouring, battering, and frying until all are done. Sprinkle with the remaining ½ teaspoon salt. Serve hot with 1 lemon cut into wedges.

In doing a batch this large, you may find the best way to serve everything hot and crisp is to return the fried artichokes to the hot oil for a moment, once they've all been fried. Drain again on paper towels and serve immediately. For 6.

Carciofi alla Parmigiana
ARTICHOKES PARMIGIANA

This rich casserole of golden-fried artichokes is layered with tomato sauce and *mozzarella* and topped with Parmesan cheese, and is another really luxurious dish that is easily put together by two cooks in unison.

FOR THE SAUCE:
1 big Bermuda onion
4 tablespoons olive oil
6 cup plum tomatoes
1½ teaspoons salt, or to taste

FOR THE ARTICHOKES:
6 medium artichokes

1 lemon
1 cup flour
4 eggs
vegetable oil for frying
1 pound mozzarella
½ cup grated Parmesan cheese
½ cup unseasoned bread crumbs

To prepare the sauce: slice the onion into the thinnest possible slivers. Put the olive oil in a big skillet, add the onions, and cook over medium heat until they are limp and translucent. Add the plum tomatoes, mashing them as they go in. Add the salt and simmer 20 minutes, or until the sauce is somewhat condensed, is darker in color, and of sauce consistency.

Prepare and fry the artichokes as in the preceding recipe. When they are drained, they're ready to layer in the casserole.

Slice the *mozzarella* as thin as possible, or grate it as coarsely as you can.

Preheat the oven to 375°.

Put a thin layer of sauce in the bottom of an ovenproof casserole, then a layer of fried artichokes, and add another layer of sauce, and finally a layer of *mozzarella*. Repeat the layering sequence until all the ingredients have been used. Cover with a generous sprinkling of Parmesan cheese mixed with bread crumbs. Bake (at 375°) for 20 minutes, or until the cheese has melted and the crumbs have turned a toasty brown.

If you want to make this dish ahead of time, fry the artichokes, let them cool on paper towels, and make the sauce, but don't assemble the casserole until it is time to bake. For 6.

225

How to Prepare Artichokes

1. A good fresh artichoke should be tightly closed and firm. The "chokes" are visible in the center of the split artichoke.

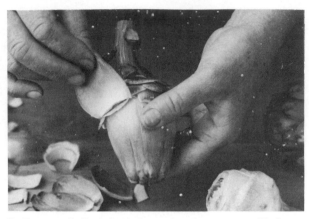

2. Tear off the tough outer leaves until they break away.

3. Peel back with a paring knife over the point where the leaves were broken off to get to the outside of the heart of the artichoke.

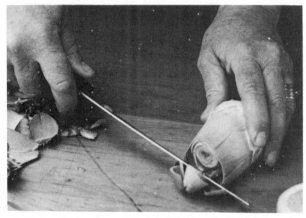

4. Cut off about a third of the top of the remaining leaves.

5. Pare all the way around the top to cut off any remaining fibrous parts.

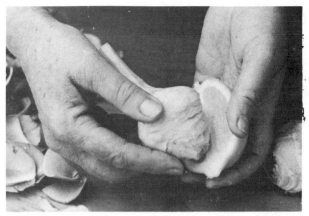

6. Rub the peeled artichoke with a lemon to prevent blackening.

7. Cut the artichoke in half, then into quarters, exposing the choke.

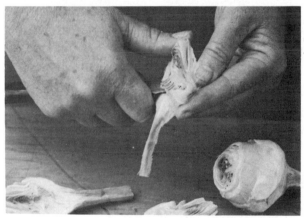

8. Scoop out the choke with a paring knife.

9. As the artichokes are cut and de-choked, put them in cold water with the juice of a lemon. Dry well and pat dry before using.

Carciofi alla Romana
ARTICHOKES, ROMAN STYLE

Roman artichokes have no choke at all, so it's easy to make a *battuto* of herbs and poke a bit of it in between the leaves before cooking the artichokes gently in olive oil and water. With patience, however, you can dechoke the available kind of these exquisite vegetables.

FOR THE BATTUTO:
6 sprigs fresh mint
1/2 clove garlic
6 sprigs parsley
1 teaspoon salt

freshly ground pepper

6 large artichokes
juice of 1 lemon
1/2 cup olive oil

Prepare the artichokes in the usual fashion (pages 226–27), but do not slice them. With your fingers, pry open the cleaned artichoke. Using the sharp point of a paring knife, cut down inside and around the thin center leaves. Then slant the knife to sever the round just cut. Scoop out the center. Next hold the artichoke under running water, and pull out any remaining bits of choke with your fingers. As the artichokes are cleaned, drop them in a bowl of water to which the lemon juice has been added.

Make a *battuto* of the mint, garlic, parsley, salt, and pepper (3–4 twists of the mill). Drain the artichokes and put a pinch or two of the *battuto* inside each one.

If you're lucky enough to find fresh baby artichokes that haven't formed a choke yet, get a dozen of them, clean them, just open a few of the leaves at random, and stuff some of the *battuto* inside.

Put 1 cup of water and the olive oil in a pot (ideally, top-of-the-stove earthenware from Italy) that has a good cover and is just large enough to accommodate the artichokes standing on their heads, stems in the air. Put in the artichokes, cover, bring to a good boil, and then reduce to medium heat.

Cook for about 20 minutes well covered, then uncover, sprinkle with a little salt, and finish cooking, reducing the liquids to practically nothing. (Pierce the heart of the artichoke with a fork or a cake tester, and when it enters easily, the cooking is over.)

Remove the artichokes and place them on a platter, still head side down. Pour over them any remaining liquid. Serve hot or tepid. For 6.

Carote e Funghi
CARROTS AND MUSHROOMS

1 pound carrots, peeled
12 ounces mushrooms, cleaned
4 tablespoons unsalted butter
½ teaspoon salt

4 tablespoons Italian parsley,
    chopped
juice of 1 lemon
white pepper to taste

Cut the carrots into julienne strips.

Bring abundant salted water to a boil, add the carrots, and when the water comes back to a boil, cook 2 minutes. Drain immediately.

Slice the mushrooms and cook 2 minutes in the butter. Add the salt. Add the cooked carrots, parsley, lemon juice, and pepper. Stir and cook 1 minute. Toss well and serve. For 4–6.

Cianfotta
VEGETABLE STEW, SOUTHERN STYLE

"Stew" is only barely acceptable as a translation of cianfotta. Assorted vegetables congregate together and bask in each other's glory when cooked this way. Almost every Mediterranean country has its own variation, and the following is native to southern Italy.

2 medium eggplants
2 or 3 potatoes (1 pound)
2 medium zucchini (¾ pound)
2 sweet peppers (yellow, red, or
    green)
2 cups fresh peeled plum tomatoes

3 onions
1 celery stalk
¼ cup olive oil
3 or 4 fresh basil leaves
1 teaspoon salt
freshly ground pepper to taste

Wash and prepare the vegetables. First halve and prepare the eggplants (page 234), and when they have been desalted, cut them into cubes; peel the potatoes, cut them into small pieces, and soak in water; cut the zucchini into rounds; core the peppers and cut them into strips; cut the tomatoes into small chunks or pass them through a food mill; cut the onions into thin slivers; slice the celery into thin slices.

Sauté the onions and celery in the olive oil in a sizeable pot or Dutch oven. When the onions are wilted, add the tomatoes, basil leaves, salt, and pepper.

As soon as the tomatoes start to bubble, add the potatoes and peppers. As soon as the peppers start to wilt, add the eggplants. Cook for 5 minutes and add the zucchini. Cover the pot and boil gently, stirring occasionally, for 15–20 minutes, or until all the vegetables are cooked but not turned to a mush. Serve hot or tepid. For 6–8.

Cipolline Agrodolce
SWEET-AND-SOUR PEARL ONIONS

Small white onions can be cooked in a pungent sauce made with brown sugar and vinegar. With their sweet-and-sour flavor, they are a favorite *contorno* with boiled beef or any of the blander meat dishes.

1 ½ pounds small pearl onions (or 24-ounce frozen package)
¼ pound unsalted butter

1 teaspoon salt
3 heaping tablespoons brown sugar
3 tablespoons wine vinegar

If using frozen pearl onions: defrost at room temperature and spread them out on paper towels to drain off as much water as possible. If using fresh onions: boil them first in salted water for 5 minutes and drain thoroughly.

Melt the butter over medium heat and add the drained onions. Cook, stirring from time to time, for about 10 minutes, or until tender. Salt and add the brown sugar, mashing it into the bubbling butter and spreading it evenly around the pan. Cook until the sugar has melted and started to glaze the onions. Add the wine vinegar, bring back to a boil, stir, and cook another 4 or 5 minutes, or until the thickened sauce clings to the onions and they are cooked through. For 6.

Fagioli Freschi al Pomodoro
FRESH SHELL BEANS IN TOMATO SAUCE

Those lucky enough to have fresh shell beans and ripe plum tomatoes owe it to themselves to make this superlative summer dish. While the beans boil, the sauce simmers, and the two finally meet and complete their cooking together.

2 pounds fresh shell beans

FOR THE SAUCE:
1 slice lean salt pork
1 onion
1 stalk celery

2 tablespoons parsley
2 tablespoons olive oil
2 pounds fresh plum tomatoes (or 4 cups canned)
2 teaspoons salt

Shell the beans and put them on to boil in about 3 quarts of water and 3 teaspoons salt.

Chop the salt pork, onion, celery, and parsley into a *battuto* and sauté it until golden in the olive

230

oil in a pan big enough to hold the tomatoes and eventually the beans.

If using fresh tomatoes: drop them in boiling water for a couple of minutes to loosen their skins, drain them, peel them, and chop them in chunks. If using canned plum tomatoes: cut them into chunks.

When the *battuto* is golden, add the chopped tomatoes and simmer for about 15 minutes, adding salt and pepper to taste. When the tomato sauce has thickened, drain the beans and add them to the simmering sauce to finish cooking. Serve hot when the beans are tender to the fork but not so soft they have started to disintegrate. For 6.

Fagiolini alla Panna
GREEN BEANS IN LEMON CREAM SAUCE

*1 ½ pounds fresh small green beans,
    or 2 10-ounce packages frozen
    French-cut beans*
4 tablespoons unsalted butter
¾ cup heavy cream
1 egg

salt
freshly ground pepper
*2 tablespoons Parmesan cheese,
    freshly grated*
¼ teaspoon freshly grated nutmeg
juice of 1 lemon

If using small fresh beans, cut the stems and tips off and wash the beans carefully. Cook uncovered in abundant salted water until they no longer taste raw but are still bright green and slightly crisp to bite. If using frozen beans, you can put them into abundant salted water without thawing and cook them as you would fresh beans. But remember that the frozen ones cook much more quickly. Drain the beans thoroughly and put them into a warm ovenproof casserole.

Add the butter and stir in all but 2 tablespoons of the cream. Cook over medium heat for a moment.

Break the egg into a small bowl. Add salt and pepper to taste, the remaining 2 tablespoons of cream, the Parmesan cheese, the nutmeg, and the lemon juice. Beat well with a fork until all the ingredients are blended and pour over the green beans. Continue cooking for 2 or 3 minutes, stirring with a wooden spoon until the cream sauce has thickened and coated all the beans. Serve hot from the casserole. For 6.

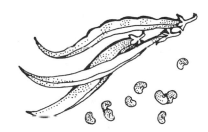

Fior di Zucchine Fritti
DEEP-FRIED ZUCCHINI FLOWERS

The delicate lilylike flowers of the zucchini are stuffed with *mozzarella* and anchovies, and then are dipped in batter and fried golden crisp: an unbelievable experience in eating, as well as practical to use what may have seemed only a decorative element in your vegetable garden. The flowers themselves are seldom seen in the market, as they're too fragile for packaging and shipping, but for those with a garden, a serving of *fior di zucchine* makes up for all the season's weeding.

18 zucchini flowers
1 pound whole-milk mozzarella
18 anchovy fillets

1 batch Pastella I *(page 219)*
vegetable oil for frying

Remove the pistils inside the flowers and cut off any discolored or wilted part of the petals. Wash carefully in very cold water and set out to dry on paper towels. Dice the *mozzarella,* and cut the anchovies into 3 or 4 pieces each. Open the petals of the flowers, put in 3 or 4 cubes of cheese, 3 or 4 bits of anchovy, or just enough barely to fill but not to overstuff.

Make a batch of *Pastella I* and gently dip the flowers in it, one by one, coating them well with the batter. Heat the frying oil to 375° (or hot enough so that a drop of batter frizzles on contact), and fry the flowers a few at a time to a golden brown. Drain on paper towels and serve hot. For 6.

Lenticchie
LENTILS

Lentils, cooked with the usual seasoning vegetables, are frequently served with sausage, but they make a good *contorno* for lots of other meats as well. Legend has it, however, that if you eat lentils on New Year's Day, you'll be rich all year long. We always serve them with a *cotechino* purchased at an Italian specialty store, just in case the children come.

Last New Year's, no one was scheduled to come for dinner but we put on a pound of lentils anyway. And then, one by one, two's and three's, the entire bunch, the children and the grandchild, and friends arrived. On went one more pound of lentils, one more *cotechino* (bought for such a grand emergency), the salad was doubled, extra leaves put in the table, more bread in the oven, and a quick trip was made down cellar for more nice bottles of Barolo. Riches indeed! MR

1-pound bag dried lentils
1 clove garlic
1 big carrot
4 plum tomatoes

1 onion
1 stalk celery, with leaves
3–4 teaspoons salt, or to taste
freshly ground pepper

Examine the lentils a handful or so at a time in order to sort out and discard any bits of chaff or stone. Wash them quickly by putting them in a sieve or colander under cold water.

Peel the garlic and the carrot, peel the onion and cut it in half, wash the celery stalk, and put everything in a big pot with the lentils and 9 cups of cold water. Add 3–4 twists of the pepper mill. Bring the pot to a boil, skim off any froth that may have formed, and reduce the heat to a simmer. Cook for about 45 minutes to 1 hour, or until the lentils are well cooked and the liquids have reduced to practically nothing. Check the liquid level toward the end of the cooking time, because a heat that's too high can reduce the liquid before the lentils are tender, in which case a bit of water must be added. For 6.

Funghi Trifolati
MUSHROOMS, "TRUFFLE STYLE"

The adjective *trifolati* in this case has been warped with age. Literally, the mushrooms should be sliced like truffles, paper-thin, but the Tuscans have changed all that by slicing them just reasonably thin, so the texture holds up under cooking. The dish is a delicate blend of mushrooms, lemon, and parsley, with salt from the anchovies binding all the flavors together.

1 pound mushrooms
½ cup olive oil
1 medium clove garlic
2–4 anchovy fillets

3 tablespoons unsalted butter
½ lemon
2 tablespoons chopped parsley

Slice the mushrooms vertically stem to top, first in half, then in quarters and so on until you have reasonably thin wedges. Put the oil in a medium-size frying pan, add the garlic, sauté it until golden (not fried), and discard it. Add the mushrooms, raise the heat, and cook quickly while stirring them. Mash the anchovies (the number depends on how salty they are), and add them to the mushrooms. Then put in the butter. When the mushrooms are tender but still firm, squirt them with the juice of ½ lemon, stir, and remove from the heat. Add the parsley, stir again, taste for salt. The anchovies should have provided enough salt, but if not add more salt. May be served immediately, or cold as an *antipasto*. For 6.

233

Melanzane a Funghetto
EGGPLANT, "MUSHROOM STYLE"

This is the best possible introduction to eggplant. Use it at its smallest size: no more than 5 inches in length, 2½ inches in diameter. This size has a tender skin, fewer seeds, less bitterness.

6 small eggplants
5 tablespoons olive oil
2 garlic cloves
1 tablespoon minced parsley

2–3 plum tomatoes, coarsely chopped
1 teaspoon salt

Most small eggplants aren't bitter as are the big ones, but just to be on the safe side, cut them in half lengthwise, salt them liberally, and let stand for 15 minutes. Then scrape away the moist salt, cut again lengthwise into 3 spears and then into 1-inch wedges.

Heat the olive oil in a large frying pan, add the garlic, and sauté over medium heat until golden. Discard the garlic, add the eggplant, and stir as they cook for a few minutes. When the eggplants have absorbed the oil, salt them and they'll release their own juices. Add the minced parsley, cook and stir for a moment, then add the coarsely chopped tomatoes. They'll add not only a bit of color but also some moisture to the sauce. Stir gently, lower the heat, and simmer for about 10 minutes, or until the eggplant can be easily pierced with a fork. (The length of time depends on the actual size and age of the eggplant.) The pulp of the eggplant should be tender but firm, the color and consistency about like a properly cooked mushroom. For 6.

Melanzane alla Parmigiana
EGGPLANT PARMIGIANA

FOR THE FRIED EGGPLANT:
4 small or 2 medium eggplants
salt
4 tablespoons flour
vegetable oil for frying

FOR THE SAUCE:
1 clove garlic
1 small onion

⅓ cup olive oil
3 cups plum tomatoes
3–4 fresh basil leaves
pinch of salt
pepper
1 cup grated Parmesan cheese
½ cup grated whole-milk mozzarella
½ cup unseasoned bread crumbs

Slice the eggplants in half, salt liberally, and let stand about 20 minutes to get the bitterness out of them.

While the salted eggplant is waiting, prepare the sauce. Slice the garlic in half and mince the onion, and sauté both until golden in the olive oil in a medium-size frying pan over medium heat. When the onion is transparent and the garlic golden, discard the garlic and add the tomatoes, basil, salt, and a few grinds of pepper. Let simmer about 15 minutes.

Scrape the now moistened salt off the eggplant and cut the halves into lengthwise slices no thicker than ½ inch. Dredge the slices in flour, coating them well, and fry in hot oil until golden brown on both sides. Drain on paper towels.

Preheat the oven to 350°.

In an ovenproof baking dish or shallow casserole, spread a layer of tomato sauce, then a layer of fried eggplant, sprinkle with some of the grated *mozzarella* and some of the Parmesan cheese. Repeat until everything is used up, finishing with tomato sauce. Sprinkle with bread crumbs and bake (at 350°) for about 15 minutes, or until the bread crumbs are toasted, the *mozzarella* melted. For 6.

Peperonata
PEPPERS WITH ONIONS AND TOMATOES

Traditionally this dish was prepared ahead of time and served cold as an accompaniment to any meat. The peppers and tomatoes had to be in season, which limited serving it to summertime. Now, however, sweet peppers are available almost year-round, so the dish can be served hot in midwinter, when it is just as appetizing. Romans, blessed with the light, dry *castelli* wines, have always made *peperonata* with wine. Southerners substitute water and wine vinegar, or just vinegar.

3 tablespoons olive oil
1 clove garlic
4–5 sweet peppers, red, green, and yellow
3 medium onions
2 cups plum tomatoes

1 teaspoon salt, or to taste
freshly ground pepper
⅓ cup dry white wine (or 3 tablespoons wine vinegar and 3 tablespoons water)

Put the olive oil in a good-size pot (with a cover) over medium heat. Cut the garlic in half, add it to the oil, sauté it to a golden brown, and then discard it. Cut the peppers open, discard their cores and stems, and slice them into long thin strips. Cut the onions into quarters and cut off the bit of core at the bottom of each quarter. Add the peppers and onions to the flavored olive oil and cook briskly, stirring constantly. As soon as they start to wilt, add the tomatoes, salt, and a few grinds of pepper. Stir well, and when the mixture is back to a boil, reduce the heat and cover the pot. Simmer for 15–20 minutes, stirring occasionally. Then raise the heat, add the wine (or wine vinegar and water), stir, and boil uncovered 5 minutes, or until the sauce has condensed a bit and the vegetables have cooked. Serve hot or cold. For 6.

Peperonata di Melanzane
PEPPERS, ONIONS, TOMATOES, AND EGGPLANT

There are French, Spanish, and Greek versions of this most Mediterranean dish, a bouquet of peppers, onions, and chunked eggplant cooked with plum tomatoes. The Italian difference is that the vegetables are cooked to the *al dente* stage, retaining shape and texture, yet exchanging flavor.

3 small eggplants
4 sweet peppers
3 medium onions
1 clove garlic
1 red pepper pod, seeded (or dash of Tabasco)
3 tablespoons olive oil

2 cups peeled plum tomatoes, coarsely chopped
1 teaspoon salt, or to taste
freshly ground pepper
⅓ cup dry white wine (or 3 tablespoons wine vinegar)

Half an hour before cooking time, wash the eggplant and cut in half lengthwise. Sprinkle liberally with salt and set aside. When the salt has drawn out the bitterness of the eggplant (about 20 minutes), scrape it away with the blade of a knife. Cut into quarters and then into 1-inch chunks. Cut the peppers open, remove the core and seeds, slice into ½-inch strips. Cut the onions into quarters or thick wedges.

Put the garlic, pepper pod, and oil in the bottom of a big pot over medium heat. When the garlic is golden and the pepper dark brown, discard them, raise the heat, and add the peppers and onions. Cook quickly, stirring, until they begin to wilt. Then add the eggplant and after 5 minutes add the chopped tomatoes (without their juice), the salt, and a few grinds of pepper, and stir well. Cover, lower the heat, and simmer for 15 minutes, stirring occasionally. When the vegetables are cooked—tender but still somewhat firm to the bite and yet easily pierced with a fork—raise the heat, add the wine, stir, and boil for 3 minutes to blend the flavors and wine in the sauce and to reduce slightly the quantity of the sauce itself. Serve hot or tepid. For 6.

Piselli alla Romana
PEAS, ROMAN STYLE

This is another dish claimed by the Romans, known for their proud use of *primizie,* the first tiny vegetables of the season, in this case, tiny new peas. Those lucky people with gardens can harvest their own new peas and make this recipe with them—that's real Italian cookery. If, however, you use the frozen tiny peas available at the ordinary American market and cook them with a hint of onion and *prosciutto* (or lean salt pork), you can achieve almost the same delicacy all year round.

2 *10-ounce packages frozen tiny*
   peas
4 *tablespoons unsalted butter*
1 *small onion*

4 *slices lean salt pork (or 6 medium-*
   thick slices prosciutto)
½ *cup dry white wine*
1 *tablespoon sugar*

Defrost the peas at room temperature for an hour or so before cooking.

Melt the butter in a deep, wide (11-inch) frying pan. Mince the onion, cut the salt pork into ½-inch strips, and sauté both slowly in the butter until they are translucent. Add the peas, wine, and sugar, and cook over medium heat about 5 minutes, or until the peas are tender. Check for moisture in the pan during cooking, and if the peas don't provide enough to keep things juicy, add a little warm water (almost but don't quite cover the peas). When the peas are tender but still firm, some of the liquid will have evaporated and the sauce, an integral part of this dish, will have thickened slightly.

If you wish to make this recipe fancier, substitute *prosciutto* for the lean salt pork. If you can't get tiny frozen peas, use the larger frozen ones, but watch out that they don't add too much moisture to the sauce. If they do, remove the peas to a hot serving dish when they're cooked, and reduce the sauce by cooking it over medium heat another 4–5 minutes. Pour the sauce over the peas and serve. For 6.

Zucchine al Sugo
ZUCCHINI IN TOMATO SAUCE

If two cooks are on hand, one can make a tomato sauce while the other slices up the zucchini. Then everybody tastes to make sure the zucchini aren't overcooked and the sauce is the right thickness and flavor. (If the ingredients are garden-fresh, there is the real danger the dish will never get to the table, having been eaten away at tasting time.)

2 tablespoons olive oil
1 big Bermuda onion (or 3 all-purpose onions)
3 cups peeled plum tomatoes
½ red pepper pod, seeded
1 teaspoon salt, or to taste
6 medium zucchini

Cut the onions into thin slivers and sauté them until golden in the olive oil over medium heat, stirring them to make sure they become translucent without browning. If using all-purpose onions, soak the slivers 10 minutes in cold water, drain, and pat dry before you sauté them. While the onions are cooking, add the half pepper pod to them and discard it when it turns dark brown. Cut the plum tomatoes into chunks and add them to the now translucent onions with the salt. Bring the mixture to a boil, reduce the heat, and simmer about 15 minutes (probably 20 minutes if you are using fresh, ripe plum tomatoes), or until the liquid has reduced and the sauce has thickened and darkened in color.

Clean the zucchini and slice into thin rounds. When the sauce is ready, add the zucchini and continue to simmer about 3 minutes, or until the zucchini are *al dente,* tender but not mushy. Taste for salt and correct the seasoning if necessary. Serve hot. For 6.

Insalatina da Taglio con la Rughetta
GARDEN LETTUCE WITH ARUGOLA

This salad, made with the earliest leaves of home-grown salad greens, follows the Italian tradition of using the first of the crop and all of the plant. When you thin the lettuce in your garden, don't throw away the thin leaves you've pulled up. Those little 2–3-inch-high greens of Romaine, Salad Bowl, or Bibb are at their sweetest and most tender.

Arugola (in Rome, *rughetta;* also known as roquette or rugola) is a sharp-tasting member of the mustard family whose leaves look rather like a dandelion's. When combined with young lettuce, the two greens bring out the best in each other. But arugola is very different from most herbs used in salads, so we advise you to try a little first: it has been known to divide families into camps, arugola lovers versus haters. It is found fresh in the American market, and its seeds are available, though you may have to order them from the catalogue of one of the large seed companies. Arugola is very easily grown in the home vegetable patch.

6 handfuls new salad leaves (about ½ pound)
5–10 arugola leaves
3 tablespoons olive oil

salt to taste
1½ tablespoons wine vinegar
freshly ground pepper

Wash the salad greens and arugola carefully, shake dry, tear into bite-sized pieces, and put into a salad bowl. Dress with the olive oil, toss, add the salt, toss again, and add the vinegar and pepper as for any other salad. For 6.

Insalata Belga e Radicchio
BELGIAN ENDIVE-RADICCHIO SALAD

3 heads Belgian endive
1 head radicchio
4 tablespoons olive oil

salt
freshly ground pepper
2 tablespoons red wine vinegar

Trim the endive by cutting in half lengthwise and taking out the small core at the base. Wash in cold water, drain, and spread out 5 or 6 leaves star-fashion on each of 6 plates.

Break off the outer leaves of the radicchio and discard. Wash and drain the rest. Place medium-size leaves at the center of the endive "star," like the inner petals of a flower. Cut leftover endive leaves into ½-inch slices and place inside the radicchio petals.

Put the olive oil in the bowl and toss with salt, pepper, and vinegar. Pour a bit of dressing on each salad. Serve immediately. For 6.

Ceci e Tonno
CHICK-PEA AND TUNA SALAD

1 7-ounce can Italian tuna fish
2 1-pound cans chick-peas
1 Bermuda onion
2–3 celery stalks

4 tablespoons olive oil
salt to taste
freshly ground pepper
2 tablespoons wine vinegar

Drain the tuna, put it in a salad bowl, and break it up with a fork. Drain and rinse the chick-peas and add to the tuna.

Slice the onion into slivers and the celery into very thin slices, discarding the leaves, and add to the salad bowl. Add the olive oil, toss well, add salt, pepper (5 or 6 twists of the mill), and vinegar. Toss again and serve with hot Italian bread. For 6.

Fagioli e Tonno
BEAN AND TUNA SALAD

A traditional summer meal that makes grand eating all year round, this salad has a host of variations, depending on how many garden-fresh vegetables are added. If made with fresh beans it has an even better flavor, but takes a bit more time.

FOR THE BASIC SALAD:
1 7-ounce can Italian tuna fish
2 1-pound cans kidney or shell beans
   (or 3 pounds fresh)
4 tablespoons olive oil
salt and pepper to taste
2 tablespoons wine vinegar

POSSIBLE ADDITIONS:
1 firm (barely ripe) tomato
1 medium Spanish onion
2 stalks celery
1 small cucumber
½ green or red sweet pepper
more olive oil, to taste

If using canned kidney or shell beans: drain them and rinse. If using fresh beans: shell and cook them in abundant salted boiling water until just tender. Do not overcook. Drain thoroughly.

Drain the tuna and put both beans and tuna in a salad bowl. Add the olive oil, salt and pepper, and toss gently. Add the vinegar and toss again. Serve with hot Italian bread.

If adding the summer vegetables, cut the tomato into quarters, sliver the onion, slice the celery and cucumber into very thin slices, and core the pepper and cut into long thin strips. Add the beans and tuna with 1 or 2 more tablespoons of olive oil, a dash more salt, and 2 or 3 more twists of the pepper mill. For 6.

Insalata Russa in Galantina
RUSSIAN SALAD IN ASPIC

Chilled summer vegetables, seasoned with tart mayonnaise, glazed with gelatin, and decorated with slices of hardboiled eggs and pickles: this salad comes in two versions, one for *festa* and one for everyday. It uses either fresh or frozen vegetables, the cook's choice and the season of the year dictating which. Since this is a case of the more the merrier as far as vegetables are concerned, we have included corn, which is not in common use in Italy.

2 hardboiled eggs
2 medium all-purpose potatoes
1 cup corn kernels (or ½ 10-ounce package frozen)
2 cups peas (or 10-ounce package frozen)
2 cups cubed carrots

2 cups French-cut green beans (10-ounce package frozen)
2 cups mayonnaise (pages 216–17)
1 tablespoon lemon juice (if using commercial mayonnaise)
1½ envelopes unflavored gelatin
2 cups beef (or chicken) stock

Scrub well the all-purpose potatoes (not the baking kind). Then cook them, whole and unpeeled, in boiling salted water until just tender to fork. Drain, cool thoroughly, peel, and cut into tiny cubes.

Bring a big pot of salted water (1 teaspoon to the quart) to a boil and put in the corn. When it comes back to a boil, add the peas and carrots. When the pot boils again, put in the green beans and cook the whole thing until the beans are just tender but still crisp and colorful (about 5 minutes). Drain everything in a colander and let it cool and dry.

Prepare 2 cups of mayonnaise. (If you use commercial mayonnaise, add the lemon juice and stir well.)

Put ½ an envelope of unflavored gelatin into 4 tablespoons of cold water in a small saucepan. Stir and then put over low heat, stirring carefully until the gelatin crystals have melted. Cool and stir into the mayonnaise.

Make the aspic with 1 envelope of gelatin dissolved in 2 cups cold beef or chicken stock and heat

as above. The stock can be made with 2 bouillon cubes and water, if you don't have the real thing. Cool by placing the pan over a big bowl full of ice cubes, so that you can watch its developing thickness and use it at the right moment.

Mix all the vegetables with the mayonnaise. Chill a big serving bowl or good-size mold.

When the aspic has cooled to the point at which it is almost syrupy and thick, pour some in the bottom of the chilled mold and swirl it around to coat the bottom and sides. Put the lined mold in the refrigerator a moment or two to set it. Slice the eggs into thin slices and arrange them decoratively on the aspic. Pour in more thickened aspic, then half the vegetables. Pour some aspic around the edge of the bowl, filling any cracks. Add the rest of the vegetables and finish with any aspic that may be left. Cover and chill in the refrigerator for at least 2 hours.

When it's time to serve, dip the bowl or mold into warm water for a few seconds, cover with a big plate, and turn it over. The *insalata russa* now rests in all its chilled glory on a serving plate.

That's the *festa* way of making Russian salad. If you want to put it together with less ado about something, you can eliminate the aspic. Mix all the vegetables and the thickened mayonnaise. Shape it on a serving platter and decorate with hardboiled eggs and Italian pickles. Chill, covered with plastic wrap, for 2 hours. For 6.

Pomodori con Basilico
TOMATO SALAD WITH BASIL

A salad of almost ripe, thinly sliced tomatoes, coarsely chopped fresh basil, olive oil and vinegar: it's simple if you have the proper elements. The final flavor depends on having fresh basil and summer tomatoes, just picked and not quite fully ripened. They must be still slightly green, only pale pink on the bottom, firm to touch, but red on the inside. Tomato fragrance and flavor are at their height at this stage, which explains why a lot of us grow tomatoes, now that we're so far from the Italian markets where they arrive on the very day they're picked.

It is frequently served with a piece of fresh Italian bread so you can get up all the juices at the end.

6 medium-size, underripe tomatoes
4–5 fresh basil leaves
2 tablespoons olive oil

1 tablespoon wine vinegar
salt to taste
freshly ground pepper

Cut the tomatoes in half, then quarters and eighths and so on, until you end up with ¼-inch wedges. Spread them out on a deep platter or wide shallow bowl. Break the basil leaves into bits and sprinkle them over the tomatoes. Sprinkle with salt and 2–3 grinds of the pepper mill, and add the oil and vine-gar. To avoid turning the tomatoes over, tilt the dish up on one side, and with a big spoon scoop up the dressing and baste the tomatoes over and over to get the essence of basil thoroughly mixed with the oil, vinegar, and tomato juices. Let stand about 15 minutes before serving. For 6.

243

Insalata di Riso
RICE SALAD

Turin's gift of a summer salad is made with rice, tuna fish, eggs, capers, and olives, all tossed with olive oil and abundant lemon juice. Also included are the Italian pickled vegetables (carrots, cauliflower, cucumbers, and others) that are frequently found in the United States labeled "Giardiniera"—they are sour rather than sweet. Traditionally, seasonal fresh vegetables are used as well, but American frozen mixed vegetables are the perfect substitute, adding the proper color and texture as well as flavor. This recipe serves 6–8 generously.

2 cups long-grain rice
2 hardboiled eggs
2 anchovy fillets
½ cup black and green olives
1 cup Italian pickled vegetables, optional
2 tablespoons capers
½ green sweet pepper

½ red sweet pepper
10-ounce package frozen mixed vegetables (2 cups)
7-ounce can Italian tuna fish
½ cup olive oil
juice of 2 lemons
salt to taste
freshly ground pepper

Cook the rice in at least 6 cups of salted water and drain in a colander the minute it's done, rinsing the cooked rice with cold water to wash off any remaining liquid and to separate the grains. Drain thoroughly and put it in a big salad bowl.

Chop up the hardboiled eggs and anchovies and add them. Cut the olives in half and add them along with the pickles (if you are using them) and capers. Slice the peppers into thin, thin strips and add them.

Cook the mixed frozen vegetables until tender, but be careful not to overcook them. Drain them and add to the rice mixture.

Drain the tuna fish and break it up with a fork before adding it to the bowl. Pour in the olive oil, enough to dress the salad well. Add the lemon juice, taste for seasonings, and adjust if necessary before tossing again. Chill for at least half an hour and serve. For 8.

V

DOLCI
DESSERTS

Any native Italian or anyone who has ever been to Italy knows that Italian sweets, all of them, rank right up at the top in any international list of lovely desserts. Probably most world travelers have tasted *Crostata, Monte Bianco*, and *Zuppa Inglese,* and have enjoyed that mixed offering of taste and texture that only pastry can provide.

Many, many pastries are made daily in thousands of pastry shops up and down the peninsula, and are sold at a modest price. Preparing them is not necessarily complicated, but it is time-consuming. Hence, in most families, when it seems to be time to set aside the omnipresent fruit and to crown a meal with an especially festive dessert, someone is sent to the pastry shop.

Yet the tradition of homemade desserts is long, and most families have a number of favorite recipes for cakes and cookies that go back generations. Some of them call for ingredients not always found around the proverbial corner. Some do take a lot of time, and that's not easily found either. We've chosen recipes that can be made at home and aren't always time-consuming to prepare. Some have stood the test, not only of generations but also of various rather makeshift kitchens where practical limitations were overcome by the wish to make a proper dessert to culminate a proper feast. In fact most family sweets do go with feast days, whether it be the celebration of a saint, a child, a republic, or a labor day. Some just represent the need to get together, family or friends, and enjoy a special morsel. With this group of recipes we invite you to treat yourself to some of the most delicious of Italian traditions.

Ciliege Sotto Spirito
PRESERVED CHERRIES

After two years in America, we returned to Rome with our three little boys to celebrate Christmas with Papà and Mamma Romagnoli. For the first time I was really plunged into the extended feast of *Natale.* Mamma brought forth her cherries, three to each glass, a tiny goblet with a bit of the liqueur in it as well.

The dinner had a fish course, a meat course, and condiments from Cremona and Modena; the salad was dressed with Balsamic vinegar, the real stuff.

Cousins and their cousins showed up. Papa kept going down to the garage to get more extension leaves for the table as well as more bottles of Lambrusco. Each year one of his friends would send up cases of the sparkling wine which no more resembles today's import than the man in the moon. It was like a good champagne, only dark red, and went marvelously with the meat.

In the end we were 24, and the children slipped away from the table to play under the decorated tree from Papà's garden. We had demolished 2 or 3 huge *panettoni.* The talk went around; a maid, donated by my sister-in-law, cleaned up and joined us before the end of the feast. Teasing, praise, attention to the little boys, a cheer for the parents. I remember it all, reflected forever in a tiny crystal goblet with a cherry. MR

1 1/2 pounds Bing cherries
1/2 cup sugar
6 cloves
3-inch stick of cinnamon

2 cups vodka, or enough to cover the
  cherries
1 quart jar with a good seal (steril-
  ized)

When you buy cherries for this kind of preserving, be sure they are not dead ripe. Choose very firm, red Bing cherries, fresh enough so that their stems are still bright green and well attached to the fruit. Wash the cherries and spread them out on a clean towel to dry. When they are dry, cut off the top of each stem, leaving just 1/4 inch. (Don't use cherries without stems, because they tend to fall apart in the jar.)

Put the sugar in the bottom of the jar, add cloves, cinnamon, and cherries. Give the jar a shake or two to settle the fruit, and pour on enough vodka to completely cover the cherries. Seal tightly and let stand at least 4 weeks before serving. Makes 1 quart.

Aranci alla Siciliana
ORANGES SICILIAN STYLE

Peeled seedless oranges are sliced thin, dressed with lemon juice and olive oil, and sprinkled with black Sicilian olives. A dash of salt brings out all the flavors.

6 seedless oranges
6 tablespoons olive oil
½ teaspoon salt, or to taste

24 black olives, Sicilian or Greek
juice of ½ lemon

Peel the oranges, taking off as much of the white inner peel as possible. Slice into thin rounds, and spread out on a large serving plate. Sprinkle with olive oil and salt (to your taste, but ½ teaspoon is the average amount).

Marinate the olives in the juice of half a lemon, 10–15 minutes. Distribute the olives over the orange slices. Tilt the plate, and with a large spoon scoop up the olive oil and juices and baste the oranges. Press down gently on some of the slices, so that more juice mingles with the oil. Baste a bit more and serve. For 6.

Mele Cotte
BAKED APPLES

½ cup raisins
½ cup white wine
6 baking apples

6 tablespoons marmalade (orange,
*   cherry, or apricot)*
¼–½ cup sugar

Preheat the oven to 350°.

Put the raisins to plump and soak in the white wine. Wash and core the apples, making sure all the seeds are removed. Butter a baking dish that is just large enough to hold the apples and put them in. Put some raisins in the bottom of the well in each apple, add a tablespoon of marmalade (more if you desire), and then put in the rest of the raisins, filling each well. Sprinkle with the sugar, and pour the wine in which the raisins soaked into the bottom of the baking dish.

Bake for half an hour (at 350°F), or until the apples are soft and puffy and the wine has mingled with the apple juices to make a splendid semithick sauce in the bottom of the dish. Baste with the sauce and serve hot or cold. For 6.

Pesche Ripiene
STUFFED BAKED PEACHES

6 large freestone peaches
1 large egg
½ cup confectioners' sugar
4 Italian macaroons (or 2 ounces

slivered almonds plus ½ teaspoon almond extract)
½ cup dry white wine

Preheat the oven to 375°.

Wash the peaches, dry them, and cut them in half. Remove the stones. With a spoon scrape out the red pulp around the hollow and save it. Beat the egg and sugar until pale yellow and fluffy.

If using macaroons *(amaretti):* crush them and add to the egg and sugar along with the peach pulp. Mix well. If using slivered almonds: toast them in the oven (as it is heating) 10 minutes, and then crush or mince them on a chopping board.

Add to the egg and sugar along with the peach pulp and the almond extract.

Fill the centers of the peach halves with the prepared mixture. Butter a baking dish just large enough to accommodate the peaches and put the halves in. Sprinkle with the wine and bake (at 375°) for half an hour. Baste the peaches with the syrup in the bottom of the pan and return them to the oven for another 10 minutes. Serve warm. For 6.

Granita di Caffe
COFFEE ICE

FOR THE ICE:
3 cups very strong Italian coffee
15 teaspoons sugar

FOR THE WHIPPED CREAM:
1 cup all-purpose cream
3 teaspoons sugar, or to taste

To get the right flavor, use an *espresso* coffee pot and Italian-roasted coffee.

While the coffee is still hot, pour it into a large Pyrex pitcher, stir in the sugar, and keep stirring until it has dissolved. Let the coffee cool a bit, and put it into a shallow pan in the freezer section of the refrigerator. After about an hour (depending on how cold the freezer really is), stir the contents of the trays with a fork, breaking up the crystals of frozen coffee that will have formed around the edges. Freeze another hour, stir again with a fork. By now the coffee is nearly completely frozen.

Freeze for another hour, stirring at the halfway point and at the end. The *granita* is ready for serving when it's all frozen in crystals, and is neither solid ice nor runny. If left in the freezer beyond this stage, it loses its characteristic texture of tiny particles of coffee ice, and should be broken up with a fork in a bowl before serving.

To serve, whip the cream, adding the sugar. Take 6 glasses, put a tablespoon of whipped cream in the bottom of each glass, add to it ⅙ of the *granita,* and top each serving with 2 tablespoons or so of whipped cream. For 6.

249

Monte Bianco
RICED CHESTNUTS WITH WHIPPED CREAM

Boiled chestnuts, flavored with vanilla and rum, whipped and sent through a potato ricer, make the *monte* (mountain), which is capped with whipped cream for the *bianco* (white) of this rich and elegant dessert.

If you can find dried, peeled chestnuts, you can save time by eliminating the first boiling. Or, if you can find purée of chestnut put up with no flavorings, just start your recipe by mashing up the canned purée until it is smooth. Then proceed to add the sugar, rum, or brandy. We don't recommend flavored puréed chestnuts, as invariably they taste of practically nothing but sugar.

FOR THE CHESTNUT PURÉE:
2 pounds chestnuts
1 ½ teaspoons salt
1 cup warm milk (approximate)
5 tablespoons confectioners' sugar
1 jigger brandy or rum (or 1 ½ teaspoons vanilla)

FOR THE WHIPPED CREAM:
1 cup all-purpose cream
1 teaspoon vanilla
5 tablespoons confectioners' sugar

Score the chestnuts with a sharp knife and put them to boil in water to cover. Add the salt and cook at least 25 minutes, or until soft. Drain, shell, and peel off the inner skin as quickly as possible (because they peel more easily while still warm).

Put the chestnuts back into a saucepan over very low heat. Add some warm milk and mash them with an ordinary potato masher. At first they tend to break up into pea-size pieces, but gradually they turn into a purée. Add more milk, a little at a time, and keep on mashing until all the lumps are gone.

When the chestnuts are a smooth, thick purée, add 5 tablespoons of sugar and the rum or brandy (or the vanilla, if you wish to substitute it for the liquor). Mash a bit more, and then pack the purée into either a cookie press with a ricer disc or into a potato ricer. Press all the purée through, letting it fall either into individual dessert dishes in little mounds, or make one big mound on a serving plate. Chill thoroughly.

Whip the cream, adding the vanilla and the sugar. Using a pastry bag, decorate the mounds (or mound) of chestnut purée with whipped cream as snow would cover a mountain peak. For 6.

Zabaglione

One of Italy's most famous and favorite sweets is from the Piedmont. Made with beaten eggs and Marsala, it is served either warm or chilled in small glasses. It's also considered a great restorative, so much so that it's part of the language: a losing soccer player is greeted with jeers of "Go get yourself a *zabaglione!*"

6 egg yolks
6 tablespoons sugar

12 tablespoons Marsala wine

A round-bottom copper bowl is ideal for making *zabaglione.* Use the bowl as the upper part of a double boiler. If you don't have one, simply use an ordinary double boiler. Put the egg yolks into whichever container you are using, add sugar, and beat until very pale and fluffy. Then put the container in hot but not boiling water and keep on beating, using a whisk or the blending speed of an electric beater. Add the Marsala a little at a time and keep on beating until the mixture thickens to the consistency of a light batter.

Remove from the heat, beat a few moments longer, and pour into dessert glasses. It can be served lukewarm or, and we think it's much better, cold. For 6.

Tirami Su
"PICK-ME-UP"

This "pick-me-up" is just that. The *Zabaglione* for a restorative, the sugar for quick energy, the biscuits for crunch. Our first taste of the *Tirami su* was up north of Venice on a cold, rainy, miserable January night. In a small fireplace-cheered restaurant called Gigetto's we had samples of wild mushrooms in every cooked form imaginable. Then Gigetto came around with his *Tira*. So restored were we that Franco insists it was not a rainy night but the stars were large in the sky as we wound our way back down the hills to Treviso.

Gigetto said I could use *Pan di Spagna* instead of the biscuits if I wanted to or lady fingers as long as they were the ones with a bit of crust to them. The softies, available everywhere, fall apart, said Gigetto, under the espresso and then you have to pick up the pick-up.MR

1 pound fresh mascarpone cheese*
¼ cup extra fine sugar
2 tablespoons light rum
2 dozen champagne biscuits**
1 cup freshly brewed espresso coffee, cooled

1 4-egg recipe Zabaglione *(page 251)*
2 tablespoons unsweetened cocoa powder
strawberries for garnish, optional

In a food processor, plastic dough blade in place, mix on/off the mascarpone, sugar, and rum until smooth, about 3 pulses.

On a serving plate arrange 6 biscuits side by side, flat side up. Moisten slightly with ⅓ of the espresso. Spread with ⅓ of the cheese mixture over the biscuits. Repeat this layering 2 more times, finishing with the cheese. Cut the 6 remaining biscuits in half lengthwise.

Make a 4-egg batch of *Zabaglione* and pour it over the top of the dessert and around the sides. Press the 12 biscuit halves into the *Zabaglione* to make a fence around the layers. Sprinkle with cocoa. Decorate with strawberry fans in the top corners of the *Tirami su.* For 6 to 8 servings.

*available in superior cheese stores, imported from Italy
**also called *biscotti all'uovo,* very similar to large, firm lady fingers, available in Italian and specialty food stores

Pasta Frolla
SWEET PASTRY DOUGH

This is a rich, soft, sweet pastry dough, which is the basis of many cakes and tarts, most notably *crostata.*

2 cups unbleached flour
½ cup plus 1 tablespoon sugar
7 tablespoons unsalted soft butter
3 tablespoons vegetable shortening

3 medium egg yolks
1 whole medium egg
1 tablespoon grated lemon or orange
   rind

Sift the flour and make it into a mound on your counter or pastry board. Add the sugar and turn the mound into a crater as for *pasta all'uovo.* Add the soft butter and the shortening in small dabs. Lightly beat the egg yolks with the whole egg and add them to the center of the crater. Start beating the egg more thoroughly with a fork, around and around the center, picking up the flour, butter, and shortening as you beat. Add grated lemon or orange rind. Continue beating until the flour, shortening, butter, and egg are all well mixed. Put aside the fork and work with your hands briefly until everything begins to stick together and forms a buttery soft dough. It is very like cookie dough and should not be handled excessively. Shape it into a ball, wrap it in plastic wrap, and chill it for at least half an hour in the refrigerator. When it's chilled, sprinkle the counter with flour and roll it as needed.

Crostata
SWEET PASTRY TART

This looks like any other big tart but its crust is sweeter, while its jam filling is sharper than that of similar pastries. The jams most frequently used in Italy are the pungent cherry or plum. American Damson plum comes close to the Italian, but American cherry is too sweet. Hence, we buy imported Italian jam made with *amarene,* sour pie cherries. *Crostata* can be made in a tart pan, or a rectangular cookie sheet.

1 batch pasta frolla, *chilled (see preceding recipe)*
1 jar plum or cherry jam (10 ounces approximately)

1 egg white, lightly beaten

Preheat the oven to 375°.

Divide the chilled ball of *pasta frolla* into one large and one small ball. Roll the larger ball into a round or rectangle about ⅛-inch thick and just big enough to fit your 10- or 11-inch tart pan and come up the sides. If the dough does develop a crack or two because of its richness, it can be manipulated easily and pushed together again. Fill the crust with the jam.

Put the second and smaller ball of dough on a floured surface and press it into a disc about ⅛ inch thick. Cut into strips ½ inch wide and place lattice-fashion on the jam. Brush with some of the lightly beaten egg white. Make a final long strip of dough and put around the edges of the *crostata,* covering all the ends of the lattice. Crimp all the way around. Brush with the remaining egg white.

Bake for 10 minutes at 375°, reduce the heat to 350°, and bake for 20 minutes, or until the crust is toasty, puffed up a bit, and baked through. Cool before serving. For 10–12.

Pastiera Napoletana
NEOPOLITAN EASTER CAKE

In Naples, it wouldn't be Easter without this cake made with sweet pastry crust, filled with whipped *ricotta*, eggs, and chocolate, flavored with zest of lemon and rum, and baked in an oven. The original uses whole wheat kernels (softened for 8 days and cooked in milk) and orange blossom water as ingredients. This modern version using rice is just as acceptable and certainly more feasible. Some people make it without the rice at all.

Usually, when we resurrect a recipe, we test it at least 4 or 5 times. With the *Pastiera*, however, the hue and cry was such that the tests went to 9, much to the pleasure of the now grown children who "visited" frequently at that time. So now we don't wait for Easter anymore. We use *Pastiera* as a call for all to gather for the fun of it.

1 recipe pasta frolla, *chilled (see page 253)*
½ cup long-grain rice
2 squares baking chocolate
1 pound ricotta
1½ cups sugar
3 medium egg yolks (room temperature)

1 tablespoon candied citron
¼ teaspoon cinnamon
grated rind of 1 lemon
¼ cup rum (or 1 teaspoon vanilla)
2 egg whites (room temperature)

Make the *pasta frolla* and chill it.

Cook the rice, rinse with cold water in a colander, and set aside to cool.

Melt the chocolate in a small double boiler and cool.

Preheat the oven to 350°.

Put the *ricotta* in a large bowl and beat it with an egg beater until smooth. Add 1 cup of the sugar and stir in the egg yolks one by one, mixing after each addition until blended. Add the citron, cinnamon, lemon rind, chocolate, and rum (or vanilla). In a separate bowl whip 2 egg whites with the last of the sugar until stiff, and fold them into the egg-*ricotta* mixture. Lastly, fold in the cooked rice.

Break off about ⅔ of the *pasta frolla*, roll it into a round, and place it in the bottom of a buttered 10-inch spring form pan. Spread it out carefully along the bottom of the pan, pushing with your fingers, and up the sides about 1½ inches. Pour in the beaten *ricotta* mixture. Flour the counter, roll out the remaining piece of *pasta frolla* until it is about ⅛ inch thick, cut into ½-inch strips with a pastry cutter or knife, and place them lattice-fashion on top of the *Pastiera*. Brush with a bit of slightly beaten egg white (use one of the whites left over from the *pasta frolla*).

Bake for 1 hour, or until the lattice of the *pasta frolla* is nicely toasted and the filling is puffed up like a soufflé. Cool before serving. For 12.

Bignè di San Giuseppe
ST. JOSEPH'S DAY PASTRIES

Franco's Zia Giuseppina in her advanced years held forth like a prophet on St. Joseph's Day (March 19). Tiny, rather deaf, but with 2 of the most expressive brown eyes I've ever seen, Zia would gather the younger ones around her. (The elders were relegated to card games in the next room.) In her gentle voice, Zia asked what each was doing in school and had they had enough *bignè?* In answer to the second question, our children, newly exposed to *bignè,* produced their first consumer report: when it comes to *bignè,* we want more (they got them) before we leave. And, as they waved goodbye to Zia, "We like Zia's saint alot. Maybe we could add his name to all of ours?"
MR

FOR THE PASTRY:
1 1/4 cups water
5 tablespoons butter
3/4 cup flour, sifted
4 eggs
1 1/2 tablespoons sugar
1/2 teaspoon grated lemon rind
1 1/2 tablespoons cognac
  (or 1 tablespoon vanilla)

FOR THE BAKED BIGNÈ:
1 recipe crema pasticcera (page 265)

FOR THE FRIED BIGNÈ:
1 quart vegetable oil
confectioners' sugar

Bring the water and butter to a boil in a saucepan over high heat, and the minute the mixture boils, take the pan off and add the flour all at once. Stir immediately and vigorously with a wooden spoon, putting the pan back over the heat. The mixture turns into a paste right away, and must be stirred continuously until it forms a ball and no longer clings to the sides or bottom of the pan. Keep on stirring a little more, until the paste sounds as if it were frying. Remove it from the heat and cool.

Add the eggs, one at a time, stirring each in completely before adding the next. Keep on stirring until the soft dough is perfectly amalgamated, smooth, and rather like drop cookie batter. Then stir in the sugar, the lemon rind, and the cognac (or vanilla). Cover and let stand 15 minutes in a cool place.

To bake: drop by the tablespoonful on a buttered cookie sheet, leaving at least 2 inches between them. Bake in a preheated 400° oven for 10 minutes, reduce the heat to 375° and bake another 10–15 minutes, or until golden brown in color, crisp on the outside, and nearly doubled in size. Remove from the oven, break open gently, and cool. When cooled, fill with vanilla or chocolate *crema pasticcera.* Makes 16.

To fry: heat 1 quart of vegetable oil to 300° in a deep pan and drop the dough in by the tablespoonful. It helps to work with 2 spoons, 1 for dipping up the dough and the other for scraping it off the first spoon (both should be dipped in the oil). Don't drop in more than 4 or 5 *bignè* at a time, and leave plenty of space for them to swell up. As they fry they will keep turning themselves over, once the first side is done to a toasty brown. The temperature of the oil will go up as the *bignè* cook, and since they must start at a lower than frying heat, turn the heat down after each group has cooked so that the second and third installments start, like the first, at about 300° and finish their cooking at 350°. Starting with an oil that is too hot will overcook the *bignè* outside and leave the inside undercooked.

When nicely browned and puffed up, remove with a slotted spoon, drain on paper towels, and finally sprinkle with a bit of confectioners' sugar.

Cannoli alla Siciliana
SICILIAN FILLED PASTRIES

This is a double treat from Sicily: crisp fried pastry and creamy *ricotta*. Either one could definitely stand on its own, but combined they become *cannoli*. The pastry was once fried wrapped around pieces of *canna* (bamboo cane), hence the name. Today we substitute for the cane 5-inch aluminum piping available in Italian or European cookware shops. As for the filling, this recipe calls for the addition of whipped cream to achieve the light texture of the traditional one made with delicate, fresh, Sicilian *ricotta*.

FOR THE PASTRY:
1 cup flour
¼ teaspoon salt
1 scant tablespoon sugar
1 tablespoon soft butter
¼ cup white wine
vegetable oil for frying

FOR THE FILLING:
2 cups ricotta
1 cup whipped heavy cream
3 tablespoons sugar (or more if you wish)
2 tablespoons candied fruits (or 3 tablespoons cocoa and 2 tablespoons chocolate jimmies)
1½ teaspoons vanilla

For the pastry: place the flour in a mound on a pastry board or counter. Make a well in the center, and put in the salt, sugar, and dabs of the soft butter. Add the wine and start stirring in the center with a fork. Keep on until most of the flour has been absorbed and you have a paste you can work with your hands.

Knead the paste until it is smooth and has picked up almost all the remaining flour. Roll it out no thicker than a noodle and cut into 3 ½ × 3 ½-inch squares, if using 5-inch-long, 1-inch diameter *cannoli* forms. The diagonal of the squares should not be longer than the forms, so adjust the size of the squares to the length of the forms.

Place *cannoli* forms diagonally on the squares. Wrap the pastry around the form, one corner over the other, and press the corners to hold them together. If the corners don't stick with pressure, moisten a finger with water and apply to contact point and press again.

Cover the bottom of a frying pan with about ¾ inch of vegetable oil and heat to 375°. If you don't have a thermometer, drop a bit of dough in. If it immediately starts to blister and turn a toast color, the temperature is right. Because *cannoli* cook very fast and swell in size during the process, you may find 3 is a good number to cook at a time. Put them in the hot oil and turn them carefully when one side is done. Remove as soon as they have become crisp, a uniform toast color, and rather blistered all around. The forms, naturally, get terribly hot: a pointed pliers is the easiest tool with which to lift them out of the pan. Holding the form with the pliers, a gentle push with a fork slips the fried *cannoli* off the form. Drain the *cannoli* on paper towels. Put the forms aside to cool. When cooled, rewrap and continue frying until all are done. If you want to work very quickly, have about 18 forms on hand (which is approximately what this recipe makes) all wrapped and ready before you begin frying.

Cannoli, when cooked and left unfilled, will keep crisp a day or so in a tin or a dry place.

If you want to make more than 18 *cannoli*, the recipe doubles easily using 2 cups of flour, 2 tablespoons soft butter, 1 ½ tablespoons sugar, ½ teaspoon salt, and ⅔ cup of wine. If you are kneading and rolling on a pasta machine, which is ideal for this particular dough, start at the widest gap and bring it down to the width used for *fettuccine.*

For the filling: put the *ricotta* in a bowl and fold in the whipped cream, adding the sugar as you fold. Chop the candied fruits to tiny slivers no bigger than grains of rice and fold in all but about a teaspoon. Add the vanilla.

Using a spatula or a broad knife, fill the *cannoli* first from one end and then from the other. Press the filling in gently to make sure the center is full. Scrape each end to smooth out the cream and decorate the ends by dipping them in the remaining candied fruit slivers.

If you want to make the filling chocolate, substitute cocoa for the candied fruits in the cream--*ricotta* mixture and decorate with grated chocolate or the chocolate jimmies.

The *cannoli* should not be filled too long before serving, as that softens the pastry. The filling, however, can be chilled, and both parts of this elegant dessert can be made ahead of time and assembled shortly before the meal. Makes 18 approximately.

Babà

A sweet bread baked as a big cake or more commonly as individual cupcakes soaked in a rum-flavored syrup. So perfect a sweet is this that to describe someone or something terribly good, a Neapolitan would say, "È nù babà!"

FOR THE SWEET BREAD:
½ cup golden seedless raisins
½ cup unsalted butter
½ cup warm water (110°)
1½ packages dry yeast
3 cups flour
2 eggs plus 1 egg yolk
⅓ cup confectioners' sugar

½ teaspoon salt
1 teaspoon vanilla

FOR THE RUM SYRUP:
1 cup sugar
1 cup water
¾ cup dark rum

Soak the raisins in a bowl of hot water in order to plump up.

Melt the butter over a low flame and let it cool. Heat ½ cup of water until it is hot to the touch (110°), and dissolve the yeast in it. Mix with 1 cup of the flour until you have a soft, sticky dough. Cover and let rise in a warm place for about half an hour, or until doubled in bulk.

In another bowl beat the eggs and sugar until very pale and fluffy. Slowly sift a cup of flour into the egg mixture. Add the melted cooked butter, mix well, and add the raised dough, the salt, and the vanilla. Keep on mixing until the egg mixture and raised dough are well amalgamated. Slowly add enough of the last cup of flour to turn the dough into a soft bread dough. Knead it well (using the last of the flour) on the counter until it is smooth, elastic, and soft. Punch it down on the counter, sprinkle with the plumped-up raisins, and knead them in.

The dough may be cooked in a tubular pan (8 inches in diameter and 3 inches tall is a good size) or in cupcake pans. In either case, butter the pan well, sprinkle with a bit of granulated sugar, and shake out any extra. Put only enough dough in the pan to fill ⅓ of it. Let rise 1½ hours, or until well over the edge of the pan, in a closed, unheated oven. When the dough has risen, turn on the oven and set the thermostat at 400°. Bake for 35–45 minutes if using the tubular pan, 25 minutes for the cupcake pans. The top should be a toasted brown. Test with a toothpick or a long, slim skewer; if babà is well done, the skewer comes out clean. Makes 1 8-inch in diameter babá or 12 to 16 individual cakes.

Cool babà slightly, and put it on a platter.

To make the rum syrup, boil the sugar and water over a high heat for 10 minutes, add the rum, boil another minute, and the syrup is ready to use. Pour it over the cooling babà and baste from time to time until all the syrup has been absorbed.

Frappe

When the children were little and Sunday afternoons in need of a lift, Franco would set out his flour in a mound on the counter, gather the children around, and teach them how to make *frappe*. Some were good at the early mixing; others learned quickly, not letting the dough stick. All of them became very efficient at rolling out the dough on the pasta machine.

Most fun of all was after a brief moment of cooling off time, the sampling. Each childish face had a wonderful mustache of sugar and the pleasure was as pervasive as the crunch. Of course the clean-up took a bit of effort the first few times, but eventually huge batches of *frappe* could be made without a mess, to the joy of all of us. MR

2 cups all-purpose unbleached flour
¼ cup granulated sugar
2 tablespoons unsalted butter, chilled and cut into ½-inch bits

1 teaspoon vanilla
3 tablespoons dry white wine
vegetable oil for frying
3–4 tablespoons confectioners' sugar (sifted) or more if desired

Put the flour, sugar, and butter in a food processor bowl with the steel blade. Process on/off until the butter is blended. With the motor running, add the vanilla and the wine and keep processing until the dough either clings together nicely when pinched or forms a ball at the end of the blade, about 2 minutes.

Work the dough briefly with your hands and then roll it to the thickness of a dime with a rolling pin or with a pasta rolling machine. Cut in diamond shapes or 8-inch-long strips and tie them in loose knots.

Fry the dough in hot (350°) vegetable oil until golden and puffed. Drain on paper towels and dust with confectioners' sugar.

Serve hot or cold, accompanied by hot chocolate for children or, for adults, a good white or slightly sweet red wine or champagne.

Meringata

Just a very few years ago, during one of our touch-the-touchstone trips to Italy, friends served us a spectacular dessert: layers of toasted almonds, shards of crisp meringues, and a cloud of what felt like semifrozen, still frothy, but obviously whipped cream, a hint of vanilla, and tiny little meringues to top the layers. It was a boon to an otherwise rather ordinary day in Milano out of season. Our hostess said in no uncertain terms, "No one in their right minds would reconstruct this dessert. I bought it from so and so's store." That was like waving a red flag in front of the proverbial bull: we wanted to duplicate the dessert and so we did, changing it slightly, but making it work for people who love dessert and the making of same. MR

FOR THE MERINGUES:
1 cup egg whites, room temperature
2 cups granulated sugar
½ teaspoon cream of tartar
½ teaspoon salt
1 tablespoon vanilla
butter and flour for the cookie sheet

FOR THE CREAM:
½ cup water

2 packets (tablespoons) unflavored
 gelatin
1 quart whipping cream, chilled
sugar to your taste
1½ teaspoons vanilla

FOR THE LAYERING:
3½ ounces almond slivers, toasted,
 chopped coarsely

Butter the cookie sheets with as little butter as possible and then wipe off excess with a paper towel. Flour the cookie sheets, shake off the excess, and let stand.

For the meringues: beat the egg whites with the salt and cream of tartar until the bubbles are small and uniform. (This stage is reached more quickly if you can use an unlined copper bowl for beating.) Continue beating and begin to add the sugar, about ¼ cup at a time, until it is all in. As the mixture gets firmer and more glossy, continue to beat. When it really holds its shape in a swirl, add the vanilla, keep on beating another 4–5 minutes. You can feel the mixture really firming up and the sugar will have melted completely.

Using a spatula or a pastry bag fitted with a wide nozzle, make 3 discs of meringue about 9–10 inches in diameter or to fit a spring form pan and your dessert plate. Any leftover meringue may be dropped from two spoons into tiny meringues for use as decoration. Bake the discs and tiny meringues at 250° for 1½ hours or until they lift off the sheet easily. Keep in a cool, dry place, covered, until time to make the *meringata*.

For the cream: melt the gelatin in cold water and heat in a double boiler over simmering water until dissolved. Allow to cool.

Put the cream in a chilled bowl and whip it (chilled whip or beaters recommended) until frothy. Start to add sugar a tablespoon at a time until the taste you wish has been achieved. Beat again for a moment and pour the cooled, melted gelatin into the vortex of the whipped cream, add the vanilla, and when incorporated, stop beating

For the layering: place one of your meringue discs in a plastic-lined spring form pan. Coarsely chop the other two discs on a chopping board with a large knife until reduced to ¼-inch bits. Spoon about ⅓ of the whipped cream onto the first disc. Sprinkle with ⅓ of the chopped meringue mixed with one third of the almonds. This layer should not be skimpy. Spread with ⅓ more of the cream and make another layer of nuts and meringue bits.

Make a final layer of the whipped cream and top it with a final layer of nuts and meringues. Decorate with the tiny meringues around the edge of the top layers.

Cover the whole thing with plastic wrap and place in the freezer for at least 2 hours and then ½ hour or so in the refrigerator. Take the sides off the spring form pan and lift up the *meringata* and place it on a serving platter. Pull the plastic out from under. Cut with a sharp knife that has been dipped in hot water. For 10.

Pan di Spagna
SPONGE CAKE

Literally, the name means "Bread of Spain," but in the very beginning it was probably called *pan di spugna,* or sponge bread. A light, bright, versatile yellow cake, it is delightful by itself as well as part of other desserts.

My father's first introduction to *Pan di Spagna* remains a portrait of a modern St. Christopher. Gamely, he had come for our wedding. Enthusiastically, he had heard all the plans, the menu, the time table, the chapel with ceilings by Rafaello. Even the guest list split right down the middle, half Italian and half American. Cane in hand, he had walked briskly with Mother reviewing the whole Roman panorama. "But what about the cake?" he asked.

"Ah," I replied knowingly, *"Pan di Spagna."*

"What's that?" he asked.

"Sponge cake, bread of Spain."

"Oh, no, no, no. No Spanish bread at this wedding!" he exclaimed.

After some explanation about versatility and frostings, what's in a name, and layers of special cream, he simmered down. But he insisted on going to the pastry shop: "I want to taste the filling, see the decorations, count the layers."

I translated dutifully and would have blown up if I hadn't felt his fierce pride, his only daughter among five sons was finally marrying. "A foreigner, yes," I'd heard him say, "but his father is an architect. He speaks French." As I recall, we drove through Rome's rainy streets, my father holding the cake gingerly and asking "Are you sure it's what you want?"

I never asked if he meant the cake or the marriage. I wanted and got both.

MR

5 *large eggs (room temperature)*
1½ *cups sugar*
1½ *cups unbleached flour*

1 *teaspoon vanilla*
½ *teaspoon grated lemon peel*

Preheat the oven to 350°.

Separate the eggs, putting the yolks in a large bowl and the whites in a smaller but still adequate one. Add the sugar to the yolks, and beat until pale yellow and the consistency of a good frosting. Beat the whites until they stand stiff in peaks. Gently fold the whites into the yolks, using a flat spoon or spatula, putting in a bit at a time and slowly turn-ing the batter over and over until the egg-sugar mixture is all absorbed. When folding, be sure to go all the way down to the bottom of the bowl and around the edges.

Sift the flour 3 times, fold it in slowly a bit at a time. By now the batter has doubled in bulk. Fold in the flavorings.

Butter and flour 2 9-inch layer cake pans or 1

8-inch square pan. Pour in the batter and bake; layers take approximately 20 minutes and the square pan takes 30 When done, the cake should be toasty and crisp on top, and a toothpick comes out clean when stuck into it.

Layers usually don't rise above the pans' edges, and can be turned upside down to cool. The square cake rises above the edge and unless you have a special rack, must be cooled face up. Either way, *pan di Spagna* must be cool before you work with or cut it. For 10–12.

Crema Pasticcera
PASTRY CREAM

This is a basic pastry cream; it can be either vanilla with a hint of lemon flavor or all chocolate.

4 tablespoons sugar
4 egg yolks
4 tablespoons flour
1 teaspoon vanilla

2⅔ cups milk
2 ounces unsweetened baking chocolate, grated (or 1 teaspoon grated lemon peel)

Put the sugar, egg yolks, flour, and vanilla in a saucepan and stir hard and fast with a wooden spoon until the mixture is smooth and light yellow, and all the sugar has dissolved (which has happened when you can't hear it grating on the sides of the pan).

In another saucepan heat the milk to scalding (it will form a skin on top just before it boils). Slowly pour the hot milk into the egg mixture, stirring constantly over medium heat. Keep stirring (always in the same direction to prevent curdling) and cooking over medium heat until the mixture starts to boil and thicken and coat the spoon. Add the vanilla. Lower the heat at this point, add either the chocolate or the lemon peel, and continue cooking for another 4 minutes or so until the *crema* is really thick, the consistency of pudding. Remove from the heat and put a piece of plastic wrap right down on the surface of the *crema* to prevent a skin from forming as it cools.

The *crema* is ready to spread when it has cooled to room temperature. It may also be made hours ahead of use and stored in the refrigerator, but if you do that, bring it to room temperature before spreading.

To make a batch that is half chocolate and half vanilla to use in *zuppa Inglese:* divide the cream into 2 saucepans just as it starts to thicken. Add 1 ounce of grated unsweetened chocolate to one of the pans and ½ teaspoon grated lemon peel to the other. Reduce the heat and continue cooking and stirring both pans for about 4 minutes, or until the *crema* is of pudding consistency. Cover and cool as above. Makes enough for 1 *zuppa Inglese* or 1 recipe of *bignè.*

Zuccotto
FLORENTINE MOLDED CAKE

Zuccotto, literally, means "skullcap," such as that worn by the Roman Catholic clergy, made of slender silk triangles sewn together to form a half sphere. The dessert, generally, has been made with sponge cake or *Pan di Spagna*, cut into rectangular slices and then put in a spherical mold. The inside was whipped cream with almonds and chocolate bits while the triangular designs were made with sifted powdered sugar and cocoa. Having tasted a number of regional versions, we finally decided on the classic Florentine recipe. The triangle design comes from the cut of the *Pan di Spagna* and the only interference with the ingredients comes with the choice of liqueurs and the addition of unflavored geletin in the whipped cream. The gelatin makes *Zuccotto* a bit firmer (not to be frozen, just chilled), easier to cut, and a very reliable dessert that can be made hours ahead of dinner time.

3 layers Pan di Spagna, 10-inch diameter, about ½ inch thick
⅛ cup Amaretto
⅛ cup brandy
1 cup (4 ounces) toasted almonds, chopped
¾ cup (5 ounces) semi-sweet chocolate, chopped coarsely
3 cups whipping cream

2 packets unflavored gelatin (2 tablespoons, approximately)
1 cup confectioners' sugar
4 squares (4 ounces) bitter baking chocolate, melted and cooled
2 teaspoons vanilla
2 tablespoons cocoa for sifting over final product (optional)

Line a 2-quart bowl with plastic wrap (the diameter of the bowl should be about 9–10 inches). Out of one of the cake layers, cut a circle to just fit the bottom of the bowl. Save 1 layer and cut remaining cake into triangular slices about an inch wide at the widest end. Place the slices crust side to the bowl around the inside of the bowl, small point pushed right up to the circle of the cake. You may want to cut off that point to make the pieces fit perfectly. Sprinkle all the slices and the circle with the Amaretto and brandy.

Put the gelatin in ¼ cup of water, heat in a double boiler, and when melted set aside to cool to room temperature. Whip the cream until it is medium thick. Keep on beating and pour the cooked gelatin into the whipped cream. When the cream is thick and the gelatin completely absorbed (a matter of seconds), whip in the sugar. Then fold in the chocolate bits and the almonds and divide the cream into two bowls. Fold the melted chocolate into one of the bowls. Add 1 teaspoon of vanilla to each bowl.

With a spatula, spread the white cream over the cake slices in the bowl and onto the center cake-circle and into the cracks. Fill the center of the now forming mold with the chocolate cream. Cover the chocolate cream and the entire surface of the mold with the last layer of cake.

Place plastic wrap over the entire surface of the cake and chill in the freezer 2 hours. Remove to the refrigerator. When it is time to serve, unmold on a platter. If you wish, decorate with a fine sifting of cocoa. For 12–16.

Zuppa Inglese
LAYERED SPONGE CAKE WITH PASTRY CREAM

Zuppa means soup and *Inglese* means English. This dessert vaguely resembles a glorified English trifle, and many people consider this the reason for its name. We prefer to believe the source is the vernacular distortion of *inzuppare* (to soak, to drench) and of *intriso* (medley), which in some Italian dialect sounds like *Inglese.* There are many regional versions of *zuppa Inglese,* but the ingredients remain basically the same. The two most common versions are the layered *zuppa* and the *zuppa* in a mold. The latter sometimes uses *savoiardi* (ladyfingers) instead of *pan di Spagna* (sponge cake). Rosolio, a red Italian liqueur made of rose essence and spices, is commonly used for color and flavor. As for the other liqueurs, the choice is dictated by preference or by what is available in the family pantry.

1 recipe Pan di Spagna *(pages 264–65) for layered* zuppa: *bake 2 round layers; for molded: 1 square*
1 recipe crema pasticcera, *half vanilla and half chocolate (page 265)*

½ cup Rosolio
¼ cup rum
1¼ cup brandy
½ ounce unsweetened baking chocolate, grated (for layered zuppa *only)*

LAYERED *ZUPPA*

Bake *Pan di Spagna* in two 9-inch round pans; prepare the vanilla and chocolate *crema pasticcera.*

(1) The first step in assembling the *zuppa Inglese* is to cut in half horizontally each round cake, making a total of four layers. Work slowly and use a serrated knife. (2) Put the first layer crust side down on a serving platter. Sprinkle with ¼ cup of the Rosolio. Spread this layer with half the chocolate *crema,* smoothing it to the edge with a wide knife. (3) Put the second layer on, crust side down, sprinkle with the rum, and spread with half the vanilla *crema.* (4) Put the third layer on, crust side down, sprinkle with the brandy, and spread with the remaining chocolate *crema.* (5) Sprinkle the cut side of the fourth and final layer with the remaining ¼ cup of Rosolio, and then put this layer on, crust-side *up.* Spread with the rest of the vanilla *crema,* and sprinkle with the grated chocolate. Chill at least half an hour before cutting

MOLDED *ZUPPA*

Bake *Pan di Spagna* in an 8-inch square pan; prepare the vanilla and chocolate *crema pasticcera.*

Cut the cake into thin (less than ½-inch) slices, and then cut all of them in half vertically. (1) Take a deep bowl (4 inches deep and 9 inches in diameter is a good size), and line the sides with half slices of cake, sponge side down. If necessary to trim the pieces to size for this first layer, reserve the scraps to fill in gaps. (2) Dribble ¼ cup of the Rosolio on the slices in the sides and bottom. Spread the bottom with chocolate *crema.* (3) Cover with more slices of cake, sprinkle with the rum, and spread with vanilla *crema,* using some to fill the cracks in the side walls. (4) Add another layer of slices, sprinkle with the brandy, and spread with chocolate *crema.* Use any remaining *crema,* chocolate or vanilla, to finish crack-filling. (5) Place a final layer of slices over the entire top, using any reserved scraps of cake to fill in gaps in what will be, when the bowl is inverted for serving, the base of the *zuppa Inglese.* Sprinkle with the remaining ¼ cup of Rosolio.

Chill for at least half an hour. Unmold by turning the bowl upside down onto a serving plate. To serve, slice into wedges as you would a layer cake. For 10–12.

VI

SVOGLIATURE
SNACKS

The Italian *svogliature,* in terms of food, can be translated as "snacks." They do stay the appetite while you are waiting for a more structured meal, but even more than that they are designed to satisfy a socio-gastronomic whim of the moment. "Let's have a pizza," is a call to friends to get together and have a good time, sharing a pizza and a few glasses of wine. Formalities, ponderous thoughts, or the worries of the day are not allowed around the table: they would definitely spoil a pizza, *calzone, crostino,* or any other *svogliature.*

Pizza

Pizza, like pasta, has been internationally elected to represent Italian cookery. *Pizza-pie* is an accepted term, even if in translation it means only "pie-pie." But a pizza is a pie, and therefore covers a multitude of variations whose common attribute is a bottom crust of bread dough baked in an oven. If the real pizza could stand up, it would surely be *pizza Napoletana:* a thin, crisp crust of bread dough, a bit of olive oil, *mozzarella* cheese, fresh, ripe plum tomatoes, a pinch of oregano, a few anchovies, and that's all.

It is fair to assume that the pizza's origins are as old as bread making. When all the loaves had been shoved in the oven, the baker would take a small ball of leftover dough, flatten it into a disc, flavor it with whatever was handy, and cook it in the hot oven. Time and imagination have produced many kinds of *pizze.* Purists tend not to recognize them and stay with the classic *Napoletana.* Yet all *pizze* should be appetizingly light and tasty, with the flavors well balanced and not overpowering.

The secrets (if they can be called that) of a good pizza are the right bread dough, the freshness of the ingredients, and most of all, the oven. Ideally this should be a wood-fired brick oven, but this is practically impossible to find today. Even in Italy, brick ovens are dying of old age and are being replaced by gas ones. *Sic transit gloria pizzae.*

This fact alone, however, should not deter anybody from trying a home-made version. With a minimum of care and a bit of love and enthusiasm, a very acceptable pizza can be produced. The following are a few guidelines:

The dough:

(1) Flour should be unbleached, all-purpose flour.

(2) Cake yeast is preferable, dissolved in lukewarm water, but dry yeast is easier to find and will work well if you use quite warm water to dissolve it (110°). Water that is too hot will let all the zip out of the yeast before it has a chance to work in the dough.

(3) Go easy on the salt. Sprinkle it on after the yeast and water have amalgamated with the flour.

(4) Knead until you have a smooth, elastic ball of dough.

(5) Roll out the dough no more than ⅛ inch thick.

(6) Pizza may be made on rounds in individual pizza stones or in pie pans, but most home pizza-makers use cookie sheets to bake large rectangular pies that will serve a crowd.

The topping:

(1) The topping or filling should not be runny, overloaded with spices, nor too complicated a combination of flavors.

(2) If you cannot find fresh *mozzarella,* use whole-milk *mozzarella* cheese, as it melts more like fresh Italian *mozzarella* and retains more of its softness on cooling.

(3) Use fresh mushrooms, not canned.

(4) Use fresh (if possible), very ripe, peeled plum tomatoes, cut into chunks. If they're not available, use canned tomatoes (not sauce), but do not use the liquid; sometimes tomatoes are put up in a very watery juice that will make a soggy mess of a pizza.

(5) Preheat the oven to 450–475°, and keep an eye on the baking pizza the first few times you make it to correct timing if necessary.

Each recipe for the various pizza toppings that follows is enough for a full batch of dough, but if you want to make different kinds of *pizze* at one time, as we do, adjust the quantities in the toppings accordingly. We find that this system is more fun and satisfies the varying tastes of 6–8 people.

For the spur-of-the-moment decisions on pizza or calzone making, we suggest you may want to try the food processor method (page 272) as well as fast-rising yeast. Use of both can get you a pizza in the oven in about an hour. We also suggest that if the mood moves you, you may make pizza dough ahead of time (a week, a month, as you please), let it rise once, roll it, cut it in the size(s) you wish, and freeze it in plastic wrap. When defrosted, it can rise again and be manipulated, sauced, and baked.

Pasta per Pizza
PIZZA DOUGH

5 cups unbleached flour
2 packets active dry yeast

2 cups warm water (110°)
1 teaspoon salt

Put the flour in a mound on your counter or pastry board and make a well in the middle. Pour the powdered yeast in that well. Add just a bit of warm water to the yeast and start stirring it with a fork. As it gathers flour and a paste starts to form, add more water. Keep on stirring and adding water to the paste until all the water is used.

Then start working with your hands. At first the dough seems hopeless and very raggedy. But in about 2 minutes it takes on the tough shape and consistency of play dough, and it will continue to pick up the remaining flour as you knead, back and forth. Add the salt. Keep on kneading until the dough is soft, smooth, and warm. At the end of about 15 minutes you should have a very smooth ball, so light in texture you can see your handprint briefly before the dough bounces back. If, after all the original flour has been used, the dough begins to stick to the counter, sprinkle with some extra flour.

Put a teaspoon or so of olive oil in a bowl at least twice as big as the finished ball of dough. Roll the dough around in the oil until it is well coated. Cover the bowl with plastic wrap, sealing it well. Put in a warm place and let it rise until doubled in size, about 30–45 minutes under good conditions.

Preheat oven to 450°.

Punch the dough down, cut it in half, and flatten each piece out on a floured surface. Roll the pieces into rectangles to fit a cookie sheet (10×15 inches) with a border ½ inch high, or into circles to fit pizza or pie pans. Flour the pans very lightly and put the dough on them. Push the dough with your fingers up and into the corners and around the edges to make a slight border to hold any kind of topping. Now you are ready to add your topping.

Bake (at 450°), the time depending on the type of pizza. Usually it takes about 20 minutes total to get a well-baked pizza, one that's toasty and crisp on the bottom and edges.

This recipe, adapted for the American oven, produces 4 12-inch rounds or 4 10×15-inch rectangles (the size of cookie sheets).

Food processor method. With the steel blade in the bowl, place all the dry ingredients in the food processor. Turn on the motor and slowly pour 1 cup of the warm water through the tube. The mixture will turn quickly a very fine grain and begin to stick together. Add ½ cup more of water with the machine running and let it run until a ball of dough forms at the end of the blade. If the ball doesn't form in a matter of seconds, add a bit more water, slowly, and only a bit. The amount of water depends on the moisture in the atmosphere. As soon as a ball of dough forms, remove it from the processor bowl, knead it 3–5 minutes and let it rise, covered with plastic wrap in an oiled bowl in a draft-free place until double in size. Punch it down, roll it out to the size and shape you wish, and proceed with toppings.

Pizza Napoletana
NEAPOLITAN PIZZA

Possibly the pizza most familiar to all of us is made with a layer of slightly crushed, ripe plum tomatoes and grated *mozzarella* cheese, salted with anchovy fillets, and flavored with just a hint of oregano.

1 recipe Pizza Dough
olive oil
3–4 cups plum tomatoes
1 pound whole-milk mozzarella
2-ounce can anchovy fillets
½ teaspoon oregano
salt

Preheat oven to 450°.

Prepare and roll the pizza dough and brush it lightly with a pastry brush dipped in olive oil.

Cut the plum tomatoes into chunks, discarding as many seeds and as much liquid as possible, and spread them over the dough more or less to cover. Grate the *mozzarella* as coarsely as you can or chop it into tiny bits. Sprinkle generously over the tomatoes. Cut the anchovies into inch-long pieces and spread them around. Sprinkle with oregano, and dribble a bit of olive oil over the entire surface. Salt lightly.

Bake in a hot oven (450°) 20–25 minutes, or until the crust is crisp and golden, the cheese melted and blended with the tomatoes. Serve hot. For 6.

Pizza coi Funghi
PIZZA WITH MUSHROOMS AND TOMATOES

1 recipe Pizza Dough
1 pound mushrooms
olive oil
2–3 cups peeled plum tomatoes
1 pound whole-milk mozzarella
salt and pepper to taste

Preheat the oven to 450°.

Prepare the pizza dough as usual.

Slice the mushrooms as finely as possible.

Brush the pizza dough with oil, using either a pastry brush or your fingers. Cut the tomatoes into chunks and spread them out on the dough. Grate the *mozzarella* or chop finely and sprinkle it over the tomatoes. Add sliced mushrooms to cover the entire pizza. Salt lightly and add a bit of freshly ground pepper. Sprinkle with drops of olive oil, and bake about 20 minutes, or until crisp and toasty around the edges, the cheese melted, and the mushrooms cooked. For 6.

273

Pizza ai Funghi
MUSHROOM PIZZA

1 recipe Pizza Dough
1 1/2 pounds mushrooms
olive oil

1 clove garlic, minced
1/4 teaspoon salt
2 tablespoons parsley, minced

Prepare the pizza dough as usual.

Preheat the oven to 450°.

Slice the mushrooms as finely as possible, and then sauté them briefly in a big frying pan with 6 tablespoons olive oil and the minced garlic. As soon as the mushrooms have absorbed most of the oil, add the salt and the parsley, stir, and cook 1 minute longer.

Spread the mushrooms over the pizza dough, salt lightly, and dribble olive oil over the surface. Bake (at 450°) 15–20 minutes. For 6.

Pizza con Mozzarella e Prosciutto
PIZZA WITH *MOZZARELLA* AND *PROSCIUTTO*

This is a relatively nondrippy pizza which, if cut into bite-size squares, is a marvelous snack to go with before-dinner drinks.

1 recipe Pizza Dough
olive oil

1/2 pound thinly sliced prosciutto
1 pound whole-milk mozzarella

Preheat the oven to 450°.

Prepare the pizza dough as usual and brush it with olive oil.

Cut the *prosciutto* into pieces about 1 inch square and spread them on the dough.

Grate the *mozzarella* or chop it into tiny bits and sprinkle all over the pizza.

Bake (at 450°) about 20 minutes, or until the dough is nicely toasted and the cheese has melted. Cool 5 minutes or so before cutting. For 6.

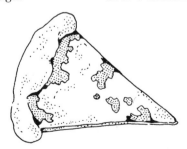

Pizza con Cipolle
ONION PIZZA

This is an old family favorite: pizza flavored with slivered onions and rosemary. Eliminate the rosemary, pepper and onion and you get *pizza bianca*, a favorite breakfast bread for our children years ago and a welcome snack for Italy's schoolchildren today.

1 recipe Pizza Dough
olive oil
1 big Bermuda or Spanish onion

1 teaspoon coarse salt
freshly ground pepper
3 teaspoons dried rosemary

Preheat the oven to 450°.

Prepare the dough as usual, spreading it out on the tins and brushing it with olive oil.

Slice the onions into thin slivers and sprinkle them over the dough. Pat lightly in order to press them into the dough. Dimple the dough here and there with your fingers. Sprinkle with coarse salt, a generous amount of freshly ground pepper, and finally add the rosemary. Dribble olive oil over everything.

Bake for about 20 minutes (at 450°), or until the dough is crisp and toasted, as will be some of the onions. For 6.

Pizza Margherita

This is a pizza for those who love the semisharp flavor of Parmesan cheese, which, blended with tomatoes, is a pleasant contrast to the *mozzarella*.

1 recipe Pizza Dough
olive oil
3–4 cups plum tomatoes
1 pound whole-milk mozzarella

¾ cup grated Parmesan cheese
salt to taste
freshly ground pepper (optional)

Preheat the oven to 450° and prepare the dough as usual, brushing it lightly with olive oil.

Cut the tomatoes into chunks and spread them around on top of the dough. Top the tomatoes with grated *mozzarella.* Sprinkle the pizza with grated Parmesan cheese as evenly as possible. Salt (and pepper, if you wish) very lightly and sprinkle with olive oil.

Bake 20–25 minutes (at 450°), or until golden, the cheeses having melted completely and blended with the tomatoes. For 6.

Scacciata
SICILIAN RUSTIC PIZZA

This is an antique recipe that we came across during a gastronomic tour of Sicily. The method is updated, of course.

5 cups all-purpose, unbleached flour
2 packets dry yeast
1½–2 cups warm water (110°)
1 teaspoon salt
⅓ cup olive oil (approximate)
½ pound caciocavallo cheese (sweet provolone may be substituted)
16 anchovies
¼ pound sliced boiled ham

2 onions (small to medium according to your taste)
3 very ripe tomatoes
3 dozen black olives, pitted
1¼ pounds prepared artichoke hearts, cooked (2 10-ounce packages frozen)
freshly ground pepper, to taste

With the steel blade in the bowl, place all the dry ingredients in the food processor. Turn on the processor and slowly pour 1 cup of water through the tube. The mixture at this time is very fine grain, just beginning to stick together. Add the ½ cup water very slowly, stopping the machine when a ball of dough has formed at the end of the blade and begun to beat about the bowl. You may need a drop or two more than 1½ cups of water, depending on the atmosphere in the kitchen.

Lift the ball of dough from the bowl, roll it in flour and knead it for 3–5 minutes or until soft, pliable, elastic, and smooth. Place about 1 tablespoon of olive oil in a bowl and put in the dough. Twirl the ball until it is glistening all around with oil. Cover the bowl with plastic wrap, place it in a warm place, out of drafts, and let it rise until double in size. Punch it down and knead it, adding about ¼ cup olive oil as you knead. When the oil is all in, divide the dough in four parts and roll out two of them to fit 2 cookie sheets (10×15), each of which you have brushed with oil.

Slice the cheese thinly. Cut the anchovies into bits, the ham into long thin julienne strips, the onions into thin slivers. Peel the tomato (if fresh), discard the seeds, and chop the rest into small bits. Chop the olives coarsely. Cut the artichoke hearts into slivers no wider than ⅜ of an inch at their widest part.

Heat the oven to 425°F.

Place the dough on the cookie sheets and cover with the sliced cheese. Spread with all the other ingredients. Sprinkle with a bit of salt and a lot of pepper. Roll out the other two pieces of dough and place to cover the toppings. Pinch the edges together and prick the tops with a fork to let steam out while cooking. Brush with olive oil.

Bake about 40 minutes. Serve hot or cold. May be made round but when served as an antipasto, the cookie sheet shape works best. The rounds are great for family style suppers, served with salad. Makes 24 antipasto servings or four round *scacciate*, about 16 healthy wedge-shaped servings.

276

Calzone
PIZZA TURNOVER

This is a pizza in disguise: the dough is the same but the topping becomes a filling. The translation of *calzone* is "breeches," but don't ask why. Perhaps because the filling should never be bigger than its breeches; if it is, you have a catastrophe in the oven.

1 recipe Pizza Dough
2 eggs
1 1/2 cups ricotta
1/2 cup grated Parmesan cheese

1/4 teaspoon salt
1/2 pound whole-milk mozzarella
1/3 pound prosciutto

Preheat oven to 450°.

When the pizza dough has risen, roll it out on a floured surface, and cut it into circles about 8 inches in diameter.

Put the eggs in a bowl and add the *ricotta*, Parmesan cheese, and salt. Mix well.

Cut the *mozzarella* into tiny cubes and the *prosciutto* into 1/2-inch strips.

Put some of the cheese-egg mixture on the center of each round of dough. Add some *mozzarella* and *prosciutto*. Fold the rounds in half to enclose the filling and press down all around the edge to seal the dough shut.

Lightly oil 2 (perhaps 3, depending on their size) cookie sheets, and put the *calzone* on them. Brush the top side of the *calzone* with oil.

Bake for 25 minutes, or until the edges are toasty and the tops golden. Serve hot. Makes 9–12 *calzone*.

Crescenti
PASTRY PILLOWS

The name *crescenti* means something that "rises" or "swells up." Made of a simple flour-and-water dough rolled very thin, *crescenti* are first cut into strips and then diagonally into pieces about 3½ inches long. In the Emilia-Romagna region, *crescenti* are served plain with *salame* or *prosciutto* and a good dry wine.

4 cups flour
2 tablespoons olive oil (or shortening)

½ teaspoon salt
½ teaspoon baking soda
oil for frying

Put the flour in a heap on your counter, table, or pastry board. Make a well in the middle and add the oil, salt, and baking soda. Add ½ cup of water to the center and mix the liquids around and around with a fork, picking up flour as you go. Keep mixing (if necessary, add a bit more water) until a thick dough forms. Put aside the fork and knead the dough thoroughly until it is soft, elastic, and uniform like pasta dough. Form into a ball. Tidy up the working surface, removing any stuck-on pieces of dough.

Sprinkle the working surface with flour and roll the dough out like a piecrust until it is as thin as a coin, as they say in Italy, or roll it out with a pasta-rolling machine. Cut into 1½-inch-wide strips, and then on the diagonal into pieces about 3½ inches long. Use either an ordinary table knife for this or a pastry cutter.

Heat the frying oil to 375°, or until a piece of dough dropped in frizzles and starts to swell on impact. Put as many pieces of cut dough into the hot oil as will fit comfortably. Turn them over the minute they've swelled on the top side and turned toasty brown on the underside. When both sides are crisp and golden, remove with a slotted spoon and drain on paper towels.

Serve hot or cold.

Supplì
RICE CROQUETTES I

Another solution for a snack or even an *antipasto* is a batch of rice croquettes. They're held together with a bit of *ragù,* flavored with nutmeg and Parmesan cheese, rolled into shapes the size of an egg, and have a morsel of *mozzarella* hidden in the center. No one we know makes the *ragù* especially for *supplì* so this recipe simply happens when you have an extra cup of sauce.

3 cups short-grain rice
3 teaspoons salt
3 tablespoons unsalted butter
1 cup ragù *(page 66)*
2 large eggs
2 tablespoons grated Parmesan cheese

¼ teaspoon nutmeg
½ pound whole-milk mozzarella
1 cup unseasoned bread crumbs
vegetable oil for frying

Combine the rice, salt, butter, and 6 cups of cold water in a big saucepan and bring to a boil. Stir, cover, reduce the heat, and simmer for 12 minutes, or until just cooked, *al dente.* Stir a couple of times while cooking. Let the rice cool to lukewarm.

Mix the *ragù,* eggs, nutmeg, and Parmesan cheese into the lukewarm rice. Cool completely.

Cut the *mozzarella* into ½-inch cubes.

Take a heaping tablespoon of rice, about the size of a jumbo egg, and place it in the palm of your hand. Put 1 or 2 cubes of *mozzarella* more or less in the center of the rice in hand. Compact the rice ball as you would a snow ball and then pat it into an oblong shape. Roll it in bread crumbs, patting gently to get as many crumbs as possible to stick to the outside. Continue until all the rice is used. Let the *supplì* rest about 10 minutes before frying.

Put about ¾ inch vegetable frying oil in the bottom of a heavy skillet (or use a frying kettle with basket insert). Bring to a high heat, lower the *supplì* one by one into the hot oil, and brown thoroughly on all sides, turning gently. Drain on absorbent paper towels and serve warm. For 6.

Supplì in Bianco
RICE CROQUETTES II

Any dish served *in bianco* means it's served or made without sauce.

3 cups short-grain rice
3 teaspoons salt
3 tablespoons unsalted butter
¼ teaspoon powdered saffron (optional)
3 tablespoons grated Parmesan cheese

2 large eggs
¼ teaspoon nutmeg
½ pound whole-milk mozzarella
1 cup unseasoned bread crumbs

Cook the rice as in the preceding recipe, adding the saffrom during the last 3 minutes of cooking. Stir in the Parmesan cheese, cool the rice to lukewarm, and then mix the eggs and nutmeg into it.

Shape and fry the *supplì* as in the preceding recipe.

Crostini
OVEN-TOASTED SANDWICHES

An extra 15 minutes is all you need to make two kinds of *crostini* for 2 that taste and look like a party. One set is layered with *mozzarella* and *prosciutto*, the other with *mozzarella* and anchovy sauce. You have to eat them with a fork.

8 slices Italian bread
6 thin slices mozzarella
3 slices prosciutto

2–3 tablespoons olive oil
2 tablespoons unsalted butter
3 anchovy fillets

Preheat the oven to 450°.

Cut the crusts off the bread and put 4 slices in each of 2 individual small casseroles that are just large enough to hold the slices standing upright. Put the slices of *mozzarella* between all the bread slices in both casseroles. Put the *prosciutto* next to the *mozzarella* in one of the casseroles. Sprinkle the 2 sets of slices with olive oil and bake until toasted (at 450°) for 15 minutes.

Meanwhile, melt the butter. Mash the anchovies and add them to the butter, heating just long enough to blend the two.

When the *crostini* come out of the oven, pour the anchovy butter over the bread slices that have only the *mozzarella.* Divide each set in half and serve some of each with a glass of cold dry white wine. For 2.

Bruschetta
GRILLED BREAD

Slices of Italian bread, brushed with olive oil and even more lightly touched with garlic, toasted over hot coals: this may be the ancestor of America's garlic bread. Those who wish to forego the garlic may substitute a few drops of vinegar. Both versions are usually served together when an outdoor grill is going or there's a picnic. Many people serve *bruschetta* with country dishes, or use as an antipasto with a glass of wine while waiting for the rest of the meal.

1 round loaf of Italian bread
1–2 cloves garlic (depending on the number of slices of bread used)

wine vinegar (optional)
olive oil
salt to taste

Cut the bread into slices about ¾ inch thick. Cut the garlic in half and rub one side of each slice of bread lightly with it (or sprinkle on a few drops of vinegar instead). Brush with olive oil. Place the oiled sides up on an open grill. When they are toasted, turn and grill the second sides. Add a few drops of olive oil and salt.

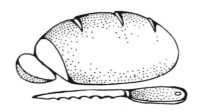

Index